THE BUILDINGS OF ENGLAND
BE 3
MIDDLESEX
NIKOLAUS PEVSNER

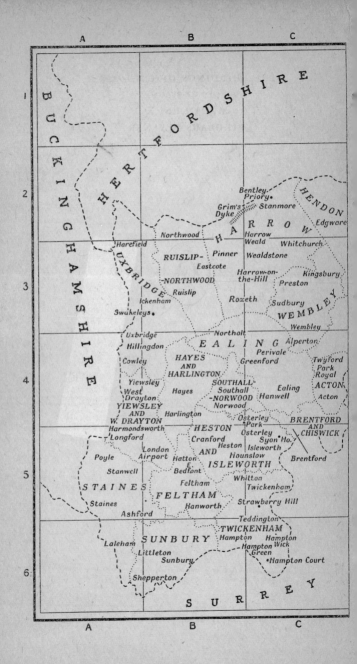

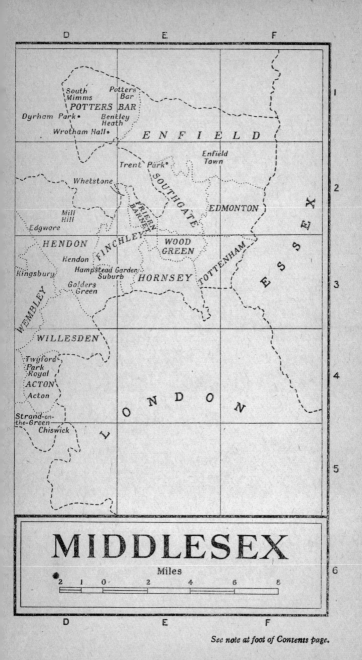

MIDDLESEX

Miles

2 1 0   2   4   6   8

THE BUILDINGS OF ENGLAND

Middlesex

BY

NIKOLAUS PEVSNER

*

PENGUIN BOOKS

HARMONDSWORTH · MIDDLESEX

FIRST PUBLISHED 1951

The author and publishers would be grateful
to any user of this book for having any errors
or omissions pointed out to them
in as much detail
as possible

MADE AND PRINTED IN GREAT BRITAIN
FOR PENGUIN BOOKS LTD
BY WILLIAM CLOWES AND SONS LTD
LONDON AND BECCLES

CONTENTS

*

*

The map on pages 2–3 shows all those places, whether towns, villages, or isolated buildings, which are the subject of separate entries in the text. The index on pages 203–204 gives references to the map square in which each place mentioned will be found

TO A.L.

*

FOREWORD

My first debt of gratitude is to Dr Gertrude Bondi for extracting and compiling most of the facts on which the following pages are based. She was greatly helped by the Middlesex volume of the Royal Commission on Historical Monuments (H.M.S.O., 1937), by Mr H. S. Goodhart-Rendel's manuscript notes on Victorian churches and Mr T. D. Kendrick's manuscript notes on Victorian glass which Mr Goodhart-Rendel and Mr Kendrick kindly placed at my disposal. The collection of photographs at the National Buildings Record was also a great help. Moreover, by the courtesy of the Ministry of Town and Country Planning, who have a statutory duty to compile lists of buildings of architectural or historic interest, I have had access to unpublished lists and much other information collected by the Chief Investigator of the Ministry and his staff. Since, however, these became accessible only after I had completed my touring of Middlesex I could but pick out what was new to me and seemed important enough for inclusion. I have marked all additions from the Ministry lists by the sign MTCP and put them into brackets. Similarly, information coming from Mr Goodhart-Rendel is marked GR, and information from Mr Kendrick TK.

Many rectors and vicars of churches and owners of houses had to be pestered with letters for information on minor points, and most of them have been sympathetic. Some have gone to much trouble in the interests of this book. With regard to houses it must be stated emphatically that their appearance in these pages does not mean that they are necessarily accessible to the public. Finally the work of compilation could not have been done if my wife and Miss Marjorie Stearn, who was then my secretary, had not, day-in and day-out, driven an obstreperous vintage 1932 car through the county.

31 December 1950

INTRODUCTION

Since London was taken out of the County of Middlesex in 1888 and made into a separate county, Middlesex has remained a torso. It has now no real capital; Brentford is hardly more than an outer suburb of London, and the County Council and Quarter Sessions meet in Westminster. Nor has Middlesex a cathedral or any large ecclesiastical establishment. What there was of monasteries and nunneries in the Middle Ages, for instance Syon of the Brigittines, Bentley Priory, Stanmore of the Austin Canons, Harmondsworth of the Brethren of the Holy Trinity, and so on, was on a small scale, and has left very little visible evidence.

Down to the early C19 the character of the present Middlesex was wholly rural in the N, and along and close to the Thames a mixture of villages and country houses of Londoners, ranging from Cardinal Wolsey's Hampton Court to Alexander Pope's villa at Twickenham and Osterley Park owned and superbly furnished by Child, the Banker. Southgate could still be called a 'sweet village' by Leigh Hunt, and Byron could still sit in Harrow churchyard and enjoy the unimpeded view towards Eton and Windsor. But in the villages Londoners had appeared by then; Chiswick Mall, Strand-on-the-Green; Montpelier Row, Twickenham, Gentlemen's Row, Enfield, and suchlike terraces were obviously built for them.

The work of the C19 and the first half of the C20 has been to convert this scattered and leisurely pattern into one of a close, uniform, and predominantly urban and suburban kind. If Greater London can be divided into a centre and three circles of suburbs, the first comprising such parts as Marylebone, Southwark, and Stepney, the second the outer fringe of the solidly built-up London, and the third the looser more recent outer growth, then Middlesex contributes a great deal to the second and third circles. Between Hammersmith and Chiswick there is no visible break anywhere, nor is there between Chiswick and Acton and Acton and Ealing, or between Paddington, Kilburn, and Willesden, or Stoke Newington and Tottenham. It is all dense, firmly knit London. Further out Edmonton, Finchley, Hendon, and even Edgware are entirely under the attraction of the great metropolitan magnet, and one has to travel as far as Enfield or Uxbridge to reach relatively independent town existences, and as far as Harefield to the NW and beyond Hampton to the W to feel really in the open country.

The outer London fringe is partly dormitory suburbs, chiefly put up by speculative builders between the two wars, partly recent industry, partly utilitarian open spaces. As to the latter, the chief areas are the airports of Heathrow, Heston, and Northolt and the waterworks demesne W and NW of Hampton village. Industry has added to the old Tottenham–Edmonton strip close to the river Lea two smokeless ribbon developments, along the Great West Road and the Western Avenue. Dormitory suburbs have, as everywhere round London, followed the progress of electric transport. In Middlesex the chief feelers are the Edgware Line, the Bakerloo Line with its two branches to Stanmore and Watford, the Central Line to Ruislip, and the Piccadilly Line to Uxbridge and Hounslow. Population figures show the difference which the opening of these lines has made to villages.

All these recent developments have tended to level out or modify original geographical and social characteristics, and it has become hard to visualize the natural state or even the medieval state of Middlesex. The county lies in the valley of the river Thames on ground very gradually rising to the N, especially to Brockley Hill, N of Stanmore, and to South Mimms. Harrow Hill is an isolated eminence. Forests covered much of the N parts, notably Enfield Chase which still in John Evelyn's time was 4,000 acres in size and stocked with 3,000 deer, and Finchley Common of 2,000 acres in the Middle Ages. Hadley Wood and Trent Park are now the only remains of all that.

Geologically the county is all London clay, the material that has gradually filled the bottom of the London Basin.

Church building was in the Middle Ages of flint rubble with Reigate stone dressings, or of Kentish rag; domestic building used timber framing. Later brick became the favourite material, as Hampton Court testifies so superbly.

Earlier than Hampton Court there is hardly anything in Middlesex of more than local importance. A History of Art and Architecture in England prior to Henry VIII could afford to omit Middlesex entirely. Still – a brief survey of what is most rewarding of all periods may in the context of this book be justified.

No prehistoric remains need singling out. Grims Dyke is probably Saxon, a defence against raiders rather than invaders. The Romans perpetuated their stay by nothing of aesthetic value, although by such impressive enterprises of engineering as the Ermine and Watling Streets, two of the main roads through the county. Ermine Street runs N through Tottenham, Edmonton, and Enfield and on to Newark and York. Watling Street goes straight NW from Marble Arch through Edgware, St. Albans, and so to Chester.

Norman Middlesex is best represented by the elaborate doorway of Harlington, the well preserved nave arcades of Laleham with short circular piers, and the fonts of Hendon and Hayes, the first square with interlaced arcading, the second drum-shaped with leaf decoration. There is a good deal more minor material which will be mentioned in its place.

The C13 is on the whole poor. At Harrow the cruciform plan can be extricated from later accretions, at Hillingdon and Hendon fragments of the decoration of the chancels survive, the corbel at Hillingdon with stiff-leaf foliage being of metropolitan quality. Then there are an odd piscina at West Drayton, the sedilia at Hayes, a solitary two-storeyed chapel with lancet windows at Moor Hall, nr. Harefield, and two poorly preserved small wall paintings of c. 1300 at East Bedfont.

For the later Middle Ages the harvest is more plentiful. Of church towers there are any number; spires are rare (Harrow, Stanwell). The towers were in the C18 every now and then made more acceptable by the addition of a playful little cupola, no bigger than the medieval staircase turrets (Harmondsworth, Hillingdon, Uxbridge, West Drayton). A good C14 chancel is at Stanwell, a pretty group of tiny village churches with weather boarded bellcotes near Greenford (Perivale, Northolt), and interior ensembles at Harrow and Uxbridge. In both these churches roofs must be mentioned specially; at Uxbridge (s aisle; as at Harmondsworth N chapel) of the hammerbeam type, at Harrow (nave) simply with tie-beams on curved braces. Good though much restored timberwork also appears in the two porches of Hayes and Harlington. Willesden has quite an impressive C14 door with cusped tracery, and Littleton an excellent elaborately carved C15 row of twelve choir stall backs, said to come from Winchester. The parclose screen at Littleton is also uncommonly rich and with its fantastic latest Gothic archshapes unparalleled in the county.

But the best place in Middlesex to appreciate the very end of medieval church architecture and decoration is South Mimms. Here a much less interestingly designed parclose screen divides off a chantry chapel of the Frowyk family. Two members of the family have rich canopied tombs in the church, and they are a most instructive study in the introduction of Renaissance motifs into a Perpendicular *ensemble*. The Frowyk Chapel also has the best range of stained glass in Middlesex, and indeed the only stained glass of importance (with the exception of the Flemish glass of *c*. 1600 at Tottenham).

As regards monuments there is again nothing better than the Frowyk tomb of *c*. 1540. The other canopied monuments of the early C16 are all of one, rather shallow, unambitious type (Edmonton, Harefield, Harlington, Norwood). Of brasses there is plenty, dated *c*. 1370 (Hayes) and later; but few are of a high aesthetic standard. The most accomplished is that of Lord and Lady Strange at Hillingdon, 1509.

Finally one C15 font deserves special mention, that at West Drayton with its carvings of the Crucifixion, the Pietà, etc., and then we can leave the churches and pass on to domestic architecture. The only monastic remains are at

Syon House, an undercroft of the Brigittine nunnery of *c.* 1440–50.

The magnificent Barn at Harmondsworth, the seventh largest in England (Cholsey, Berks, not preserved, and Abbotsbury, Dorset, come first) should, strictly speaking, be called monastic as it belonged to a Priory. Other good barns such as at Ruislip and Headstone nr. Pinner, formed part of manors or farms. Headstone Manor gives one now the most convincing impression of the late medieval manor house with additions not later than when such estates were still going concerns. The house is of brick, but most of the surviving farmhouses in Middlesex are half-timbered. Particularly pretty examples will be found at Pinner, Ruislip, Stanwell, and Harmondsworth.

On the largest scale early Tudor domestic architecture appears at Hampton Court, and here at last we have a monument of first-rate national importance, a plan larger and more sweeping than any other of its date in England and so proudly symmetrical as we do not expect to find before the Elizabethan age (cf., however, on a smaller scale, Sutton Place, nr. Guildford; Barrington Court, Somerset; and Thornbury, Gloucestershire, all of the early c16 and with symmetrically designed fronts), a hall and a chapel of the most spectacular workmanship, and, in a few odd details such as the terra-cotta medallions of Roman Emperors by *Giovanni da Majano* and the coat of arms of Henry VIII, some very early examples of architectural decoration in the new Italian fashion (1521).

More of these terra-cotta medallions have been found at Hanworth House, and at West Drayton a somewhat mutilated gatehouse remains of the country house of the Paget and then de Burgh families, a mansion of approximately the same date as Hampton and on a comparable though no doubt smaller scale.

The step from early to later Tudor or from Henry VIII to Queen Elizabeth is marked by one exquisite piece of decoration, the fireplace from Enfield Palace still essentially of the playful Early Renaissance, but already with strapwork details, and by the two large houses of Syon and Osterley, of

identical plan with a large square inner courtyard and four
outer corner turrets with bulbous cupolas. Bruce Castle at
Tottenham shows the more customary E-plan, and Southall
Manor House Elizabethan picturesque grouping and half-
timbering at its best.

Only one piece of c16 church architecture deserves a
word : the brick tower of Littleton church. Two or three
more oddments and we have finished with the Tudor style.
They are the large barn belonging to the Hampton Court
Mews, the Hampton Court Stables with their boxes divided
(late in the c17) by Tuscan columns, and two school buildings : at Enfield, mid c16, and at Harrow, the original
nucleus of Harrow School. The date of this, however, is
1611, so that it really belongs to the Early Stuart Age, as incidentally does yet another school, Lord Knyvett's at Stanwell, 1624, a larger more expensive building originally than
Harrow, but now a village school.

Otherwise the first half of the c17 is – as everywhere – less
conspicuous for church architecture than for church monuments. Of the former Shepperton of 1614 and Great Stanmore of 1632, now in ruins, and the towers of Hillingdon
(1629) and Staines (1631) can be pointed out, of the latter
there is a series as good as any in the centre of London. The
richest display of funeral monuments altogether is at Harefield ; the little church is a storehouse far too little known. It
has its c17 – c18 fittings still fairly complete, notably a combined pulpit and reader's desk, and the chancel is cramful
of monuments ranging from the heavy four-poster *baldacchino* of the Countess of Derby (1636) to the early c19.
The church is in its wealth of costly monuments an exception in its part of the county. On the whole it is very noticeable that the riverside villages were more patronized by the
nobility and gentry than the churches in the rural N.

As far as the early c17 is concerned the most noteworthy
monuments are at Cranford (1612), Stanwell (1622), and
Hillingdon (1637), with kneeling figures facing each other,
at Hayes (1612), Uxbridge (1638), and Enfield (1646) with
figures semi-recumbent propped up on their elbows, at
Harefield (cf. above) and Stanmore (1639) with recumbent

figures, and at Hayes (1615), Greenford (1637), Ruislip (1638), Tottenham (1644), and Twyford (1637 and 1660) with busts in niches. It is in these latter particularly that the evolution from the robust Jacobean to the more courtly Carolean style can be followed impressively and instructively. The style of *Inigo Jones* makes its first appearance in the ornamental work of the Coston tomb at Greenford, that is in 1637.

Earlier than that, however, and yet far more severely classical is the *Inigo Jones* gateway now in the gardens of the Chiswick Villa. It was not originally at Chiswick but comes from Beaufort House, Chelsea. Also connected with the Inigo Jones style are the three most important mid-C17 houses in the county: Boston Manor, Brentford, with rainwater heads of 1622 and 1623, Swakeleys, Ickenham, of 1629–38, and Forty Hall of 1629–36. Swakeleys is Jacobean in plan and externally of a type earlier than, say, Raynham in Norfolk, that is essentially pre-Jones. Internally it has features of pure Jones style which must be by the King's Surveyor himself, if they are *c.* 1638, or else must be later. Boston Manor is puzzling; it has still steep straight Jacobean gables, a Jacobean porch, and wonderfully rich Late Jacobean plaster ceilings and fireplaces (only matched in Middlesex at The Priory, Tottenham, where they are dated 1620), but its windows and cornice are so classical that one can only assume a 'face-lifting' about 1650 or later. One gets the same impression at Forty Hall, where the exterior can hardly be much earlier than, say, Eltham Lodge, Woolwich, of 1663, whereas the fireplaces and ceilings fit the documentarily certain date of 1629–36 quite well.

In fact the style of the façades of Forty Hall comes already quite close to the accepted domestic style of the Wren period as exhibited in Middlesex, for example by other houses up Forty Hill or by York House, Twickenham, and the Rectory, Shepperton. Proportions, however, tend to become slimmer as we leave the Inigo period. There are many groups and terraces of houses in this style (The Butts, Brentford; The Mall, Chiswick; Gentlemen's Row, Enfield; Hampton Green; Square at Shepperton; Montpelier Row,

Twickenham). A few churches were also rebuilt in the early C18, in the plain, solid, comfortable style of the period : Isleworth (1705) (destroyed, alas, during the Second World War), Cranford (1710), and Twickenham (1713). Of church furnishings the most notable are those of Hampton Court Palace chapel, and then the luxurious communion rails of Littleton and Harefield of foreign origin, the equally sumptuous altar of Harefield, and the much more homely pulpit at Harrow (1708). No church monuments of first quality were erected in Middlesex during these years (Hornsey, 1680; Harlington, 1695; Hendon, 1703; Isleworth, 1705).

The outstanding piece of architecture in Middlesex between 1690 and the early C18 is of course the new parts of Hampton Court, designed by *Wren* and decorated by the court artists, some as brilliant as the woodcarver *Grinling Gibbons* and the smith *Tijou*, others as pedestrian as the painters *Verrio* and *Laguerre*. After Wren's death *William Kent* added here and there : the early Gothic Revival details of 1732 and some fireplaces, etc. *Kent* also appears in Lord Burlington's important job, the Chiswick Villa, so chaste outside and so sumptuous inside, which stands at the beginning of the Palladian style in England. It also stands at the beginning of the Picturesque Movement, as its gardens had all the characteristics of the new irregularity and whimsicality. It was a movement away from the grand, French formality of the gardens of Hampton Court, just as the villa itself was a demonstration against the Baroque, as represented in Middlesex on a scale comparable to Chiswick at Arnos Grove, Southgate, 1719, on a more courtly scale in the octagon of Orleans House, Twickenham (by *Gibbs*, 1730), and on the grandest scale at Canons, the Duke of Chandos's Palace of which now only the church of Little Stanmore with its wall paintings and funeral monuments evokes an echo.

Another early Palladian house is Marble Hill, Twickenham, another very early picturesque fragment Pope's grotto, also at Twickenham. *Isaac Ware* was one of the later representatives of Palladianism, and he designed Wrotham Park for Admiral Byng in 1754. At the same time *Horace Walpole* was remodelling his cottage at Strawberry Hill and converting it into a Gothic castle which was to become famous all over Europe. He was still busy on his Rococo-Gothic when *Robert Adam* converted the interiors of Osterley Park and Syon House in a brilliant neo-classical taste, whose delicacy and finesse is, however, not far from the Rococo. *Adam* also appears in Middlesex with the Shakespeare Temple in Garrick's garden at Hampton and the Child Monument at Heston of 1782. The sculptor there is *van Gelder* (also Hanwell, 1806). Other Georgian sculptors whose names appear are *Andrew Carpentier* (Little Stanmore), *W. Powell* (Hampton, 1731), *Rysbrack* (Twickenham), *Hayward* (? Harefield), *Flaxman* (Harrow, 1815), *Bacon* (West Drayton, 1793, 1800), *Bacon Jun.* (Harefield, Friern Barnet, etc.), *Westmacott* (Perivale, etc.), *Thomas Banks* (Ickenham, 1820).

Church building went on in the course of the C18 on a small scale (towers: Laleham, 1732, and Sunbury, 1752; churches: Teddington, 1753, Edgware, 1764, and Feltham, 1802). More activity started after the Church Building Act of 1818 had set aside one million pounds for the purpose. It was administered by Commissioners, and the type of Commissioners' Churches, cheap and Gothic, is easily recognizable in Middlesex, London, and everywhere. Their stock brick, their somewhat starved thinness, their papery walls with very little of projections or mouldings, their tall narrow windows, their interior galleries appear also in those churches of *c.* 1825–30 which were altered or rebuilt with other than Commissioners' money. Examples of the style in Middlesex are (amongst many) Staines, 1828, and Hampton, 1831.

Of Late Georgian secular architecture it is sufficient to mention the stately Uxbridge Town Hall of 1789 and a small number of private houses such as Grovelands at Southgate by *Nash* in the classical manner, Pitzhanger at Ealing by *Soane* in his inimitable personal manner, and Berrymead Priory, Acton, and Twyford Abbey (by *P. Atkinson*) in the Gothic manner. All these belong to the ten years between 1797 and 1807.

Now for the Victorian period, of course specially well

stocked in a county so close to London and so much part of
London. Church designs by most of the leading architects
(*Scott, Butterfield, Teulon, Brooks*) appear, but none of their
major works. The most characteristic examples of the
various stages of development between 1840 and 1900 are
St Andrew's, Kingsbury, brought there from Wells Street,
W 1, where it had been built and furnished as one of the fore-
most examples of Early Victorian ecclesiological zeal, then
All Souls, Harlesden, Willesden, 1879, by *Tarver*, with a
most original octagonal centre, and finally St Peter, Ealing,
by *Sedding* and *Wilson* with all the freedom and happy
imagination of the best in the nineties. The busiest architect
amongst the late Victorians and Edwardians was *Caroë*.
Good early *Morris* glass is at Southgate, and Victorian
sculpture worth recording at Harlington (*Lucas*) and Stanmore (*Boehm*).

In secular architecture High Victorian earnestness (and
gloom) reign supreme in the buildings of Harrow School.
Large Victorian villas can best be seen at Harrow Weald,
varying from the Harrow School style to the picturesque
and a little bogus half-timbered neo-Tudor of *Norman
Shaw's* Grims Dyke. *Norman Shaw* at his very best can be
studied in the plan and some of the buildings of Bedford
Park, Acton, the first of the garden suburbs, or rather the
first middle-class estate taking into consideration the ameni-
ties of free planning, variety in architecture, and the
relations of trees to buildings.

The garden suburb movement is represented in Middlesex from its beginnings at Bedford Park to its climax, the
Hampstead Garden Suburb by *Parker & Unwin*. The
centre of this is one of the most successful groups of buildings designed by *Lutyens*. Amongst architects busy in the
suburb *Baillie Scott* was the most original.

Finally the style of to-day is represented excellently by
Charles Holden in the many stations of the London Transport system, built chiefly between 1932 and 1937. The
most recent batch of stations was finished too late for
inclusion in this volume. The County Council is responsible
for a number of soundly planned schools, chiefly in the west

parts of the county. These were designed between the two wars by *W. T. Curtis & Burchett* and after the war by *C. G. Stillman*. None of his schools was completed in time to be mentioned in the following text, but two may at least be referred to here, the Junior and Infant Schools at East Bedfont (Hatton Road) and Twickenham (Powder Mill Lane).

Of modern public buildings the best is the Town Hall at Wembley begun in 1935. Modern churches have appeared at North Harrow and Watling, Hendon. Modern private houses are rare, but the comeliest type of prefabricated houses erected in England after the Second World War, that designed by *Frederick Gibberd*, has been chosen for various housing schemes. Factories are on the whole atrociously bad, Modernism at its showiest and silliest. The Guinness Brewery at Willesden (*see* Twyford) by *Sir Giles G. Scott* is an exception.

A final paragraph on the printed sources from which the information in the following pages is derived. By far the most important is the Middlesex volume of the *Royal Commission on Historical Monuments* which was published in 1937. This is very detailed and reliable as far as it goes, but does not take in any monuments later than 1714. So Mr M. S. Briggs's *Middlesex, Old and New*, 1934, is indispensable. In addition the *Victoria County History* (vol. 2), Lysons's *Environs of London* (1795) and *Parishes of Middlesex* (1800), the *Little Guide* (by J. B. Fish, 1906), *Kelly's Directory* (1899 and 1922), J. Tavernor Perry and others' *Memorials of Old Middlesex*, the volumes of *Country Life*, the *Transactions of the London and Middlesex Arch. Soc.*, the *Home Counties Magazine*, and much local literature have been used.

NOTE

MIDDLESEX

*

ACTON

The parish of Acton had 1,425 inhabitants in 1801, 3,150 in 1861, 17,000 in 1881, 37,000 in 1901, 71,000 in 1931, 68,000 in 1949. In the early C19 there was nothing but a village near where the parish church stands, and a few outlying hamlets and scattered houses and farms. During the second half of the C19 London swamped Acton and converted it into a suburb. Of the village nothing is left.

PARISH CHURCH ST MARY, first mentioned in 1240. Rebuilt 1865 by Messrs Francis, tower 1877. Many wall tablets were transferred from the old church. The only more ambitious ones are to Frances Trotman † 1698 (unusually handsome scrolly cartouche with angels' heads) and to Sir Robert Adair † 1790 (sarcophagus with above medallion to Lady Constance Adair † 1769). – PLATE. A flagon, chalice, and patens, all richly repoussé and ornamented, and all by *T. Bird*, said to have been given by Lady Dudley 1638–9. The flagon is the largest in the county.

ST MICHAEL, Bedford Park, *see* p. 25.

ST PETER, Southfield Road, 1914, by *W. A. Pite*, plain and reasonable Early Christian-type basilica without campanile.

ACTON HILL METHODIST CHURCH, 1907, by *Gordon & Gordon*, with a characteristic tower with a marked batter to the corner buttresses, and Gothic detail of the free style typical of about 1900.

TOWN HALL, High Street, 1939, by *R. Atkinson* and *W. G. Cross*, indifferent.

PASSMORE EDWARDS LIBRARY, High Street, 1899, by *M. Adams*, in this architect's typical rather bulging Baroque paraphrase of the accepted Tudor of the Late Victorian decades.

MINISTRY OF PENSIONS, The Vale, 1914, by *West*. A strictly utilitarian block, flat-roofed with quoins, impressive by sheer size.

ACTON TOWN L.T. STATION, 1933, one of the excellent station buildings by *Charles Holden*, functional yet not without elegance. This one has three two-light windows (cf., for example, Sudbury Hill, Sudbury Town, Northfields) and a long curved ground-floor canopy.

CHISWICK PARK L.T. STATION, 1933. The canopy here is in axis with the ticket hall which has a curved front with five large windows. Details such as mouldings are standard in all Mr Holden's later stations.

PARK ROYAL L.T. STATION, 1935–6, a more complex group with a circular ticket hall, a tall tower, and a curved shopping arcade. Not by Mr Holden; architects *Day, Welch, & Lander*.

ELECTROFLO FACTORY, Park Road, by *Adie, Button & Partners*, 1937. An example of the contemporary idiom without any embellishment whatsoever. Mr Richards calls it diagrammatic.

GOLDSMITHS' ALMSHOUSES, Churchfield Road East, 1811. A long two-storeyed yellow brick building with two wings coming forward towards the street. At their ends and in the centre modest Ionic features. The whole, thanks to two old cedar trees, makes a very pretty picture.

Of the large houses in the borough nothing survives except an OBELISK, Churchfield Road East, opposite Goldsmiths' Almshouses, erected to the memory of James Radcliffe, Earl of Derwentwater, beheaded in 1716 for his share in the 1715 Rebellion. The obelisk stood in the Derwentwater grounds in Horn Lane.

Of smaller houses the only specially enjoyable is BERRY-MEAD PRIORY, immediately behind the Town Hall, 1802–4 with additions of *c.* 1850; castellated Gothick with plastered walls and picturesquely asymmetrical interior.

Other houses:

THE ELMS, High Street, by Twyford Crescent. Georgian; red brick, five bays, with four giant pilasters carrying a pediment. Lower straight wings to left and right.

THE GRANGE and EAST ACTON HOUSE, East Acton Lane. Late Georgian.

ACTON GREEN. On the S side, in Hardwick Road, several small Late Georgian houses.

BEDFORD PARK, just N or Turnham Green Station. Archi- 63a tecturally the most important part of Acton. Bedford Park is the earliest of planned garden suburbs. Before its date there had been planned picturesque villages of the type of Edensor (Derbys.) or Blaise Hamlet, nr. Bristol, but no garden suburbs in our sense. The initiative came from Jonathan T. Carr (1845–1915). He chose *Norman Shaw* to be his designer. Work started in 1875. By *Norman Shaw* is the layout with its curved streets, its carefully preserved old trees, and its novel variety of detached, semi-detached, and terrace houses. The liking for red brick and the dominant motifs of the houses are also Shavian: Dutch gables or tile-hung gables, much use of decorative tiles, white window casements, white little oriels, cosy porches, etc. As early as 1880 William Morris commented on the 'quaint and pretty architecture' of Bedford Park and the preservation of trees. The *St James's Gazette* (17 Dec., 1881) was less complimentary, commenting on the houses of Bedford Park 'Where men may lead a chaste correct Aesthetical existence'. The arty character of the early population of Bedford Park is familiar from G. K. Chesterton's *The Man who was Thursday*.

To go into architectural detail, some of the houses are by *Shaw*, others by *M. Adams* and *E. J. May*, that is the young *Shaw* followers of the seventies whom one also meets in Chelsea and Hampstead. Yet other houses by *E. Godwin* (of Whistler's house in Chelsea). *Shaw* kept for himself the principal group of church, inn, and bank. The TABARD INN is at the corner of Bath Road and the Common. It has tile-hung gables and very original shallow-curved completely glazed bay windows. To its left follows a sedate Dutch-looking brick house and then the BANK with a ground floor all windows and an upper floor with a repetition of *Shaw's* favourite motif of Sparrowe's

House at Ipswich. Opposite is the church of ST
MICHAEL AND ALL ANGELS, 1880. It forms one composition with the parish hall, begun 1887, by *M. Adams.*
Outside the church *Norman Shaw* is at his very best, in-
exhaustible in his inventiveness. The combination of a
Perpendicular ground floor with upper features taken
from the C17 and C18 comes off most happily. The red
brickwork gable with cross and clock, the charming lantern over the crossing, and the bold white timber balustrade at the foot of the high roof should be specially
noticed. The interior is light and spacious. Against the W
wall a painting of Peter's Denial of Christ by a Dutch follower of *Caravaggio.*

Of individual houses three in SOUTH PARADE deserve
mention: No. 1, Melbourne House with Bedford House
behind it in The Avenue, the survivors of a small group
of Georgian houses N of the Green; No. 2, a modern
newcomer, by *Dugdale & Ruhemann,* 1938; and, last but
not least, No. 14, by *Voysey,* 1889 (with an added lower
wing of 1894). This is one of *Voysey's* first houses, designed evidently in conscious opposition to the red-brick
cosiness of the suburb. It is rough-cast and shows proudly
its bare grey walls and the robust stone dressings of the
horizontal windows. The far projecting eaves are carried
on elegant thin iron brackets.

ALPERTON

L.T. STATION by *Charles Holden,* 1933. One of that excellent set of designs produced in 1932 and 1933 which
did so much to establish the modern idiom in Britain.
Modest, functional, yet not without elegance. Com-
parisons with such other Piccadilly Line stations as Sudbury Town, Sudbury Hill, Oakwood will repay; the same
motifs are every time subtly modified (the right mixture
of standardization and variation).

ASHFORD

One of the least rewarding Middlesex villages.

PARISH CHURCH ST MATTHEW, 1858–65, by *Butterfield*, but with little to disclose the power of the designer of All Saints, Margaret Street, London. The exterior might have been more eventful if the tower, standing s of the s aisle, virtually on its own, had been completed as originally intended by the architect. The bald interior has little to recommend it. – PLATE. Chalice by *E. Pearce*, 1711; Paten, 1715; large Chalice and Paten, 1812. – BRASS to W. Goode † 1522 and wife. The site of the Norman chancel E of the present church is marked by a floor slab preserved in the churchyard.

ST MICHAEL, Fordbridge Road, 1928, by *Sir Giles G. Scott*. Incomplete.

CLOCKHOUSE FARM, NE of the church in Clockhouse Road. A brick front behind two magnificent monkey-puzzle trees, the side front of the house half-timbered.

WELSH CHARITY SCHOOL, 1857, by *Henry Clutton*. Gothic, not Clutton's French Renaissance. A long stone front with ten steep gabled dormer windows and three-light windows. The centre with a richer Gothic entrance; influence from Ruskin's favourite Venetian. In the entrance hall a niche with a life-size figure of Albert Edward Prince of Wales (later Edward VII) as a handsome boy in a kind of *Veronese* dress, surrounded by Gothic foliage.

BENTLEY HEATH

Outside the gates of Wrotham Hall the Church of HOLY TRINITY, 1865, by *S. S. Teulon*, rather raw red brick with dark and light brick window arches and an odd little bellcote, and a row of cottages of 1864. Cottages and church erected by the second Earl of Stratford.

BRENTFORD

Although Brentford is the county-town of Middlesex, it has no county hall of the representational kind that all other counties possess. The county council meets in London, and

the quarter sessions are held in London. The combined
population of Brentford and Chiswick in 1947 was 59,000.
Brentford's landmark is the MINARET of the Grand Union
Waterworks erected in 1867 close to the entry of the road
from Chiswick into Brentford. The village (or rather the
villages of Old Brentford and further w New Brentford)
then develop along the road rather than along the Thames.
The church stands on the road, over a quarter of a mile
from the river. The little market square (with a C19 TOWN
HALL, refronted recently) is on the opposite side of the
road. The river Brent runs close to market and church, and
the ford was between them.

PARISH CHURCH ST LAWRENCE. The W tower is C15,
low, of Kentish rag, with diagonal buttresses and embattled. The body of the church dates from 1764, a plain
brick box, probably designed locally. The interior was re-
done in 1889 with deplorable tall octagonal E.E. timber
piers. – FONT. C15, plain. – PLATE. Large Chalice and
Paten, 1689; Flagon by *D. Willaume*, 1709; two chalices,
1795, by *R. Makepeace*. – MONUMENTS. Damaged miniature brass to H. Redman † 1528 (kneeling in profile with
Trinity higher up in centre). Redman was Chief Mason
of the King's Works and probably the designer of the
original Hampton Court. – John Middleton and wife †
1628, wall monument with figures kneeling opposite each
other. – Thos. Hardwick † 1829 (the architect), neo-
Greek tablet with very elongated urns on the short
flanking pilasters.

ST GEORGE (by-the-gasholder), 1887, by *A. Blomfield*,
tower 1913. Against E wall of aisle Last Supper by *Zoffany*, coming from the old church of *c.* 1770: rather a
weak and woolly picture.

ST FAITH, Windmill Road, 1907, by *Bodley*. The interior
has the austerity of a friars' church, long nave, straight-
ended chancel, piers without capitals, pointed arches,
plain clerestory and wagon-roof with tie-beams across
(all thoughtfully and feelingly detailed).

THE BUTTS. The best part of the village, just N of the
market square, a short street leading into a spacious rather

rural square with pollarded lime-trees. Of the houses the best are BEAUFORT HOUSE, *c.* 1700, and No. 26, somewhat later.

The main N road is Half Acre with NEW GROVE MANSIONS, neo-Greek, with Doric porch on the r., and then on the same side CLIFDEN HOUSE (Museum), much larger than the others, seven bays, pediment, little Ionic porch connected into one composition with the window above, second quarter C18.

By the Thames FERRY HOUSE, Ferry Lane, late C17. Much added to.

Farther away from the village are the larger properties, chiefly Gunnersbury on the NE and Boston Manor on the NW.

GUNNERSBURY PARK. The greatest attraction is now the park. Of the house built by Inigo Jones's pupil *John Webb* nothing is visible any longer. The two main houses side by side are C19, the one further S by *Sidney Smirke c.* 1834, the other one a little grander looks *c.* 1850, when the Rothschilds bought the estate. The detail here is going rather weakly Dixhuitième. *Smirke's* detail is still classical, as is that of the dignified orangery SW of the houses. NW a large temple by the circular pond, with a tall Tuscan portico *in antis*, dating probably from the time when Princess Amelia, George III's aunt, lived here (estate bought 1760). E of the houses a sham-medieval lodge (damaged in the war) with a garden with castellated walls. Some of the planting of the park is supposed still to be *Kent's*.

BOSTON MANOR. A plain rectangle of four by five win- 46b dows, dated 1622 on three rainwater heads and 1623 on a plaster ceiling inside. The property belonged to the wife of Sir William Reade at the time. The exterior is brick with three plain straight gables on the long and two on the short sides. Niches in the gables. Three storeys with a modillion cornice above the second. On the NE side an elaborate Jacobean porch. Inside equally elaborate plaster 43 ceilings in three rooms, and an elaborate fireplace. While 42 these are typical of their period, in fact if anything a little conservative, with their close strapwork, leathery cartouches and arabesques, the outside windows on the ground floor have triangular (NE and SW) and segmental pediments. There is a decided contrast between this quiet, harmonious, and correct Italian motif and the Jacobean character of the rest. None but Inigo Jones himself would have used such pediments and such a cornice in England in 1622. They became accepted only after the Restoration. It should therefore be considered whether the house was not externally altered when it passed to the Clitherow family in 1670. At that time outbuildings, for example a pigeon house, were erected to the N.

No. 71 BOSTON MANOR ROAD. Two good houses of *c.* 1700, one of them with a Roman Doric porch.

L.T. BOSTON MANOR STATION, by *C. Holden*, 1934, with its somewhat jazzy tower not as successful as the neighbouring slightly earlier stations at Acton Town and Northfields.

CHISWICK

Old and New Brentford, with which Chiswick now forms a single borough (population in 1949, 60,000), are treated separately under Brentford.

The parish of Chiswick had 3,275 inhabitants in 1801, 6,500 in 1861, 15,600 in 1881. It is the typical development of the Outer Circle of Greater London. The change from village to suburb belongs to the second third of the C19. What distinguishes Chiswick from, say, Ealing or Acton nearby, is that of its existence independent of London much more survives, and what survives is of a high quality, aesthetically, historically, and picturesquely. The centre was the village church close to the river. From it Georgian and earlier houses extended NW for some 150 yards and NE along the river for half a mile to join up with the Hammersmith Mall. Another ribbon of Georgian development started from Kew Bridge and went SW (Strand on the Green). Between these two extended the grounds of a few large houses (Grove House, Sutton Court, etc.). Only one of these now remains : Chiswick House.

PARISH CHURCH ST NICHOLAS. First visitation of a church at Chiswick 1252. Rebuilt C15; the W tower by a vicar of 1416–35. It is of three stages with diagonal buttresses and battlemented top. Rebuilt 1882–4 by *J. L. Pearson*, who incorporated into his chancel the windows made by *Burges* for a projected rebuilding in 1861. Their robust design contrasts with *Pearson's* sensitive and competent neo-Perpendicular. Comfortably broad aisles, nearly as wide and nearly as high as the nave. – PLATE. Chalice on baluster stem, 1747; set of 1785 given by the Duchess of Devonshire. – Of MONUMENTS the most interesting is in the S chancel chapel: Sir Thomas Chaloner † 1615; alabaster with Sir Thomas and his wife kneeling and facing each other across a praying-desk. They kneel under a semicircularly projecting canopy with curtains hanging down and held up by two bearded armed servants. Pyramidal top with small standing allegorical figure. – Above the S door Thomas Bentley † 1780, by the younger *Scheemakers*, casket-shaped, with portrait-head and cherubs with inverted porches l. and r. In tower Sir Richard Taylor † 1716, Charles Holland, the actor † 1769, by *W. Tyler*, pyramidal epitaph with bust and inscription by Garrick, and others of C17 and C18. – In the churchyard urn on tall pedestal for William Hogarth † 1764, and little mausoleum in Soanian style for P. L. de Loutherbourg the painter, designer of moving scenery and panoramas, and faith healer, † 1812. – Buried in the church are also Lord Burlington and William Kent; *see* below.

ST MARY MAGDALEN, Bennett Street, 1848, by *J. C. Sharpe*; later enlarged. Modest with odd little polygonal turret on the N; tasteless but jolly.

CHRIST CHURCH, Turnham Green, 1843, by *Scott & Moffatt*; chancel later. An early work of the most successful Victorian architect, who proves himself already in this essay in E.E. interpretation a competent if uninspired performer.

OUR LADY OF GRACE AND ST EDWARD, Chiswick High Road, corner of Duke's Avenue, 1904, by *J. Kelly*.

Dignified red-brick front of Roman C17 type. Steeple by *Sir Giles G. Scott*, 1930.

CHISWICK HOUSE. It is a matter of taste whether one regards the grand manner of Chiswick House or the intimate manner of the Mall as the chief attraction of Chiswick. Originally most of the villages around London exhibited both these qualities (cf. Kenwood and Church Row at Hampstead, Marble Hill and Montpelier Row at Twickenham, etc.), but few now can vie with Chiswick for aesthetic merits of both kinds. The 3rd Earl of Burlington (1694–1753) had returned from Italy in 1719, taking home a great enthusiasm for Palladio's noble and cool style, and *William Kent* (1684–1748), a young painter who was to be his chief protégé and executant. The Chiswick estate had been acquired by the 1st Earl in 1675. There was a large, irregular Jacobean house on it. The 3rd Earl began remodelling the grounds in 1717 if not a little earlier. The villa was started early in the twenties w of the old house, and in 1726 work on its interior decoration was going on. *Kent* designed the decoration, but as for the villa itself it was most probably Burlington's own unaided effort. Its strictly Palladian style is due to Burlington's studies at Vicenza, caused in the first place, it seems, by an interest kindled in him by *Colen Campbell*, the author of *Vitruvius Britannicus* (vol. I, 1715). The garden we owe to *Kent*. It was the first ambitious design in the new style of the Picturesque.

55a   Chiswick Villa was originally not as isolated as it is now. It was a modern addition to the Jacobean building and just as such perhaps specially demonstrative of the change of taste. A suite of three rooms by *Burlington* was the connecting link. Its low walls have crenellated tops with ball finials, an unclassical motif, but one found in *Palladio*. It is repeated slightly further to the E, where a gateway from Beaufort House, Chelsea, was erected which was attributed to *Inigo Jones* himself, the one native architect whom Burlington could fully accept. The gateway is rusticated and has severe Tuscan columns supporting a Doric frieze and pediment. Inscriptions record that it was built

by *Inigo Jones* in 1621 and given by Sir Hans Sloane
(Lord of the Manor of Chelsea and originator of the British
Museum's natural history collection) to Lord Burlington
in 1738. The villa itself is a rectangle of nearly square
shape, with an octagonal central hall surrounded by three
rooms on the entrance side, four on the garden side, and
two large ones connecting the two suites.

The house is evidently modelled on *Palladio's* famous
Villa Capra or Villa Rotonda, but it is by no means a copy.
Recent research (Professor Wittkower) has in fact proved
that Burlington assembled details from various Palladian
sources, the N front with its three Venetian windows from
Scamozzi's Villa Pisani, the semicircular windows, the
side elevations, and certain features inside from
Scamozzi's Villa Molin, the rusticated ground floor and
the two-column deep portico on the S front from Palladio's Villa Malcontenta (or Mereworth, or Gibbs's St
Martin's in the Fields) and so on. More important than
this variety of features of generally Palladian character is
it to point to those in which Burlington (and Kent) de-
viated from their pure originals in the Baroque sense of
their period. The N staircase leading up to the portico is
far more spectacular and complex in design than Palladio
would have tolerated, the two flanking statues of Palladio
and Inigo Jones (presumably by *Scheemakers*) are highly
melodramatic in attitudes and draperies, the break in the
evenness of the spacing of the columns in the portico is
derived from the French C 17, and the four identical porticoes of the Villa Capra are replaced by only one. With
the same intention of replacing all-round symmetry by
more determined direction, the interior has not Palladio's
four identical rooms in the corners of the square block,
but square rooms on one side and round ones on the other.
The Gallery, moreover, has two apsidal ends, a feature
not to be found in the Villa Rotonda.

While the general design of the building no doubt belongs to Burlington himself, it may be assumed that Kent
influenced him in introducing such Baroque modifica-
tions. The interior decoration is wholly *Kent's*; see such

M.—2

characteristic motifs as the bold relief of the ceiling of the
SE corner room and its fireplace, the scrolly, heavily gar-
landed fireplaces of the NW and SW rooms, etc.

After Lord Burlington's death the property went to his
son-in-law, the 4th Duke of Devonshire. It remained in
the possession of the family until the Chiswick Borough
Council acquired it in 1929. The 5th Duke employed
James Wyatt in 1788 to add wings, in keeping with the
central block. That necessitated the sacrifice of Burlington's central E and W sitting-rooms. Wyatt's E wing incorporates Kent's drawing-room in the little wing connecting the former Jacobean house with the Burlington
Villa. At the time of writing the Borough Council had
just begun pulling down these wings – an ill-advised
compliment to the purity of Burlington's original design.

Burlington's gardens were originally laid out by *Bridgman* and *Kent*, the two originators of Picturesque landscape gardening. Bridgman's connexion with Chiswick is
only assumed on the strength of Whately's testimony
(1801) and of similarity of style between Chiswick and the
original layout of Stowe. The essence of the Chiswick plan
which makes it typical of the first stage of Picturesque layout is that the main avenues were still all straight and that
winding paths are introduced only in the thickets between
them. Their windings also are not as gentle as later on,
but rather of a Rococo capriciousness. The grounds
which had been for long in a neglected state are now in
course of restoration. Even as it was at the time of
writing, some of the main axes could be traced, especially
the short avenue with its vases, sphinxes, and busts facing
the portico, and the long and grand avenue on the N
which originally had four lines of presumably lime or
horse-chestnut trees. This avenue leads to a semicircle
with statuary from which three straight radiating avenues
crossed the wilderness to NW, N, and SW. Only the latter
remains and ends in a rusticated little very Kentian pavilion, now housing a bust of Napoleon. Due E from the
semicircle is a sub-centre with a solitary Tuscan column
on which a copy of the Venus de Medici used to stand.

It corresponds to an obelisk due W of the semicircle. This stood in a basin and had on its left the 'Bagno', according to Colin Campbell's *Vitruvius Britannicus* Burlington's earliest design, done in 1717, a miniature version of the Pantheon type, round and domed with an Ionic four-column portico. Of the garden furnishings there is now only one more obelisk in the SW corner of the estate close to the Kentian entrance from Burlington Lane. The major landscape effects are now more easily recognized than the smaller *finesses*, namely the long mount on the SW to hide the villa from the lane and enable visitors to see the Thames, and the artificial river running N–S, from which the earth for the mount was excavated. It is this river with its Palladian bridge (probably by *Wyatt*) and its grotto seat at the S end that gives us now the most vivid idea of the picturesqueness of the original design.

In 1812 the Duke of Devonshire bought an estate adjoining on the E. This is where some C17 walls still remain, and where a magnificent avenue of horse-chestnut trees stretches along, and a conservatory faces a large amphitheatre of flower beds. The alterations and additions are often ascribed to *Paxton*, but there seems to be no documentary proof of this.

CHISWICK MALL. The impression is still almost wholly 53 that of the riverside village for wealthy Londoners. The river is unembanked here; hence the small front gardens between street and water. Coming from the Hammersmith boundary we pass SWAN HOUSE, NORFOLK HOUSE (early C19, taller than the others and more pretentious), then, after some indifferent C 20, the splendid group of *c.* 1730 façades: MORTON HOUSE, STRAWBERRY HOUSE (with a pretty late C18 porch on the slenderest of columns), WALPOLE HOUSE (pure *c.* 1700 on the garden side; excellent railings and gate on the river side). After this group a stretch of no importance except for GREENASH, built 1882 by *J. Belcher* for Sir John Thornycroft (whose famous wharf lay just S of the church) in a wildly Shavian manner, with its high double gable breaking all Georgian good manners concerning skyline.

Off the Mall in Chiswick Lane a plain terrace of four three-storeyed C18 houses called MAWSON ROW. Between Chiswick Lane and the church another good group: THAMES VIEW and LINGARD HOUSE *c.* 1700, originally one house, SAÏD HOUSE, Victorian but Georgianized, EYNHAM HOUSE and BEDFORD HOUSE, also originally one, with one common four-bay pediment, mid C18 with later additions (and a Gothick gazebo in the garden), WOODROFFE HOUSE, late C17 and forbiddingly severe, and the later, cement-rendered VICARAGE.

CHURCH STREET. A similarly rewarding walk is from the Vicarage N to Burlington Lane, now wide and of the character of a bypass road: VINE HOUSE on the r., LATIMER HOUSE on the l., with its attached pavilion used on the ground floor as a coach-house. Opposite some earlier cottages and the weatherboarded BURLINGTON COURT. More Georgian houses on the r., and on the l. the six recessed cottages of LAMBS YARD.

CHISWICK SQUARE. Off Burlington Lane, only a few yards W of Church Street. It is a kind of forecourt to BOSTON HOUSE. The whole group is of late C17 date, a composition like The Albany or Derby House in London, complete with the iron gates to Boston House.

HOGARTH HOUSE, Hogarth Lane; late C17, in bad repair, but to be restored.

STRAND ON THE GREEN. Another riverside ribbon of the same period as the Mall, more intimate, because instead of a road there is only a pathway between the houses and the water. The houses are on the whole more modest too, chiefly cottages now resolutely prettified. The best group is Nos 64–8 with ZOFFANY HOUSE and SPRINGFIELD HOUSE. Nos 52–5 is a taller more self-possessed early C19 group with pediment. The fat E.E. railway bridge cuts oddly across the lane and its houses.

Of the hamlet by Sutton Court only one cottage, LITTLE SUTTON COTTAGE, Sutton Lane, and a row of very plain former ALMSHOUSES next to it exists.

CHISWICK HIGH ROAD. Little of any note survives: Nos 1–21 are of *c.* 1830–40, a unified composition with giant

pilasters at the ends and in the centre, a total of nineteen
bays. AFTON HOUSE by Duke's Avenue is an example of
the wealthier house of *c*. 1800. An early C19 house in
HEATHFIELD TERRACE faces Turnham Green.

TOWN HALL, Turnham Green, 1876, by *W. J. Trehearne*;
Italianate.

CHISWICK BRIDGE, 1933, the art applied by *Sir Herbert
Baker*.

CHISWICK STATION (Southern Section), by *Tite*, 1849;
a typical late-classical, plain and decent station building
with a Tuscan porch. KEW BRIDGE STATION is similar
in character. CHISWICK PARK L. T. STATION, 1933;
see Acton.

SANDERSON'S FACTORY, now Alliance Assurance, Barley
Mow Passage, E of Turnham Green, 1902, by *Charles
Voysey*. His only factory building, and a clean and charming design. White glazed brick with ground floor and
dressings in dark blue brick. Large horizontal segment-
headed windows, and buttresses ending with flat 'mortar-
board' projections like wooden bedsteads in the Arts and
Crafts taste. A tall parapet curves gracefully between
them.

COWLEY

The village does not to-day appear as a coherent whole. The
church is separated from the main street by the railway, and
the main street runs without noticeable break from Uxbridge
(or rather West Hillingdon) into Yiewsley.

PARISH CHURCH ST LAURENCE, a small flint rubble
building of C12 with a C13 chancel and a timber bellcote
of 1780. The interior has a white ceiled roof with king-
posts. Of the windows the three lancets at the E end and
the typical two-light window of *c*. 1300–20 in the S wall
are worth mentioning. The two-storeyed W gallery is
recent and quite picturesque. – PEWS in chancel and
SCREEN with some C15 or early C16 fragments. – PLATE.
Flagon, 1709; two salvers, 1723, 1739. – BRASS to Walter
Pope † 1505 and wives on N wall of chancel.

The main street has a number of nice if not outstanding
houses: (from N to S): COWLEY GROVE, plain Late-
Georgian; COWLEY COTTAGE, early C 18; COWLEY
HOUSE, about the same time with additions; THE
BEECHES, THE OLD HOUSE, with pretty late C18 door-
way.

Further S at Cowley Peachey opposite each other THE OLD
COTTAGE and BARNACRE, both half-timbered. The
early C16 E side of the Old Cottage is specially characteristic.

Also at Cowley Peachey, on the main West-Drayton–Uxbridge road, four modest brick cottages of 1947, uncommonly finely detailed, with the typical slight roof-
pitch of the 1940s. By *F. R. S. Yorke, Rosenberg &
Mardall*.

CRANFORD

Cranford House, a seat of the Earls of Berkeley, built mostly
c. 1710–20, was pulled down shortly before the Second
World War. So the church lies now all on its own, with only
the stables close to it, and reached from the village by a drive
and across a humped bridge. There is great charm in this
solitude.

PARISH CHURCH ST DUNSTAN. There is also great charm
in the church itself, an aisleless little building of an all-
over length of less than 70 ft. It has a C15 W tower and
chancel of flint rubble; but the top storey of the tower is
brick-built of 1716. The nave also is of brick, with a
doorway with an intermittent ashlar surround and a
heavy big keystone. Inside there is nothing of architectural distinction, but a number of monuments, so many
of them as to dominate the impression completely. In
the chancel Sir Roger Aston and wife, 1611–13, by *William Cure*, Master Mason to the King, reconstructed
standing wall monument, tripartite on the Venetian
window scheme. In the arched centre kneels Sir Roger
(who was Keeper of the King's Wardrobe) and opposite
him his two wives. Two daughters kneel in each of the

outer compartments, and a fifth lies small in front of her
father. The monument is of 'alabaster, tuche, rance, and
white and black marble', as stated in the agreement. –
Against the other chancel wall is the tomb-chest of Elizabeth, widow of Sir Thomas Berkeley † 1635. She is por-
trayed in white marble lying in her shroud. A little to the
W in the chancel the simple tablet to Thomas Fuller (of
the *Worthies*) † 1661, vicar of Cranford. In the nave
against the N wall a large epitaph to William Smythe,
who married a Berkeley and died in 1720: a portrait
medallion with two seated cherubs at the foot of a large
inscription plate flanked by columns and with a shell top
(cf. Bishop Fowler, Hendon). Opposite an equally large
plain monument to Pelsant Reeves † 1727. – E of this a
Spanish early C17 PAINTING of the Immaculate Conception brought by a Rector of the church from Cuzco,
Peru. – STAINED GLASS. E window with Crucifixion,
etc., by *Kempe*, 1895. – Amongst the VESTMENTS of the
church is a mid C17 Chasuble and a C17 purple Cope
with thick floral embroidery. – PLATE. Chalice and
Paten, 1639; Flagon, 1649; Paten, 1650; Paten, 1698.
Some minor Late Georgian houses (Stansfield House,
Avenue House, Sheepcote House) are situated along the
road from Cranford Village to Cranford church.
(COACH AND HORSES INN, Bath Road. C18 yellow brick
with added C19 wing. MTCP.)

DYRHAM PARK

House of various dates; the noteworthy part is to the E,
with a curiously heavy detached portico of Tuscan
columns and far projecting timber pediment. It must be
c. 1800 and looks as if it might be inspired by Inigo Jones's
St Paul's, Covent Garden, or direct by Vitruvius's description of the Tuscan temple. The gateway on the St
Albans road is monumental with an arch flanked by
Tuscan columns and a low urn on top silhouetted against
the sky. The date 1736 usually assigned to it is too early.
Its style is of the third third of the C18. S of the gate

outside the grounds is KNIGHTSLAND FARM, a good C16
farmhouse faced with brick in the C18. Inside on the first
floor late C16 wall paintings of folk-art naïveté. They
represent the story of the Prodigal Son.

EALING

The borough of Ealing now includes Greenford, Hanwell,
Northolt, and Perivale (qq.v.). Its total population in 1949
was 119,000. The parish of Ealing had 5,000 inhabitants in
1801, 12,000 in 1861, 25,750 in 1881, 47,500 in 1901,
117,700 in 1931. These figures show that Ealing was a large
independent village in the early C19 and that London began
to submerge it after 1850. It shared this fate with its neigh-
bours, especially Acton, but compared with Acton Ealing
was luckier in that its chief urban growth took place away
from the old village. This lies s of Broadway from the
Green to St Mary's Church, at right angles to the main
present-day artery, that is the Uxbridge Road and Broadway. This development explains why Ealing has two
central parish churches.

PARISH CHURCH ST MARY. Of medieval origin, rebuilt
1866–73 by *Teulon*. An unfortunate end to the pleasant
backwater of Ealing, N of it. Teulon's building replaces
a modest red brick box of 1729–39 which must have
looked just right in its position. The new church is
domineering and coarse (some may say robust) with its
elephantine somewhat institutional-looking tower, its
large bare London stock brick walls and insensitive Early
Gothic detail. The interior is also large and bare with galleries on three sides and tall iron shafts of stove-pipe type
to support the open timber roof. – PLATE. Seal-topped
Spoon, 1598; Chalice with unusually elaborate repoussé
decoration (Holy Family, Woman of Samaria), 1674;
similar Paten, Flagon, and two dishes, 1684; Ciborium,
1717; Almsdishes, 1773. – MONUMENTS. Some wall
tablets of late C18 and early C19 dates, especially in the w
parts. In the nave on the N wall brass to R. Amondesham
of c. 1490.

CHRIST CHURCH, Broadway, 1852, by *Sir George Gilbert Scott*. Kentish rag and Bath stone, with w spire, ambitious and dull, of correct Late E.E. style, that is with geometrical tracery and plenty of naturalistic carving of capitals and corbels inside. *G. F. Bodley* added some quiet decoration.

ST PETER, N end of Mount Park Road, designed 1889, begun 1892, by *J. D. Sedding* and his pupil *H. Wilson*. A very original design with an enormous w window divided into three lights, not by mullions but by buttresses. The tracery shows the revived sympathy of Art Nouveau for the flowing lines of the early C14 Decorated. Narrow turrets l. and r. of the window with spirelets. Tall steep-pitched roof. Along the roof runs at half its height a series of depressed arches connecting turrets. These turrets are in fact the top ends of the piers inside sticking up through the roof, a logically and aesthetically convincing novel idea. Interior spacious with aisles holding a gallery on low wide depressed arches. The gallery has E.E. openings. An E tower with spire was originally planned.

PITZHANGER MANOR (Ealing Public Library), in Walpole Park, just S of Broadway. Bought by *John Soane* in 1801 and built for himself. The exterior completed 1802. The s wing was allowed to remain from the previous building which had been designed by Soane's master, *George Dance* the Younger, in 1770. The wing is very plain outside and contains inside two rooms, the dining-room and (above) the billiard-room. Both have delicate stucco decoration of Adam style. The dining-room has on the N an apsed niche between the two doors. Soane pulled down the rest of the house and gave its new centre a grandiose scale of which he alone in England was capable. The contrast between the actual size of a small villa of only three bays and the scale of the design is surprising every time one compares an illustration of the house with the original. Also typical of Soane is the contrast between the bare walls and the grand Ionic order of Portland stone set in front of it like a screen. The idea of the detached order with strongly projecting entablature over each column came from Adam's early design at Kedleston, Derbyshire, and of course originally from the Arch of Constantine in Rome. Soane had used it himself just before in the Lothbury Court of the Bank of England. The entablatures carry standing terra-cotta statues (as they do at the Bank) placed against a windowless attic half the height of the ground floor. The centre is raised yet higher. No roof shows: Balustrades emphasize the severe rectangularity of the design. Inside, the entrance hall is tiny, but full of interest with its sequence of a tunnel vault, a raised lantern, and another tunnel vault. The best rooms are the front parlour (now the Librarian's Room) in which a very shallow dome is supported in the corners by four caryatids. The caryatids stand flat against the wall, and the elegant segmental arches with their spandrels touching the corners in a point have all the brittle thinness and precision so typical of Soane. The back parlour has an equally shallow groined vault continued at the back in a flat segmental tunnel vault. The exterior towards the park on the w has instead of columns flat strips without bases or capitals. Towards N where the new lending library now stands Soane had a court with an exedra to display as an artificial ruin some antique architectural fragments. In the basement was the Monk's Parlour. All these features Soane was to repeat or develop in his later town house in Lincoln's Inn Fields. He sold the Ealing manor in 1811.

L.T. STATIONS. EALING COMMON of c. 1930 is of the type of the Morden Line Extension, no longer period-revival, but in its bare concrete forms a little bleak compared with the immediately following NORTHFIELDS, 1933. This is the type of Sudbury Hill, Sudbury Town, Acton Town, etc., elegant without being fussy, a straight ground-floor canopy and the higher ticket hall block at right angles to it with one large, wide window. Both stations are by *Charles Holden*, Northfields in co-operation with *S. A. Heaps*.

HOUSES. From Pitzhanger Manor s to the church there still survives a stretch never systematically rebuilt. It exhibits a variety of plain Georgian houses (Greenacres, St Mary's near the Manor House, Ealing Court Mansions, Westfield House by the church) and of early C19 classical, Gothic, and Jacobean features. THE PARK, a side street to the E, was laid out by *S. Smirke* in 1846. There are also a few cottages of C17 and C18 to S, N, and NW of the church.

Apart from this centre of Ealing village there were nuclei of houses by Haven Green, on Hanger Hill, and at Little Ealing. At Haven Green nothing survives, on Hanger Hill is OLD COURT and BEAU SEJOUR (largish with a porch of late C18), at Little Ealing opposite each other two convents, originally Rochester House and Place House.

ROCHESTER HOUSE, simple red-brick block of six bays with two storeys and attic storey. The windows are segment-headed.

PLACE HOUSE (or EALING PARK), late C18 or early C19. Low and long; nine bays with pediment over the centre and an Ionic one-storeyed colonnade all along. The gardens were famous in Victorian times. The remaining octagonal garden pavilion is Georgian.

EAST BEDFONT

East Bedfont although on the main London–Staines road has been lucky in avoiding the complete destruction of its former village character. The road only skirts the spacious Green, and the small church lies comfortably back from the traffic, screened by plenty of trees and partly hidden by a perfectly crazy outsized display of topiary (old yews trimmed into initials, the date 1704, and peacocks).

PARISH CHURCH ST MARY. Nave as well as chancel incorporate enough of the Early Norman building to prove that this was of the rather N than S English type of, say, Escomb, County Durham, very long, narrow, and aisleless. In the N chancel and S nave walls Norman windows with their deep internal splays remain. So does the Norman doorway of two orders, one with simple leaf, the other with zigzag motifs. The chancel arch also is Norman (the only one in Middlesex) with zigzag decoration.

The chancel was extended in the C15, a shapeless N transept added in 1829, and in 1865 a S porch and a pretty S tower with its upper part of timber. The building is of ironstone rubble with ashlar dressings. The roofs are C15. The most important feature of the interior is a C13 recess of two bays with pointed arches, the one in the E corner of the N wall of the nave, the other round the corner in the E wall. In the recess are two WALL PAINTINGS of the late C13, representing the Last Judgment (Christ in Glory surrounded by angels; placed in a quatrefoil frame, the Resurrection of the Dead below) and the Crucifixion. Both paintings are in red line on red background. There is nothing else in the country to emulate them – no doubt London work. A small Flemish RELIEF of the Crucifixion of *c.* 1530 is in the nave. In the chancel (W wall) an unusual MONUMENT: a wooden panel darkly painted with coat of arms to record W. Weldish † 1640. – PLATE. Chalice and Paten by *J. L. Langford*, 1719; Paten on foot, given 1756.

To the E of the church a few nice Georgian houses; to the SW, No. 735 in the STAINES ROAD, a two-gabled Tudor brick house, redone *c.* 1700; to the N PATES MANOR FARM, C16 with later additions and a weatherboarded barn. Outside Bedfont on the Staines Road towards Homerton is the FAIRHOME ESTATE, by *C. Hewitt*, 1934, a nice neo-Georgian group of low-rental houses, one- and two-storeyed with Dutch gables. A well in the centre and a community hall at the back.

EASTCOTE

PARISH CHURCH ST LAURENCE, Bridle Road, 1932–3, by *Sir William Nicholson*. Brick; a pleasant interior with Tuscan columns, round arches, and wagon-roof.

The centre of Eastcote is the crossing of Eastcote High Road and Field End Road. Close to the crossing are several bigger houses, notably EASTCOTE HOUSE (an insignificant whitewashed Georgian exterior covers some C16 and C17 remains inside) and HAYDON HALL, Joel Street (a sound late C17 brick house of seven bays, with hipped roof and simply adorned doorways.

Towards E, W, and especially S many good farmhouses and outbuildings survive, scattered amid modern domestic development.

In the High Road E of the main crossing EASTCOTE GRANGE, large, gabled, and weatherboarded, with C16 and C17 work and much recent restoring; then RAMIN, with a half-timbered overhang towards the street; and in Catlin's Lane, ST CATHERINE'S FARM, half-timbered, with a weatherboarded barn. W of the main crossing, also in the High Road is OLD BARN HOUSE, originally perhaps c. 1500, then EASTCOTE LODGE of 1888, a typical example of *George & Peto's* Dutch revival, the style called by Mr Lancaster Pont Street Dutch, and derived of course from Norman Shaw. Further W HIGH GROVE, Early Georgian brick with many late C19 alterations. – Field End Road makes the best show of old buildings in the parish; nothing spectacular, but much that is attractive. The start is EASTCOTE COTTAGE by the main crossing, then a London stock brick METHODIST CHAPEL of 1847, PARK FARM, THE BARNS, THE RETREAT (fine half-timbered barn), FIELD END HOUSE (early C19), FIELD END LODGE (an exceedingly pretty farmhouse with an E end with typically close early timber framing), and FIELD END FARM (with an uncommonly high C16 barn). Immediately S of this a C20 shopping parade intrudes. FIELD END PRIMARY SCHOOL, by *H. V. Lobb*, 1946–7, is a good example of up-to-date County Council school planning – more half-timbered cottages in Wiltshire Lane further N, especially Old Cheyne Cottage, Ivy Farm, and Cherry Cottage.   33b

EDGWARE

Edgware in its present appearance is, like its neighbour Hendon, of which borough it now forms part, the result of the London Transport extension from Golders Green to Edgware. This was opened in 1925. Edgware had a population of 1,576 in 1921, 5,352 in 1931, 17,523 in 1939.

The village can still be recognized quite plainly along the High Street, that is the Edgware tract of Watling Street. There is a number of cottages here, not remarkable in themselves but well worth preserving as a record of the parish's rural past. The church lies at the crossing of Watling Street with the street from Whitchurch to Mill Hill.

PARISH CHURCH ST MARGARET. A C15 W tower of Kentish rag and Reigate dressings with diagonal buttresses and a NE turret, higher than the battlemented parapet. The rest of the church is of brick, and dates from 1845 with aisles added 1928. The interior is plain and has no monuments of special importance. A BRASS in the chancel is to Anthony Childe, 1599, a tiny babe in swaddling clothes. – PLATE. Chalice, 1562, that is of early date, as plate in Middlesex goes; Patens of c. 1557 and 1715.

Up Watling Street, in Stone Grove, are the DAY ALMSHOUSES, 1828; symmetrical, cement-rendered, and gabled, with cement barge-boarding. The minute ATKINSON ALMSHOUSES, 1680, a little higher up were badly bombed in the Second World War.

(At Newlands NEWLANDS GRANGE and BROOMFIELD LODGE, both early C19, stuccoed. MTCP.)

BROCKLEY HILL, where Watling Street leaves Middlesex, was the site of the Roman SULLONIACAE. Not much is so far known of this settlement. An obelisk of moderate size recording it was put up by W. Sharpe, secretary to the Duke of Chandos. It is now in the grounds of the Royal National Orthopaedic Hospital.

L. T. STATION, by *Charles Holden*, 1925. A good example of the generally neo-Georgian character of the Holden stations before c. 1930. The same type is modified on the other stations of the Northern Line between Brent and Edgware.

EDMONTON

Edmonton, just like Tottenham, its southern neighbour, lies along the Roman Ermine Street, W of the Lea Valley. Travelling N from Tottenham Green, the Tottenham High Road develops without any break into Fore Street and then

Edmonton Broadway and the Hertford Road. The two nuclei of older building are Upper Edmonton Green and Silver Street as a spur to the w, and Lower Edmonton Green with Church Street and the church also to the w. The population of the parish (which is now a borough) was 5,000 in 1801, 11,000 in 1861, 23,000 in 1881, 62,000 in 1901, 78,000 in 1931, and 106,000 in 1949; a typical outer suburban development.

PARISH CHURCH ALL SAINTS, Church Street. The external appearance is characterized by the contrast between the c15 Kentish rag w tower with angle buttresses at the w corners and a higher stair-turret in the SE corner, and the tall N aisle (there is no clerestory) and chancel, refaced in yellow brick in 1772. There must have been a c12 church here originally; for fragments of a Norman doorway with voussoirs exhibiting (from outer to inner order) small diaper, beakhead, several zigzags, are built into the w wall. Inside, the slim octagonal piers of moderate height and the arches between nave and N aisle are c15. The roofs require special attention: c15 in the vestry and the nave, c16 in the N chancel aisle, and c17 in the N aisle (flat and divided into sixteen panels with patterns of ribs forming alternatingly a cross and a lozenge. – PLATE. Especially good set of 1880; Chalice of neo-Elizabethan style of 1854. – MONUMENTS. Brass to J. Asplyn, G. Askew, and their wife, c. 1500, tiny figures on an inscription tablet; N. Boone and wife † 1523, the figures and inscription plate larger; E. Nowell, wife, and children † 1616. Kirton(?) Monument, c. 1530: Niche in s wall with Late Perp panelling in the shallow jambs and voussoirs above tomb-chest with quatrefoils; straight cornice with crestings; the brasses of the back wall are missing (cf. Norwood). Many minor monuments of c17 and c 18. The churchyard surrounds the church. Charles Lamb † 1834 and his sister are buried in it.

CHARLES LAMB'S COTTAGE still exists, just NE of the church, and another neglected cottage, VICARAGE COTTAGE, just E of the church.

ST ALDHELM, Silver Street, 1903, by *Caroë*; very typical of this architect. Brick, low with tall steep-pitched roof, a playful turret on the crossing, and Gothic detail.

ST MICHAEL BASSISHAW, Hertford Road, 1901, by *Caroë*. Comparison of this much bigger church with St Aldhelm brings out the features which are characteristic of Caroë's Gothic. The contrast between the aisles so narrow that they are only passages and the wide nave is quite impressive, and the exterior again sports a playful NW tower and another over the chancel.

CONGREGATIONAL CHURCH, Snell's Park, 1849, by *Francis Pouget*. The yellow brick of early C19 Gothic but prettified by the five gables over the bays of the aisle and the Dec. tracery and finials.

FORE STREET AND HERTFORD ROAD. Typical suburban arterial roads, shopping areas alternating with residential areas. Of pre-Victorian building a good deal survives, but so scattered that only rarely a coherent impression can be gained. Two cottages and a slightly larger house of *c.* 1700 at the very S end of Fore Street really form part of the Brook Street end of Tottenham High Road. After that there is a gap until SILVER STREET is reached. At the NW corner is ANGEL PLACE, a pretty terrace of two-storeyed cottages with Georgian door surrounds by Pymme's Brook. Then odd houses: 231, 238, 258–60 (all Early Georgian). Then the Green with a few altered cottages and bits of Georgian or pre-Georgian brickwork. In Hertford Road an ambitious Regency or Early Victorian terrace with grand pilasters to centre and corner pavilions (altogether nearly sixty bays).

In SILVER STREET, S of Pymme's Park, is a pretty row of cottages, brick and weatherboarded.

There was once quite a number of large houses in their grounds to the W of Edmonton. At the outbreak of the Second World War only two of value remained, Pymme's and Salisbury House, and Pymme's was burnt in 1940.

SALISBURY HOUSE, a manor house of *c.* 1600, now lies in the middle of between-the-wars suburban houses, its rugged and neglected walls and gables in a poignant contrast to their primness. The ground floor is brick, the projecting upper storey timber-framed. The gables again project. The whole is a higgledy-piggledy group, with a stair-turret, an oriel window, some weatherboarding, and so on.

On BUSH HILL stood several large houses. Now there is only HALLIWICK, featureless late Georgian. In SILVER STREET past Pymme's on the s side is the St David's Hospital incorporating MILFORD HOUSE, also early C19, with a symmetrical nine-bay front and iron verandahs.

ENFIELD

Leaving the City of London by the Roman Ermine Street, that is going straight north, one does not reach the country until one has passed through Enfield. Yet one feels for the first time at Enfield to be in a town and not a suburb. The present area of the borough (population in 1949, 111,000) covers of course far more than Enfield Town. It includes even within its solidly built-over quarters several former villages and hamlets. This is particularly noticeable on the E where the Roman and the main medieval street ran just on the edge of the Lea escarpment, crossing from s to N Ponders End, Enfield Highway, and Freezywater before reaching Hertfordshire and Waltham Cross. The town proper has its High Street at right angles to Ermine Street further W, and its market place close to the crossing of this axis with the town's main N–S axis (London Road–Silver Street–Baker Street). In the following pages the town itself is described first, its feelers E (Enfield Highway), NE (Turkey Street), NW (Clayhill), and N (Forty Hill, etc.) afterwards, the rural parts of the Borough in the end, that is Trent Park and Cockfosters, and the remaining sites of lodges of Enfield Chase.

PARISH CHURCH ST ANDREW. A town church, not a village church, situated on the N side of the market place and visible from it in its full length. Overall length about 120 ft, W tower projecting, the rest, nave and chancel and N and S aisles, forming a complete rectangle. From the market place the tower of ragstone rubble appears in contrast to a s aisle rebuilt in brick in the early C19. The brick wall forms a fine background to the several stately late C18 and early C19 sarcophagi and monuments in the churchyard. From the N the church walls are also rubble. Aisles, nave, and tower are all battlemented. Inside, the oldest part is the chancel with a C13 window towards where now the s chapel is. Nave and choir belong to the same period as the tower: late C14. The nave has quatrefoil piers and arches both moulded and chamfered. The upper walls are rubble, the clerestory is early C16. The chancel is lower, and above the chancel arch a Crucifixion was painted in 1923 by *Powell's* of Highgate. – BREAD SHELF in N chapel *c.* 1630 with three columns supporting an entablature. – ORGAN CASE of 1752, exceedingly good of its period. – PLATE. Silver-plated copper set of 1786. – MONUMENTS. Joyce Lady Tiptoft † 1446, brass plate with effigy under three little gables, all with concave sides. The brass is on a tomb-chest with heraldic shields in diagonal cusped panels. The monument is surmounted by a canopy of *c.* 1530 with a four-centred arch and a straight top cornice. – Robert Deicrowe † 1586, Robert Middlemore † 1610, Francis Evrington † 1614, all epitaphs with kneeling figures. – Martha Palmer, 1617, by *Nicholas Stone*, upright cartouche flanked by the graceful, very swaying, and very Mannerist figures of Faith and Charity. – Sir Nicholas Raynton (of Forty Hall), Lord Mayor of London †1646, his wife and family: standing wall monument in three stages; on the plinth the kneeling minor figures facing each other, above the recumbent wife turned over towards us, and immediately above her on a higher shelf Sir Nicholas also recumbent, his cheek on his hand; top with broken pediment. – Thomas Stringer † 1706, standing wall monument with bust in armour under a tent-canopy with heavy opened draperies, the whole against a backpiece with entablature and broken pediment. Is it by *Bird*?

ST LUKE, Browning Road, 1899–1903, by *J. Brooks*. Conventional E.E., chiefly brick, the distinguishing feature being a two-aisled transept showing outside in two half-timbered gables. A shingled turret over the crossing.

ST MARY MAGDALENE, Windmill Hill, 1883, by *Butterfield*. Indifferent outside, but with a rich polychrome interior culminating in the chancel.

ST MICHAEL, Chase Side, 1874, by *Carpenter & Inglelow*. Unfinished.

GRAMMAR SCHOOL, immediately W of the church. Mid C16, brick, two storeys, with three E dormers with four-light windows all of brick. The other windows modern. Stair-turret on the W. Inside one large schoolroom on the ground floor (cf. Harrow).

The 'High Street' of Enfield is called The Town in its E part, Church Street in its W part. In THE TOWN there still remain one weatherboarded house and, opposite, the former Vestry Offices, Late Georgian, with a tiny polygonal façade as if it were a toll house.

GENTLEMEN'S ROW is the best street of Enfield. Its N part is completely preserved; Nos 9–23 are all old, and all of moderate or small size. The details point to the early C18. No 17 is the cottage in which Charles Lamb stayed in 1827. No. 11 is weatherboarded and sticks out with its gable far in front of the others. The whole group is highly picturesque and varied. The S of Gentlemen's Row has a modern villa with garden to which its owner has added an annexe housing the precious remains of EN-FIELD PALACE which he bought to secure them for Enfield when the so-called Palace was pulled down in 1927. The style is earliest Elizabethan. The remains are a splendid fireplace, wood panelling, and a plastered ceiling 41 with thin ribs separating plain panels each with just one badge or emblem. The development from here to the ceilings at Tottenham of 1610 and Boston Manor (Brentford) of *c*. 1622 is illuminating.

SILVER STREET and BAKER STREET. Much of pre-Victorian dates remains, but nothing of special interest (Fox Hall, 90 Silver Street, Baptist Chapel of *c*. 1840, Enfield Court, very altered).

ENFIELD HIGHWAY (E of Enfield).

ST JAMES, Hertford Road, 1831, by *W. C. Lochner*; chancel
   1864. A characteristic yellow brick church of its date, that
   is of Commissioners' type, thin and cheap with a narrow
   towered front, shallow buttresses, and battlemented
   throughout.

EAGLE HOUSE, High Street. Mid C18 brick, with good
   iron gate and eagles on the gate posts.

35b FLOUR MILL, Lea Valley Road, a delightful *ensemble*, probably mainly of the early C19. Brick house of the miller
   surrounded by white and dark weatherboarded sheds of
   different heights. The elevated part of more recent cor-
   rugated iron painted dark red. The Mill lies in the river
   meadows.

TURKEY STREET (NE of Enfield):
The Turkey Street–Clayhill E–W line is the boundary of
   urban building. Turkey Street is all villagey in its houses
   and open to the S. Nothing of particular importance.

CLAY HILL (NW of Enfield).
Old village lane with two country inns: the ROSE AND
   CROWN, brick cottages, and the FALLOW BUCK,
   weatherboarded. Suburban development has started en-
   croaching. Several pleasant largish houses are left, notably
   HILL LODGE, rambling stuccoed early C19 with flat roofs;
   WOODBURY, Italianate *c.* 1860 of London stock brick
   with robust detail; BRAMLEY HOUSE, Georgian brick
   much added to; LITTLE PIPERS, picturesque with
   barge-boarding and hood-moulds to the windows; THE
   FIRS, Georgian but recently refaced.

FORTY HILL and BULL'S CROSS (N of Enfield):
A lane with several exceptionally good houses. Starting from
   the S there is first some good C18 ironwork by the corner
   of Clay Hill, then the HERMITAGE, a perfect example of
   its date 1704. Six bays, two storeys, hipped roof, and door
   surround with rusticated Tuscan pilasters. The Hermitage is followed by the OLD BAKERY, symmetrical and
   weatherboarded. A little higher up on the other (E) side

WORCESTER LODGE, same date and style as the Hermitage. Between this and Elsynge Cottage more nice houses. ELSYNGE COTTAGE is an original asymmetrical late C18 house with all windows on the ground floor of the Venetian type, all windows on the upper floor semicircular. After this the gates of FORTY HALL appear on the W side. 47a The house lies back in extensive grounds. It does not belong to the lane as the others do. Its architectural importance is considerable. It was built by Sir Nicholas Raynton between 1629 and 1636. Its plaster ceilings and the screen in the Hall correspond to that date, that is are still in the Jacobean tradition. It is true that by 1620 already Inigo Jones had broken with this tradition, but his style did not penetrate beyond the court before the middle of the C17. Inside Forty Hall only the large shell motifs of the Hall Screen show an acquaintance with the new classical Italian ideal. But outside, the square house of brick with $2\frac{1}{2}$ storeys and a hipped roof above a modillion cornice appears to belong to the late C17. Alterations were made to the house by the Wolstenholmes in 1700. Does the exterior and especially the porches and the central window with its Corinthian aedicule above the S door belong to these alterations? The quoins and broad flat window surrounds on the other hand look as if they might be very progressive work of 1630.

Further N is JESUS CHURCH, 1835, by *Thomas Ashwell*, according to the patron's wishes designed in imitation of Holy Trinity, Tottenham, by *Savage* (*q.v.*). It is the Commissioners' type all over, London stock brick with a narrow front showing aisles and nave in tight section; finials on the corners of the nave. Again further N MYDDELTON HOUSE, notable chiefly because of Mr E. A. Bowles's famous garden.

TRENT PARK, 2 m. W of Enfield church. Built by Sir Richard Jebb, George III's favourite doctor and called after Trent in the Tyrol where the then Duke of Gloucester had just at that time recovered from an illness. Now belongs to the Middlesex County Council. The present appearance practically entirely of two recent building

periods: *c.* 1900 and (for Sir Philip Sassoon) 1926, etc.
The park laid out by *Repton*.

COCKFOSTERS: CHRIST CHURCH, 1839, by *H. E. Kendall*. Still the London stock brick and the lancet windows
of the Commissioners' churches, but no longer symmetrical. The tower stands on the S side just E of the W
gable. N aisle added by *Sir A. Blomfield*, 1898.

WEST LODGE, NORTH LODGE (Kilvinton Hall), and
SOUTH LODGE all look early C19, much altered. At
WHITEWEBBS (now a home for the aged) the alterations
are in the French taste of *c.* 1870. The S Lodge of Whitewebbs is an unusually pretty early C19 cottage with a
barge-boarded gable.

FELTHAM

Feltham (population of urban district 44,000 in 1949) now
consists of Lower and Upper Feltham, the former present-
ing a few traces of the old village (and its church), the latter
being C19 and C20 in character. The urban district also includes Hanworth (*q.v.*).

PARISH CHURCH ST DUNSTAN, Lower Feltham, 1802.
Brick with the typical round-headed windows and a low
battlemented tower, with later shingled spire. The interior a pleasant surprise: the pews of 1802 preserved
complete, and the wooden W gallery on Roman Doric
columns with elaborate commemorative inscriptions all in
a handsome flowing script. The ceiling is flat, the E end
has a Venetian window. In 1853 aisles were added and the
windows Normanized, of all things. – PLATE. Pieces dated
1771, 1787, 1791, and 1801, all given when the church
was built.

PARISH CHURCH ST CATHERINE, Upper Feltham, by the
station, 1880 (steeple 1898), by *Carpenter & Ingelow*.
Earnest and careful, with an impressive spire. The S aisle
not yet built.

Along and near the street connecting the two churches a few
old houses, first two nice brick cottages of *c.* 1700, then
the MANOR HOUSE (*c.* 1634?) with weatherboarded barn.

FINCHLEY

The main parts of the borough are Church End, East Finchley, and North Finchley, an urban area but still with much green surrounding it and penetrating into it. In addition there is a tongue stretching to the s and one stretching to the N. The s tongue consists of a part of the Hampstead Garden Suburb (dealt with under Hendon) and ends on the s with the Spaniards Inn (*see* Kenwood in the second London volume of this series). The N tongue reaches up to Whetstone (*q.v.*). Finchley Parish had only 1,500 inhabitants in 1801 and still only 7,000 in 1871. Thereafter suburbanization set in: 16,000 1891, 40,000 1911, 59,000 1931, 72,000 in 1949.

PARISH CHURCH ST MARY, a low, broad C15 building of rag rubble with a modest well preserved w tower. A C12 church must have been in the same spot, as in the walls inside some fragments of Norman zigzag and foliage are inserted. The interior is oddly shapeless, owing to the addition in the C19 and C20 of an inner and an outer s aisle. The one remarkable feature of the old parts (N aisle and N chancel chapel) is that the chancel is narrower than the nave and that between the two a narrow skewed bay with a low four-centred arcade is inserted. The roof of the nave is C15, flat-pitched, with moulded tie-beams and curved braces. – FONT. C13 on modern shaft; plain octagonal bowl with two pointed blank panels to each face (a C13 development of the Harlington type). – PLATE. Set of 1806. – MONUMENTS. Several brasses in the floor of the N chapel, and one in the w wall of the s aisle. – Alexander Klinge and wife † 1618, kneeling figures in profile facing each other across a prayer desk; columns on cherub corbels l. and r., cherubs and shield on the entablature.

ST LUKE, Mountfield Road, by *Caroë*, 1903–5.

HOLY TRINITY, Church Lane, East Finchley, by *Salvin*, 1849.

CONGREGATIONAL CHURCH, West Finchley, by *Tarring & Wilkinson*, 1875.

CHAPEL OF THE ST MARYLEBONE CEMETERY, East End
Road, by *Sir E. Cooper*, 1937.

CHRIST'S COLLEGE, Church End, 1857. A school building of mid-Victorian gloom, in purple brick with Tudor
diaper decoration in vitrified bricks; it towers over the so
much more modest village church across the road.

For old houses the best part is EAST END ROAD, the road
connecting Church End, that is old Finchley Village, with
East Finchley. On the s side lies the MANOR HOUSE
(now the Convent School of Marie Auxiliatrice), dated on
a rainwater head 1723, a plain and dignified brick building of three storeys and seven bays. Its only decoration is
a flat rusticated door surround and two vases on the corners of the parapet. Entrance and garden side are identical, except that a curved staircase with original iron
railings appears on the entrance side. Towards East
Finchley some more modest early C19 houses and cottages survive, for example the oldest part of the CON-
VENT OF THE GOOD SHEPHERD, a square house of three
bays with a Doric porch. Towards Church End is the
bigger AVENUE HOUSE (now a Borough Council department), rather reactionary Italianate of 1887. It is a picturesque composition with a tower and projecting eaves
on brackets. In the grounds is the sham medieval crenellated wash-house.

FRIERN BARNET

A very small urban district (population 29,000 in 1949), its
few monuments strung up along Friern Barnet Lane which
in its course and with its many old trees still reflects a
rural past.

PARISH CHURCH ST JAMES. Small church so extensively
restored in 1853 that little of original detail remains. The
s doorway is Norman, probably C12, with one order of
columns, the shafts and voussoirs and also the border of
the tympanum with zigzag ornament. The centre of the
tympanum has diapering. The E window with figures of
Faith, Charity, Hope. – PLATE. Flagon of 1655, Chalice

of 1691, Chalice of early C18 date. – MONUMENT to four sons and two daughters of R. Down by *J. Bacon Jun.*, 1804, fine and sensitive in very shallow relief with a composition of urns and on top under a pointed arch a group of angels clearly inspired by *Flaxman*.

ST JOHN, Friern Barnet Road, by *J. L. Pearson*. Begun 1891, completed after his death. An ambitious building, though not impressive in its exterior. Vaulted throughout and with a narrow ambulatory round the chancel. The style is E.E. or rather Early Gothic, cool but satisfying.

TOWN HALL by *Sir John Brown & Henson*, begun 1939. A pleasant accommodating piece of design, modern but with such traditional features as a porch on attenuated piers and a cupola. The façade is concave to embrace the side of a circus at the crossing of the two main streets of the Borough.

CAMPE ALMSHOUSES, Friern Barnet Lane, 1612. Long, straight, and low, of brick with seven tenements, their entrances grouped 2, 2, 2, 1, with four-centred tops to the doors and low windows of three lights on the ground floor, two lights above. Screened from the street by old trees.

COLNEY HATCH (L.C.C. Friern Hospital). *S. W. Dawkes's* large original group of buildings, begun in 1849, is still the centre of the mental hospital.

GOLDERS GREEN

The typical area rapidly developed after the Underground railway had reached it. Golders Green station was opened in 1907.

ALL SAINTS, Finchley Road, 1856, by *Bury*.

ST ALBAN, 1932, by *Sir Giles G. Scott*. A pleasant brick church (raked joints) with a crossing tower and quite an impressive brick interior.

CREMATORIUM, 1905, by *George & Yates*. A new chapel by *Mitchell & Bridgwater* was added in 1938.

KING ALFRED SCHOOL, North End Road, the back parts, 1934–6, by *E. C. Kaufmann* in the international style of the 30s.

GREENFORD

PARISH CHURCH HOLY CROSS. The old church, only
60 ft long, was replaced by a new building in 1939, but
left standing. It has a weatherboarded tower (cf. Perivale)
which is new, but rests on an interesting timber structure
visible from inside. The tower staircase and W gallery
seem to be early C 17. The chancel roof is C 15 with a central king-post with four-way struts (cf. Perivale). Next to
the W structure mentioned, the most noteworthy objects
in the church are the STAINED GLASS panels of *c.* 1500,
said to come from King's College, Cambridge. They are
mostly heraldic and show in the E window the arms of
Henry VIII and Catherine of Aragon, in the SE window
the arms of King's College, in the SW window the same,
and those of Eton College. There are also other motifs, the
initials T. P., T. B., and T. H., the arms of the Grocers'
Company, a little windmill, etc. – FONT. Small bowl on
four-sided baluster, 1638. The cover may be of the same
date, though its four volutes are still crocketed. – PLATE.
Chalice, 1638; two Flagons, 1640; Paten, 1661. – MONU-
MENTS. Brass in chancel: demi-figure of priest, the same
type as Hayes, Stanwell, Harlington, etc. – Some other
brasses. – M. Gardiner † 1630 and wife, the usual type
with the two figures kneeling opposite each other. –
Bridget Coston, 1637, a curious combination of the kneeling family type and the type with portrait bust in niche.
The widow kneels to the l., holding the infant John, and
behind her kneel her daughters labelled Frances, Mary,
Jane, Anne, and Philadelphia. Behind the group a little
higher up appears their late father as if he were looking
out of a window, with his cheek resting on his hand. Two
allegorical figures on the sides of the pediment hold up
curtains.

The new church was begun in 1939 to the designs of
Professor A. E. Richardson. The interior is large with a
very high open timber roof construction and sturdy posts
to separate nave from aisles. The front has a kind of tall
oriel window in the roof and a little spirelet.

BARN, Greenford Green Farm. Timber-framed and weatherboarded; probably C17.

GRIMS DYKE

The only major pre-Norman monument in Middlesex. Its date and purpose have given rise to much controversy. Most probably the dyke is Saxon and not prehistoric and served as a defence against raiders rather than military invaders. It consists of a ditch and a bank, 100 ft in total width, and well over 9 ft in height. The ditch lies consistently inside, that is to the E and S of the bank. Its siting is far from militarily judicious. Hilltops more than once lie just outside it. It can be followed from Ruislip to Harrow Weald, in a generally NE direction. The best preserved stretches are (1) E of the Pinner Hill Road parallel to the Uxbridge Road at a distance of about 750 ft to its N; (2) further E on the Uxbridge Road from just W of Woodridings Farm in a NNE direction towards the bridge across the Watford Line railway; (3) just N of Wealdwood Road running NE through the Golf Course and then turning sharp E at the N boundary of Grims Dyke, the Norman Shaw house. As for this house, *see* under Harrow Weald.

HAMPSTEAD GARDEN SUBURB

The aesthetically most satisfactory and socially most successful of all C20 garden suburbs. The conception of the garden suburb is not the same as that of the garden city. The garden city, industrially and commercially an independent unit, was first proposed by Ebenezer Howard in his book of 1898, and first realized at Letchworth, Herts., in 1903. The garden suburb goes back to Bedford Park (*see* Acton), 1875, and to Port Sunlight and Bournville. In its social character the Hampstead Garden Suburb comes nearest to what Bedford Park was in its beginnings. The population is on the whole comfortably off and ranges from true sensibility to amateur arty-craftiness. While the garden suburb is not meant to have its own factories, warehouses, etc., it yet needs a social centre to be more than a dormitory. This the Hampstead Garden Suburb has, and it is something to be proud of, as it should be.

The Hampstead Garden Suburb was founded in 1906 chiefly at the inspiration of Dame Henrietta Barnett whose Toynbee Hall experience in the East End of London had taught her the necessity of reforms in the social as well as aesthetic principles of house planning. The Trust obtained the land (less than half the present land of the Hampstead Garden Suburb). Originally (and up to the First World War) only the fringe of the Hampstead Heath Extension on the w (Hampstead Way and its closes, Wellgarth Road, and the E part of Corringham Way) and an area bounded by Wood Hatch and Temple Fortune Lane on the w, Addison Way in the N, and Erskine Hill, Central Square, Meadway, and Thornton Way in the E were built on. *Parker & Unwin* were appointed as planners (Sir Raymond Unwin was in charge from 1907 to 1915) and *Sir Edwin Lutyens* as consultant on certain buildings. Parker & Unwin had planned Letchworth a few years earlier. The Hampstead Garden Suburb is in many ways an improvement on Letchworth, and indeed as interesting and convincing to-day as it was when in its first years it influenced America as much as Germany and Holland.

The pattern of streets and squares takes the contours carefully into consideration. The Central Square is placed on the highest eminence and dominates drearier suburbs around for a good mile on all sides. Patches of wood are preserved in two places, and old trees everywhere in streets and gardens. The main streets are neither all straight nor all winding, but rectangular crossings are almost universally avoided for the sake of more interesting *points de vue*. Occasionally footpaths allow short-cuts amid dense bushes (for example w exit of Central Square); a 'pedestrian network' in embryo. A clear distinction between streets for traffic and purely residential streets appears everywhere. The Hampstead Garden Suburb was in fact the place where planners learned the benefits of closes. All houses have private gardens, but these are divided only by low hedges, never by walls (an innovation for England, though the accepted practice of the United States). Only towards the Heath Extension in the s is a retaining wall with a kind of gazebos introduced as a more formal boundary. The terrace formed in its centre and leading up to Heathgate and St Jude's is the only monumental approach; the others are less impressive, although Raymond Unwin had intended the Temple Fortune entrance in the w to be the main point of entry. Here and only here did he provide a shopping arcade. Hampstead Way, Wellgarth Road, Corringham Road, and Willifield Way (from sw to nw) are the other approaches.

The Hampstead Garden Suburb now comprises about 800 acres. Of these 317 are owned by the Trust and form the Garden Suburb proper. The land e of the Heath Extension and the original area was developed after the First World War, planned on similar lines (by *J. C. S. Soutar*), but with less control over the architecture of the houses.

Socially the conception of the Hampstead Garden Suburb was as sound as it was aesthetically. It was (entirely in the sense now universally accepted) meant to be for a mixture of classes, not for one class. Smaller houses appear in the nw and lead at the nw end, in Addison Way, to working-class (or artisans') flats (by *Unwin*). There is also a 'college', that is a quadrangle for single working ladies (Waterlow Court at the w end of Heath Close; by *Baillie Scott*), and another quadrangle for the Aged (The Orchard, between Hampstead and Willifield Way; by *Unwin*). Moreover, a mixture is provided (again exactly as demanded and executed by planners to-day) of free-standing houses, semi-detached houses, and terraces (Reynolds Close; *Unwin*) and of houses along streets and houses grouped around squares, crescents (both to be seen off Temple Fortune Lane), and closes.

As the Suburb developed, however, the mixed character gradually disappeared. The population now is very much of one kind (a fact worth serious study by to-day's planners). In this respect the Suburb has not in the end worked out as its originators projected. Some other disadvantages have also shown themselves with the growth of the Suburb and the growth of London around. Shops are too far away.

The Central Square, in spite of its public buildings, has never become a real social centre, because not only shops, but also cinemas, pubs, cafés have been refused admission. Institute education and divine worship have not proved to be as much of a permanent and non-intermittent attraction as the social reformers behind the Suburb had hoped for. The lack of any public transport anywhere through the Suburb has also proved a serious snag.

Yet, in spite of these objections to the plan and development of the Hampstead Garden Suburb, it has been of the greatest importance in the history of c 20 town-planning in England. It seems indeed as if, with its principle of eight houses to the acre, it was the starting-point of a new type of town-planning legislation.

To turn to individual buildings now, the most conspicuous ones are all in the Central Square: the two churches, the two parsonages, and the Institute, all by *Lutyens* and all designed about 1908–10. The parish CHURCH OF ST JUDE is one of Lutyens' most successful buildings. It exhibits all his best qualities and even turns that 'naughtiness' or wilful originality which often mars his late buildings into a decided advantage. The church has a nave and aisles covered by a huge roof starting uncommonly close to the ground. It is broken by very tall dormer windows of aedicule form. This discord between medieval and Baroque features is what Lutyens must have enjoyed as much as, say, Norman Shaw before him in the church of Bedford Park. The façade (added later but to the original designs) also shows it. The tall spire over the crossing has also most original features, reminiscent of Byzantine and early Tudor brickwork. It looks magnificent whatever the distance it is viewed from. Inside the discord perhaps goes too far. The church is tunnel- and dome-vaulted, which leads to a painful conflict with the open timber lean-to roofs of the aisles. The FREE CHURCH is a variation on the same themes, with the same roof and dormers and façade, but a low dome instead of the spire. The IN-STITUTE is more conventional neo-Georgian. The houses surrounding the square all appear a little too low. They deprive the square of an otherwise well-established urban character, and are too much like a mere screen around the public buildings. *Lutyens* also did the houses along the s end of ERSKINE HILL which leads up to the Square, of a fine restrained late c17 formality, in grey brick with red-brick dressings. The even more formal approach from the s, up Heathgate, has houses by other architects, also handling late c17 and early c18 forms (Nos 1 and 4: *J. C. S. Soutar*; No. 6: *Quennell*).

But neo-Georgian or neo-William-and-Mary are not the characteristic style of the Hampstead Garden Suburb (as they are of the later Welwyn Garden City, Herts). The architects who designed most of the other houses, headed by Sir Raymond Unwin, believed in a free and comfortable neo-Tudor brick architecture which has indeed stood the test of forty years splendidly. The brick-work is sensitive throughout, of uneven surface and varying in colour from grey to dark purple-reds. The roofs are usually steep-pitched and with many gables. These qualities run through most of the Hampstead Garden Suburb architecture. Even greater unity is achieved, where the same architect designed a whole close or square. Where that is not the case, each design has its own individuality, but control by the Trust secured a general harmony of character all the same. Space does not permit to run through the streets individually. All that can be done is to single out some architects and say where chararacteristic work of theirs can be found.

Unwin: Shops at Temple Fortune, Heath Close, Reynolds Close, The Orchard (between Hampstead Way and Willi-field Way). The other architects most widely employed were *Geoffrey Lucas* (60–82 Hampstead Way, 9–37 Willifield Way) and *Crickmer* (66 Willifield Way and on to 40–6 Temple Fortune Hill; also development opposite). – *Baillie Scott:* only two jobs, but both masterly: Waterlow Court, w end of Heath Close, with low arcades on four sides of a lawn and a gabled and bellcoted central feature opposite the entrance, 1909. – 22 Hampstead Way and 6–10 Meadway, the most picturesque

group in the suburb. – Voysey, the originator of so
many elements to be seen in the Suburb, did not himself build anything. But his style is clearly recognizable,
for example in *Bunney's* 7–13 Meadway, less in the same
architect's 2–7 Linnell Close. – *Dawber*: 38–48 Temple
Fortune Lane, 20 Hampstead Way, 5–6 Ruskin Close. –
Curtis Green: 135–41 Hampstead Way. – *Town-
send*: 2 Temple Fortune Lane. – *Morley Horder*:
121–3 Hampstead Way. – The first five years of the
Suburb had, with the exception of Lutyens's work, been
exclusively of the Tudor variety. Neo-Georgian or rather
neo-William-and-Mary with usually five bays, a centre
entrance with or without a pediment and a hipped roof
came in with No. 19 Wellgarth Road, by *C. Cowles
Voysey*, 1912; No. 12 Turner Close, by *Quennell*,
1912; and No. 16 Hampstead Way, by *Bunney*, 1912.
It became the accepted style for the wealthier houses
after the First World War and can be seen at its best in
Wildwood Road (*by C. H. James* in Fairway Close Nos 1,
2 and Fairway House, in Wildwood Road itself Nos 32
and 32A, 56–60, by *C. Cowles Voysey* Nos 34, etc., by
R. Atkinson No. 48).

HAMPTON

The village (now included in the Borough of Twickenham)
lies beyond Hampton Court, separated from the Palace by
the large Green which in its character and function is so
much an appendage of the palace that it is treated under
Hampton Court. Hampton village itself really begins only
where its own manor house, Hampton House, lies. The
church is the centre, streets reach out from it to N, W, and E.

PARISH CHURCH ST MARY, 1831, by *E. Lapidge*, who
built several churches in the neighbourhood. The usual
plain yellow stock brick building with lean lancet windows and a W tower without unnecessary adornment.
Inside S and N galleries and tall quatrefoil piers reaching
right up to the roof. Nothing mysterious, nothing en-
thusiastic. In 1888 *Sir Arthur Blomfield* added a sumptuous but hard short sanctuary in the E. – PLATE. Cup and

Paten of 1704, Almsdish of 1707, Flagon of 1780, Beadle's Staff of 1821. – MONUMENTS. Sybil Pane † 1562, in sw lobby, standing wall monument of four-poster type, the lower part of the columns and the tomb-chest with strapwork decoration, recumbent effigy, the body hardly modelled at all. Long inscription ('Pen here is brought to home, the place of long abode | Whose vertu guided hath her shippe, in to the quyet rode', etc.) on tablet under simple, unadorned (that is early) pediment; strapwork scrolls on l. and r. – Mrs Thomas † 1731 designed by *Archer* and signed by *W. Powell*, in s aisle. A noble composition, though the figures of the semi-reclining mother and the seated daughter are not very sensitive. Behind the figures a grey obelisk, the whole in an altar framing. – George Tilson † 1738, in sw lobby, with above the long inscription an enterprising putto on a highly asymmetrical cartouche. – Capt. A. Ellick, Comptroller General of the Coastguards † 1853, by *Bedford*, with a coastguard mourning by the Captain's coffin. Many more tablets of similar dates on the galleries. In the churchyard a clumsy bare pyramid to John Grey of Dominica † 1795.

ST JAMES, Park Road, New Hampton, 1864, by *Wigginton*. Exceedingly ugly, but with the punch of which the sixties were capable.

Several nice cottages in THAMES STREET. At its very end the Italianate waterworks start with a tower and palatial offices (*see* Sunbury). HIGH STREET and CHURCH STREET also have several old cottages and smaller houses. The only buildings in Church Street which deserve individual notice are THE OLD GRANGE, with two gables of the 1630 type, with concave curves carrying straight pediments. A fireplace inside appears if anything older than 1630. Immediately N of the old Grange is ORME HOUSE, early C18 with a contemporary pediment and door hood both brought in from other places. Further N more pleasant Late Georgian property.

E of the church is HAMPTON HOUSE, the manor house, bought 1754 by David Garrick and for him altered by *Robert Adam* first *c.* 1755 and then 1772–4. The result is

M—3

aesthetically unsatisfactory; the detail, especially the attenuated pilasters, are Adam, but no unity of composition is achieved. Close to the river and separated from the house by the road is Garrick's Shakespeare Temple, a little octagon with a deep Ionic portico, built, perhaps to *Capability Brown's* design, to house *Roubiliac's* Shakespeare of 1758. On towards Hampton Green ST ALBANS on the r., only a bare wall from the street, Georgian with some C17 features inside. Then more recent riverside houses amongst which the Swiss Chalet of Messrs Hucks and Son, Marine Engineers, deserves mention. It was brought over *c.* 1899 and looks wonderfully incongruous. Past the chalet the Green is soon reached (*see* Hampton Court).

HAMPTON COURT

History. The manor belonged to the Order of St John of Jerusalem, until it was bought by Wolsey in 1514. He was the coming man in English politics, just under forty years old. His King, Henry VIII, was twenty-three. Wolsey's father had been a butcher at Ipswich. The boy had unbounded ambition and exceptional ability. He went into the church, found patronage with several noblemen, and in 1507 became one of the Chaplains to Henry VII. Henry VIII took him over and made him Almoner. Then in 1513 he was elected Dean of York. From that day his rise was unparalleled. Bishop of Lincoln in 1514, Bishop of Tournai in 1514, Archbishop of York in 1514, Lord Chancellor in 1515, Cardinal in 1515, Papal Legate in 1518, Abbot of St Albans in 1521 and Bishop of Winchester in 1528. He also farmed three more English bishoprics for foreign occupants. His income was estimated in 1519 at about £100,000 a year (in 1925 value), and just before his fall at £350,000. Where at a great Royal pageant the Archbishop of Canterbury appeared with 70 servants, Wolsey brought along 300.

When the King's sister had a household of 44, and his eldest daughter of 65, Wolsey's counted 429. He had a sumptuous town house, north of the Palace of Westminster, which Henry VIII later converted into the Palace of White-hall. He founded a school at Ipswich (which never deve-loped) and a college at Oxford (which became the cele-brated Christ Church), and built himself three country seats of which Moor Park (Herts.) was the most luxurious, but Hampton Court was infinitely the biggest.

'Why come ye not to Court?' wrote the satirist Skelton

> To wyche court?
> To the Kynges Courte?
> Or to Hampton Court?
> Nay, to the Kynges Courte,
> But Hampton Court
> Hath the preemynence.

Wolsey's Hampton Court was the grandest of all houses built in England at the time, at least 300 by 550 feet in size, compared to the contemporary Chambord of Francis I with its 315 by 420 feet. This unashamed display was one of the many things irritating the King, and when Wolsey in 1529 decided to make a present of the house and its furnishings to Henry VIII, it was too late. In the same year he was de-prived of all his lands and belongings, and in the next year he died after his arrest for high treason.

Wolsey's palace consisted of the present w front (without the wings), the Base Court and its buildings, the Clock Court (with buildings in the N and S different from the present ones), the buildings round the Master Carpenter's Court, and some more further E, the Chapel and the cloisters w of the chapel. It seems that the E part had none of the sym-metry which will be noticed in the w façade and the Base Court. Wolsey's master mason was most probably *Henry Redman*, who also appears on Wolsey's work at Christ Church, Oxford.

Henry VIII spent more on Hampton Court than on any other of his palaces, except perhaps Greenwich. Five of his six queens were at Hampton, and Edward VI was born there. Henry added the Great Hall, remodelled Wolsey's structures round Clock Court, built a new court, where now Fountain Court is, and buildings to the N and E of Chapel Court. He also added the two wings to Wolsey's w façade. His master mason during these years was *John Molton*.

The palace was used by Mary, Elizabeth, James I and Charles I. James I held his Hampton Court Conference here in 1604 to settle controversial church matters. But of building little was done until William III appeared. Elizabeth added a small range s of Wolsey's s range of Clock Court; that is about all. Under the Commonwealth the palace was not sold but kept for Cromwell's use. Charles II busied himself on the layout of the garden, but on the buildings his work is nowhere found.

William and Mary, however, who did not like residing in Whitehall, decided to make Hampton Court their Versailles. *Wren* started work in 1689 and by the time William died the structural work was complete on the new Fountain Court with its E and S frontages to the gardens, and on the new s range of Clock Court and the new Orangery. Painting and furnishing of the Staterooms continued under Anne, and the Banqueting House was built.

Minor work was done under the first two Georges, chiefly on interiors; for example the State Rooms to the NE of Fountain Court. The entrance from the Clock to the Fountain Court is dated 1732 and was designed by *Kent*. At about the same time the N front towards Tennis Court Lane was heightened.

George III did not use Hampton Court, and since then no monarch has resided here. Apartments were divided off and granted 'by grace and favour' to servants of the Crown. There are at present forty-five of these.

In 1771–3 the Great Gatehouse in the middle of the w front was rebuilt. In 1882 it was rebuilt again. Otherwise the C19 did little to Hampton Court (infinitely less than to Windsor Castle). The State Apartments were opened to the public two years after Victoria, young and public-spirited, had ascended the throne.

Exterior Courts and Ground Floor Rooms. The main approach is now from the w, that is Hampton Green, through the TROPHY GATES built by George II. Wren regarded the Lion Gates N of the Wilderness as the principal entrance on the land side (*see* p. 84). The Trophy Gates lead into the Outer Green Court, with the river on the r. and the CAVALRY BARRACKS of the last third of the C17 on the l.

The front of Wolsey's building with Henry VIII's wings (*c.* 1536) and the Great Gatehouse, originally two storeys higher, is reached by means of a bridge across a moat. The bridge was built under Henry VIII and dug out in 1910. The King's Beasts on the parapet are new. The façade, nearly 400 ft wide, is the grandest of its date in Britain. Its perfect symmetry seems to belong wholly to the Renaissance, just then entering England in the learning of Erasmus, More, Grocyn, Colet, and in the art of Torrigiani at Westminster Abbey.

Wolsey indeed began to build almost exactly when Francis I started on Chambord. But to remember Chambord makes it at once clear that Hampton Court still holds fast to the Gothic style. Not only is every detail Perpendicular (with the exception of the two terra-cotta medallions which were not originally here, but at the Whitehall; on these medallions *see* below) but the conception of an outer wall with a tall symmetrical gatehouse also needed no Italian introduction to England. It existed already in the mighty front of Harlech before 1300. Bodiam is a well-known example of *c.* 1400. Others survive in old engravings, and such gatehouses as Oxburgh in Norfolk of 1482 are very similar to Hampton. The St Aldate's façade of Wolsey's Cardinal College in Oxford, now Christ Church, also exhibits the same scheme as Hampton Court. The French C14 was familiar with it too (*see*, for example, Charles V's Louvre). So the composition of the Hampton Court front cannot be taken as a sign of the coming of Italian principles; it is much rather one of many Northern parallels to the new sense of order which in the South chose antiquity as its ally. The shape of the gatehouse, the oriel window set into it (with a panel with the arms of Henry VIII), the texture of the dark mauve brick to its l.

and r. with its diapering of vitrified brick (the gatehouse itself has unfortunately a harsh C19 red colour), the free spacing of the windows, and the fantastic shapes of the chimneys (renewed without exception) can all be regarded as typically Perpendicular and typically English.

The BASE COURT is entered through the two contemporary doors of the Gatehouse and under a renewed vault. It is perfectly square and surrounded on the N, S, and W by ranges of only two-storeyed battlemented 'lodgings' for retainers or guests. The two stair-turrets of the Gatehouse were renewed by Queen Elizabeth in 1566. The Gatehouse opposite is known as Anne Boleyn's Gateway, because alterations were done to it while she was queen. It forms, however, part of Wolsey's original work which extended around Clock Court and to the E and NE of it. The Base Court with its bolder and more regular shape was only conceived a few years later. Anne Boleyn's Gateway is crowned by a pretty C18 cupola. It has an oriel window like the Great Gatehouse and two more terracotta medallions of Roman Emperors. For the medallions *Giovanni da Majano* was paid £2 6s. each in 1521. He made eight in all, which are now set into both sides of Anne Boleyn's Gateway and into the E gatehouse of Clock Court. Those of the Great Gatehouse (*see* above) and two at Hanworth probably come from the so-called Holbein Gate at Whitehall. The medallions are, except for the tomb of Henry VII in Westminster Abbey, the earliest example of the Italian Renaissance in England. The Base Court is 168 by 166 ft as against, for example, the 264 by 261 ft of Tom Quad at Christ Church. And as Tom Quad has the one poignant asymmetry of the higher college hall on the r., so the uniformity of the Base Court is broken by the bold W front of the Great Hall with its large Perpendicular window appearing on the left of Anne Boleyn's Gateway.

48 The CLOCK COURT delights with its variety of heights and forms after the relative uniformity of the Base Court. Its W side carries on the motifs as before. The porch of the Gatehouse is the same as its W front except that there is no

oriel window and instead the Astronomical Clock made by *Nicholas Oursian* in 1540. It shows the hour, the day, the month, the number of days since New Year, the phases of the moon, and (an eminently characteristic addition) the times of high water at London Bridge. Very different from this w side of Clock Court is the view to the N, where the sheer wall of the Great Hall rises with its cellars with small windows, then a large expanse of unbroken brickwork, and then the five four-light transomed windows with four-centred heads. The windows are separated by narrow buttresses rising in three steps. The E bay of the hall has a vast oriel window with five transomes. The cellars are early Wolsey work. The Hall itself was completed by Henry VIII in 1536. On the s side of the Court the Wolsey range is hidden by the spectacular somewhat operatic appearance of *Wren's* work. He kept the Tudor brick wall with its windows, turret, and bay windows (which is therefore uncommonly well preserved) and placed in front of it a colonnade of Portland stone with coupled columns (*à la Perrault's* Louvre Colonnade) and a weighty entablature with cornice and balustrade. Two trophies raise the horizontal line of the balustrade and end in vases. The large round-headed windows above the colonnade on the l. are like the brickwork around them, of course also of Wren's period. The rubbed brickwork of the court is worth special noting and touching. Between colonnade and Hall stretches the E side of Clock Court with its entrance feature looking oddly Victorian, although it is an exceedingly early example of the Gothic Revival (more than fifteen years older than the beginning of Walpole's remodelling of Strawberry Hill). The pointed arch of the doorway, the ceiling inside plastered to imitate Gothic vaulting motifs, the pretty tablet above the doorway and the window above it are all *Kent's* design of 1732[1]. Most of the brickwork is of the same period.

1. Inside, on the first floor, in a private room, is an elaborate Neo-Jacobean plaster ceiling, also of the Kent period – again an amazingly early date.

At this stage, that is before passing on to Wren's work where it stands on its own, it is advisable to trace back one's steps and look at the N front of the palace, pass through the inner courtyards between that front and Base Court and Clock Court, and enter some of the Tudor rooms there preserved.

The N front, nearly 700 ft long, faces Tennis Court Lane. The buildings on the N of the Lane are of no importance. But the palace itself is on this side (with the exception of the W end remodelled early in the C18, the easily recognizable C19 insertions l. and r. of the E Kitchen and the heightening of the E parts in the C18), entirely of Wolsey's and Henry's time: first the gabled part N of the Master Carpenter's Court, then the Kitchens projecting their clusters of chimneys, and after a while the E Kitchen doing the same. From the turret soon after that the N range of Chapel Court starts, higher and duller. But the whole is an outstanding example of the Tudor style, where it had no reason to give up utilitarian freedom of composition.

Henry VIII's NW wing of the main W façade can be entered in its middle, and one can walk through the Lord Chamberlain's Court, the Master Carpenter's Court, the Great Hall Court, the Round Kitchen Court, and on into the Chapel Court, all the time parallel with the line of Tennis Court Lane. The Lord Chamberlain's Court is much altered and of no interest, the Master Carpenter's Court a good example of little-restored Wolsey brick and of rambling Tudor composition (*négligé* as against the court ceremonial of the W front and the Base Court).

From the Master Carpenter's Court the N Cloister leads straight on, skirting the little Great Hall Court. To its S is the basement of the Great Hall: the KING'S BEER CELLARS (entry from the W, from the Base Court). A large household in the C16, that is before the introduction of coffee, tea, or cocoa, consumed an amount of beer inconceivable to-day. The beer cellars are divided into two by a cross-wall supporting the central hearth in the Hall above (*see* below). Their total length is 100 ft. They are divided into nave and aisles by two rows of octagonal oak

posts. In the Cellars are now exhibited some pieces transferred from other parts of the palace, for example exquisitely carved ALTAR RAILS of about 1630, made for
the Chapel.

The Beer Cellars are followed by the WINE CELLAR, below
the great Watching Chamber. It has a brick vault with
plain ribs on octagonal piers. From its N exit one returns
to the N Cloister and continues N into the SERVING
PLACE by the side of the Great Kitchens. Several oak
hatches open into the Serving Place, and it is worth re-
membering the functionally sound relation of Kitchen to
Great Hall. The dais end as well as the screen end of the
Hall could easily be reached up two different stairs by the
servants receiving the dishes in the Serving Place. The
GREAT KITCHENS are an object lesson in large-scale
Tudor catering. The E room was added by Henry VIII to
Wolsey's Kitchen next door to the W. Wolsey's Kitchen
is now divided by a partition wall with C18 brick ovens.
Only one of the three fireplaces is in the room open to the
public. It is 17 ft wide. Henry VIII's Great Kitchen has
three large fireplaces. In one of these a spit is in position.
Several contemporary cooking utensils are exhibited.

Continuing along the N Cloister visitors enter the Cloisters
round the ROUND KITCHEN COURT. They are of
Wolsey's time. From the E range the CHAPEL ROYAL is 40b
reached. Its plan belongs to Wolsey, but it was altered by
Henry VIII in 1535–6. The Chapel proper is preceded in
the W by a wider antechapel (the scheme familiar from
such earlier Oxford College chapels as New College or
Magdalen). Access to the antechapel is by a doorway with
two early Renaissance panels in which Wolsey's arms have
been replaced by Henry's impaling Seymour. The gallery
of dark wood, the columns supporting it, the staircase
leading up to it and the Royal Pew above are all early C18.
This was indeed the time when the chapel was thoroughly
overhauled. There are rainwater heads outside with the
date 1711. Of the same period are the panelling of the
chapel itself and the splendid REREDOS with coupled
fluted Corinthian giant columns supporting a wide broken

segmental pediment. The carving is by *Grinling Gibbons*. The painted decoration along the top parts of the walls is contemporary but makes a very poor show compared with Gibbons's uncanny skill. The broad mighty curve of the reredos pediment is in strong contrast to the roof, with its stars of lierne vaulting and its exuberant pendants, as typical an example of English work of the 1530s as can be found anywhere in the palace. The fact that it is timber and not stone (like the Divinity School or the Cathedral Choir in Oxford or Henry VII Chapel in Westminster Abbey) will disappoint only those who know it. Of furnishings the former ALTAR RAILS have already been mentioned, the COMMUNION TABLE and BENCHES belong to the Wren period, the ORGAN was made by *Christopher Schrider*, Father Smith's son-in-law (cf. Westminster Abbey). Amongst the PLATE are a Cup, Cover-Paten, and Almsdish of 1668 and two Flagons of 1687.

THE CHAPEL COURT has on the ground floor Tudor brickwork, especially early on the E side. In the NE corner is a turret with its original lead cupola. Otherwise there are many C17 and C18 alterations.

49 We can now return to one of the entrances to FOUNTAIN COURT. *Wren* began his work at Hampton Court in 1689. It had originally been intended, it seems, to rebuild the whole palace. In the end the W parts were left intact, and Wren was free in his design only around Fountain Court, where Wolsey's buildings were pulled down. Even so, however, the W side of the Court, lower than the others, has plenty of jagged Tudor excrescences looking down on to the serenity of the work of 1689 to *c.* 1702. The Court is only 117 by 101 ft, as against, for example, the (about) 290 by 150 ft of Schlüter's Court at Berlin, the (about) 300 by 300 ft of the Louvre Court, and the (about) 300 by 230 ft of Stockholm. With its brick on the stone arcade and with stone trim to the windows it is cheerful, a little busy, and anything but grand and courtly. The piers of the arcade are square and squat, and above the long, noble windows of the main floor is a row of circular panels with wreaths and then an attic storey above—no firm subordi-

nation of everything to one ruling effect, a comfortable spreading out of little effects instead. The ground-floor arcades incidentally have semicircular arches, but the cross-vaults behind them are depressed, and this shows outside. The reason is that the floor level of the first floor inside is lower than the apex of the arches of the arcade (a typically Baroque discrepancy between what appears and what is real). Wren had done the same at Trinity Library, Cambridge, some twenty years before.

The E walk of the cloister round Fountain Court has two symmetrical apsidal recesses, the N one opening into the main entrance hall from the E side. This hall, plain with four Tuscan columns, is in the centre of the E front, and the duplication of the recesses is therefore a clever way (similar to many used before in France) to achieve symmetry when two opposite fronts of the same room have two different axes.

The E FRONT is twenty-three windows wide. It has a low 47b ground floor with boldly segment-headed windows (an early example of this in England), a main floor and small round windows above, and an attic storey topped by a balustrade (as in the fronts towards the Court rather a scattering than a pulling together of effects). The corners have quoins but no other emphasis. In the centre is a seven-bay projection and in the centre of this a further projection of three bays. So there is a convincing *crescendo* from the plain brickwork of the walls to pilasters and then attached columns. Also the wall of the whole projection is ashlar-faced. But while the *crescendo* works from outer ends towards centre, it fails in the development from bottom to top; for the main pediment is not the crowning motif of the whole. The attic storey continues behind it, and the top balustrade runs all the way through, keeping the pediment under. So from the point of view of the Grand Manner Hampton Court is infinitely inferior to Versailles or the Louvre Colonnade. The English have never been able to carry off that autocratic grandeur, and William III could do it less and wanted less to do it than almost any other British monarch. (On Charles II's gardens, however, cf. below.) To be successful in the Versailles style, the largest scale is necessary as imitators at Schleissheim, Ludwigsburg, Caserta, Stupinigi, La Granja, etc., knew only too well. With a mere 300 ft, Louis le Grand cannot be emulated.

The S FRONT shows the same qualities and shortcomings. Here again the centre with its four columns and no pediment is weak, and the sub-centres in the middle of the recessed parts a little restless. The balustrade seems more than anything to crush all impetus.

Regarding details of the two fronts the magnificent ironwork of the three E entrances compensates for much else that is missing. The sash windows here and in other places at Hampton Court are amongst the earliest in England; the sculpture in the E pediment is by *Cibber*, 1694–6. Rainwater heads towards the S corner of the E wing have the date 1691, in the S wing 1690. The two statues of Mars and Hercules in front of the S façade are by an unknown sculptor. The statues on the top balustrade have been removed.

To finish the walk round the outside of the Palace, a small Elizabethan structure with the date 1568 stands W of the S front. After that the exterior of Wolsey's work appears again, though largely hidden by the ORANGERY, built by *Wren* under Queen Anne, a very plain utilitarian building which now houses the *Mantegna* cartoons of the Triumph of Caesar. Past the Orangery one is faced with the E side of Henry VIII's SW wing of Wolsey's W façade. The buildings here are partly C18 and partly late C19. The VINE in its Vinery was planted in 1769. The main branch is now over 100 ft long.

Interiors on the First Floor. (The description follows the way from the public entrance to the public exit.)

Entry to the State Rooms is by Wren's Colonnade in Clock Court.

KING'S STAIRCASE. The Wren part of the palace has two suites of state apartments known as the King's and the Queen's Sides. Hence there are two grand staircases too, both of the same type specially popular at that time, with flights of stairs and landings occupying three sides of a square or rectangle. The centre remains free as a wide open well. The airiness of this Baroque arrangement is emphasized by the replacement of heavy stone balusters by *Tijou's* lovely wrought-iron balustrade. The paintings by *Verrio* are dull in comparison, with the insensitive way in which the compositions go over the cove and the rounded corners without any articulation.

The large KING'S GUARD ROOM is panelled and displays 3,000 pieces of arms neatly arranged under William III.

Off the Guard Room to the w a door leads down into some of the few remaining WOLSEY ROOMS. There are three here of which the westernmost is divided into two. They have some linenfold panelling, two original fireplaces, and one and a half original ceilings of great importance. For 39 these ceilings seem to be the earliest examples of that art of the plasterer which was to develop so prodigiously in Elizabethan and Jacobean days. Here for the first time do we find these fine ribs interlaced with stars, lozenges, and bands. There are no pendants, only knobs in the centre of the stars.

To the E of the Guard Room the KING'S SIDE begins. In the first four rooms the most notable decoration is the wood carving from *Gibbons's* workshop. The large paint- 50a ing of William III landing at Margate, by *Kneller*, 1697, is typical of the helplessness of English court artists when it came to celebrating the glories and triumphs of royalty. In the same room as this painting is William's Chair of State, a far more successful work of art, because of its sober functional soundness. With the KING'S BEDROOM the *Verrio* ceiling paintings begin, characteristically English 49 in their tempering of Baroque ideals. The Italian artist, schooled in France, has done in his far from masterly way what Wren did in architecture : he has made the sweeping compositions of Southern Baroque palatable in our climate by freezing all individual figures. Thus they appear as firm and fixed as a Wren column. The colours are dismally lacking in fire.

Through some smaller rooms the E front and the Queen's Side is reached. The QUEEN'S GALLERY has what is perhaps the most attractive fireplace in the palace, by *John Nost* (or rather *van Ost*), with a scrolled pediment, two cupids, two doves, and a bust of Venus, very free and playful as a composition. The tapestries are *Le Brun* designs. The QUEEN'S BEDROOM has a *Thornhill* ceiling of 1715 (*Verrio* had died in 1707) and show once more that Thornhill was the only man in England capable of some Baroque *brio*. Below the cornice are medallions of George I, the Prince of Wales, Princess Caroline, and their son Frederick. The furniture was made in 1715–16 for the Prince of Wales and is a good example of the comfort and 'middle class' commodiousness of English cabinet-making and upholstery at the time of Richardson, even when done for the court. The furniture in the QUEEN'S DRAWING ROOM was made for Queen Anne. The ceiling and wall paintings by *Verrio* glorify the Queen's justice, the Queen's power over the four quarters of the globe, and the Fleet (in the backgrounds of the scene with Prince George of Denmark as Lord High Admiral, and of that with Cupid drawn by sea-horses).

With the PUBLIC DINING ROOM a group of rooms is entered (extending N in the Prince of Wales's apartment, not open to the public) which were remodelled under George II. The same is true of the QUEEN'S PRESENCE CHAMBER and QUEEN'S GUARD CHAMBER which form the N side of Fountain Court. They should be seen in conjunction with the Queen's Staircase, as they are the beginning of the Queen's Suite, but the tour through the palace first turns S and covers the series of small rooms behind the State Rooms of the E front. This series faces Fountain Court. It is important to remember that Wren provided such cabinets for the comfort of the Royal families. Not the whole of their daily lives was spent in the larger and chilly saloons. Among the seven small rooms the first, the QUEEN'S PRIVATE CHAPEL, fitted up for Queen Caroline, wife of George II, is distinguished by an octagonal skylight. The CLOSET, next to the Chapel, and the

QUEEN'S PRIVATE CHAMBER have marble wash basins in the walls.

All the windows on the S side of Fountain Court belong to the CARTOON GALLERY, completed in 1695 for the celebrated seven *Raphael* cartoons which Charles I had bought in 1632 and which are now at the Victoria and Albert Museum. The tapestries made from them and now hanging in their place are of the C17. The fireplace has a charming, oddly Rococo-looking relief of the Triumph of Venus, by *Nost*. The COMMUNICATION GALLERY fills the W range of Fountain Court. Its chief original interest was that it housed the Mantegna Cartoons now in the Orangery (*see* p. 76). To the N of the Gallery is the QUEEN'S STAIRCASE, which ends the tour of the Apartments. It is in plan like the King's Staircase, and has like it an iron balustrade by *Tijou*. The ceiling painting is by *Kent*, dated 1735. Against the W wall is a large (Dutch?) painting of the late C17 representing the Arts and Sciences introduced to Apollo and Diana.

The Queen's Staircase incorporates in its W, N, and S walls masonry of Wolsey's time, and immediately behind the Communication Gallery on the W there are also fragments of Wolsey's original building left, fragments belonging to the very first years of his activity at Hampton Court. One room at least is very completely preserved, the one known as WOLSEY'S CABINET (accessible from the Gallery). It is only about 12 ft square, but possesses the most perfect Early Renaissance ceiling in England. The pattern is of interlaced octagons with inset squares of gold on blue. Everything is covered by small-scale ornament; but the ornament is of such Italian clarity and purity that the impression, though extremely busy, is nowhere confused. The frieze is especially delicate, but the paintings below are later, of the heavy somewhat coarse style of Leonardesque (Last Supper), Michelangelesque (Scourging of Christ) Romanism in the Netherlands. Of the linenfold panelling much is modern restoration.

The tour through the palace turns now into the N, Tudor parts, along the Cloisters to the E and N of the Round

Kitchen Court. A door leads to the upper floor of the CHAPEL ROYAL (*see* p. 73). The GREAT WATCHING CHAMBER dates from 1535 and 1536. It has a ceiling with a rib design similar to those of Wolsey's rooms s of Clock Court (*see* p. 77), but with pendants. The walls have early C16 Flemish tapestry, and the grand curved bay window glass made by Willement in 1846. This room was under Henry VIII the Guard Chamber at the entrance to the King's State Rooms which are no longer in existence.

The scale of magnificence of Henry VIII's Hampton Court can now only be judged by the GREAT HALL, erected in 1531-6, instead of Wolsey's more modest hall. It is 97 by 40 by 60 ft, as compared with the 115 by 40 ft of the contemporary hall of Christ Church, and with the 244 by 70 ft of Westminster Hall. The roofing type known as hammerbeam roofs was invented at Westminster Hall late in the C14; the roofs of Christ Church 1525-9 and of Hampton Court are amongst its proudest descendants. The designer at Hampton was probably the King's Carpenter, *John Nedeham*. The technique is wholly Gothic but the detail has the same Renaissance finesse as Wolsey's Cabinet. The Screen on the other hand is still medieval throughout. As in all English medieval halls the screen hides a passage for servants to carry food and drink through, but whereas the normal arrangement for the kitchen is to be right behind the screen passage, the size of Hampton Court made this impossible and dishes were, as has been said on p. 73, brought up from the Kitchens on the ground floor by the stair to the N of the screen passage. The stair to its s is the main entrance from Anne Boleyn's Gateway. Communication between Kitchen and High Table end, that is E end, of the Great Hall, is by the stair ending in the HORN ROOM, NE of the Hall. The bay window of the Hall has a little fan vault high up and two long slim three-light windows. There was originally a central hearth, now marked by a stone slab. The corresponding opening in the roof has been closed. The tapestries against the walls are designed by *van Orley* and woven by *Pannemaker* of Brussels, *c.* 1540.

37b
38

Churches: Harlington, Norman doorway

Churches: Laleham, Norman arcade

2

Churches: Harmondsworth, early and late thirteenth-century arcades, North chancel arcade fourteenth century

Churches: Uxbridge, fifteenth century. In the foreground the large chapel of the Guild of St Mary and St Margaret

4

Churches: Uxbridge, hammerbeam roof, fifteenth century

Churches: Perivale, tower, weatherboarded

Churches: Harmondsworth, tower, lower parts flint, upper parts brick,
c. 1500

(b) *Churches:* Hayes, porch, early sixteenth century

(a) *Churches:* Harlington, porch, c. 1500, reconstructed

Churches: Littleton, thirteenth-century chancel of flint, sixteenth-century brick tower. The early eighteenth century completed the tower and added the north chapel

(a) *Churches:* Great Stanmore, St John, *c.* 1630

(b) *Churches:* Twickenham, 1714–15, by John James.
The tower is fifteenth century

Churches: Stanmore, St Lawrence, 1715–20. Built and decorated for the Duke of Chandos

Churches: Willesden, All Souls, Harlesden, 1875 by Tarver, roof

Churches: Hampstead Garden Suburb, St Jude, 1910
by Sir Edwin Lutyens

(b) *Church Furnishings*: West Drayton, Font, fifteenth century

(a) *Church Furnishings*: Hendon, Norman font

14

Church Furnishings: West Drayton, Chalice and Paten, 1507

Church Furnishings: Littleton, Chancel Stalls, fifteenth century

Church Furnishings: Harefield, Altar Back and Altar Rails, Flemish, *c.* 1700

(b) *Church Painting:* Hayes, sixteenth century

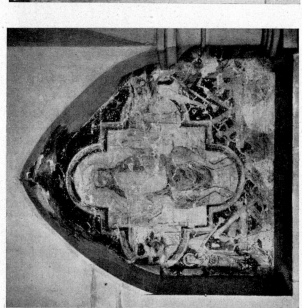

(a) *Church Painting:* East Bedfont, c. 1300

18

Church Monuments: (a) Hillingdon, Brass to Lord Strange, 1509

(b) Hornsey, Incised Slab to George Rey, late sixteenth century

19

Church Monuments: South Mimms, Henry Frowyck the Younger, 1527 (?)

Church Monuments: South Mimms, Henry Frowyck the Elder,
c. 1540 (?)

21

Church Monuments: Cranford, Sir Roger Aston, 1612

Church Monuments: Stanwell, Lord Knyvett, 1622

Church Monuments: Harefield, Countess of Derby, 1636. On the right
Lady Newdigate, 1774, probably by R. Hayward

Church Monuments: Hillingdon, Sir Edward Carr, 1637

(a) *Church Monuments:* Great Stanmore, St John, Sir John Wolstenholme, 1639, by Nicholas Stone

(b) *Church Monuments:* Ickenham, Robert Clayton, 1665

Church Monuments: Hendon, Sir Jeremy Whichcot, 1677

(b) *Church Monuments*: Stanmore, St Lawrence, Duke of Chandos, probably by Andrew Carpentier

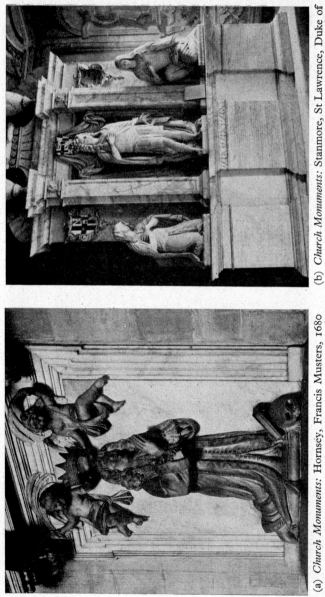

(a) *Church Monuments*: Hornsey, Francis Musters, 1680

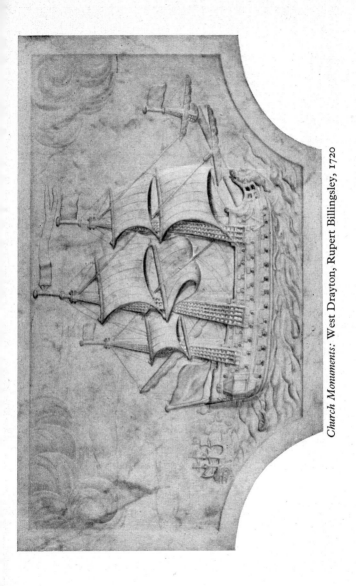

Church Monuments: West Drayton, Rupert Billingsley, 1720

Church Monuments: Hillingdon, Earl of Uxbridge, 1743

Church Monuments: Stanmore, John Dalton, by Bacon, 1791

31

IOANNI LION
PRESTONIAE·IN·PAROECIA·HARROVIENSI
MORTVO
SEXT·NON·OCTOBR·ANNO·CHRISTI·MDXCII
ET·IN·HAC·ECCLESIA·SEPVLTO
FVNDI·DOMINO·CVLTORI·QVE
ASSIDVO·FRVGI·PROBO
SAPIENTI·SINE·VIA·ET·ARTE
ET·QVIA·BONIS·SVIS·OPTIME·VTI·NOVIT
VNICE·FORTVNATO
SCHOLAE·IMPENSIS·EIVS·EXTRVCTAE
ET·AD·PVEROS·GRAECIS·AC·LATINIS·LITTERIS
ERVDIENDOS·INSTITVTAE
GVBERNATORES·MAGISTRI·ATQVE·ALVMNI
HOC·MONIMENTVM·COLLATA·PECVNIA
PONENDVM·CVRAVERVNT
ANNO·SACRO·MDCCCXV.

Church Monuments: Harrow, John Lyon, by Flaxman, 1815

(a) *Village Building:* Pinner, Tudor Cottage

(b) *Village Building:* Eastcote, Old Cheyne Cottage

Village Building: Harmondsworth, Barn

34

(a) *Village Building:* Ickenham, Manor Farm

(b) *Village Building:* Enfield, Flour Mill, Lea Valley Road

(a) *Country Houses:* West Drayton, Manor House, Gatehouse

(b) *Country Houses:* Hampton Court, Drawbridge

(a) *Country Houses:* Hampton Court, Outer Gatehouse

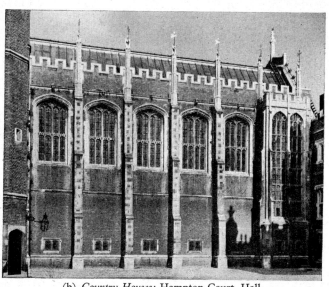

(b) *Country Houses:* Hampton Court, Hall

Country Houses: Hampton Court, Hall Roof

Country Houses: Hampton Court, Ceiling of Wolsey's Closet

(b) *Country Houses*: Hampton Court, Chapel, 1535–6.
The reredos is of *c.* 1710

(a) *Country Houses*: Hampton Court,
Medallion by Giovanni da Majano, 1521

Country Houses: Enfield, Fireplace from Enfield Palace, c. 1560

(a) *Country Houses:* Southall, 1587

(b) *Country Houses:* Tottenham, Bruce Castle, Elizabethan and late
seventeenth century

42

(a) *School:* Stanwell, Lord Knyvett's Free School, 1624

(b) *School:* Harrow, Old School, 1611

Country Houses: Boston Manor, Brentford, Fireplace, *c.* 1623

Country Houses: Boston Manor, Plaster Ceiling, *c.* 1623

(a) *Country Houses:* Swakeleys, *c.* 1630–5

(b) *Country Houses:* Boston Manor, Brentford, *c.* 1622–3, probably
altered 1670

(a) *Country Houses:* Forty Hall, Enfield, 1629–36, probably altered
c. 1700

(b) *Country Houses:* Hampton Court, East front, by Sir Christopher
Wren

Country Houses: Hampton Court, Colonnade in Clock Court, by Sir Christopher Wren

Country Houses: Hampton Court, Fountain Court, by Sir Christopher Wren

49

(a) *Country Houses:* Hampton Court, Ceiling by Verrio, King's Bedroom

(b) *Country Houses:* Hampton Court, Wood Carving by Grinling Gibbons, King's Private Dressing Room

50

Country Houses: Hampton Court, Wrought-iron Gate by Tijou

(a) *Town and Village Houses:* Shepperton, Rectory, façade of *c.* 1700

(b) *Town and Village Houses:* Twickenham, York House, *c.* 1700

The Riverside Village: Chiswick, The Mall

53

Country Houses: Hendon Place, portico, probably from Canons, early
eighteenth century

(a) *Country Houses:* Chiswick, Lord Burlington's Villa, *c.* 1720–5, the wings by J. Wyatt now pulled down

(b) *Country Houses:* Wrotham Hall, 1754, by Isaac Ware (*Copyright Country Life*)

Country Houses: Osterley Park, *c.* 1575, re-modelled by Robert Adam, 1763

Country Houses, Strawberry Hill, Twickenham, 1750–72

57

Country Houses: Syon House, Isleworth, Entrance Hall by Robert
Adam, 1763 (*Copyright Country Life*)

(a) *Country Houses:* Strawberry Hill, Twickenham, Holbein Chamber, 1759 (*Copyright Country Life*)

(b) *Country Houses:* Pitzhanger Manor, Ealing, by Sir John Soane, 1801–2

59

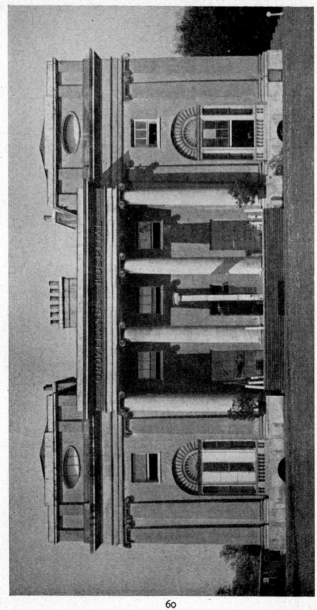

Country Houses: Grovelands, Southgate, by John Nash, 1797

Country Houses: Hanworth Club Hotel, *c.* 1800

(a) *Cottage Orné:* Hanwell, The Hermitage,
early nineteenth century

(b) *Country House:* Harrow Weald, Grims Dyke, by
Norman Shaw, 1872

(a) *Garden Suburb:* Bedford Park, Acton, designed by
Norman Shaw, 1875

(b) *Garden Suburb:* Hampstead Garden Suburb, designed by
Parker & Unwin, begun in 1907

Sudbury Town Station (London Transport), by Charles Holden, 1932

Gardens and Parks, and Buildings belonging to them. Wolsey
is said to have enclosed about 2,000 acres around his
palace. The main parts of this vast park are now the Home
Park to the E and Bushey Park to the N of the palace and
gardens.

The present appearance of both parks is, in spite of all later
alterations, that of the late C17 and the earliest C18, that is
the period of the greatest influence on all Europe of Versailles and *Le Nôtre's* immortal work there. William's
revolution was in this case indeed so unbloody that it was
no revolution at all. He followed the *Roi Soleil* just as
wholeheartedly as his more autocratic predecessor Charles
II had done when, just back from exile, he began to lay
out the gardens and park to the E of the Tudor Palace
(there was no Wren block yet) by having the mile-long
straight canal through the Home Park dug and diverting
it into a semicircle at its W end. These works appear
already in John Evelyn's Diary for 1662. The gardener
in charge seems to have been *John Rose*, a pupil of Le
Nôtre, though *Adrian May* and two French pupils of
Le Nôtre, *Beaumont* and *Le Quintenaye*, are also
mentioned. *May* was made supervisor of the 'French
gardeners' at Whitehall, St James and Hampton Court
in 1661.

But if the Home Park and Bushey Park are now the best
places in England in which to remember the grandeur of
Versailles, this is due to William III and his gardeners
George London and *Henry Wise*. The scheme was approved in 1689, and planting began immediately. They
planted the mile of the central N–S avenue through
Bushey Park to end in the S at a new *Cour d'Honneur*
planned by *Wren*. The Lion Gate is only a feeble echo
of the splendid approach of Wren's dreams. The avenue
has two central lines of chestnut-trees 168 ft from each
other and outside them four lines of lime-trees on each
side. The chestnut-trees are 42 ft apart, another 42 ft
separates them from the first line of lime-trees, and
another 42 ft lies between rows one and two of these.
Rows two and three have 66 ft in between, rows three and

M.—6

four again 42 ft. So if 42 ft is taken as the module of the composition, it would read thus:

$$m - \frac{3m}{2} - m - m - 4m - m - m - \frac{3m}{2} - m.$$

Two more lime avenues run towards the Paddock and Hampton village. The main avenue is interrupted about three-quarters down its length by a large circular pond in which in 1713 a bronze statue of Diana was placed on a high (but not high enough) rusticated pedestal. The figure had been made (according to Evelyn) by *Fanelli*, for the Privy Garden under Charles I. Its size may have been right for its original position; in Bushey Park it is far too small, and its elegant, smooth workmanship can only be appreciated by those provided with field-glasses.

The only important building inside the park was BUSHEY HOUSE, built early in the C18. Only its stables stand, a neat utilitarian structure of late Wren style.

More interesting are the stables of the STUD HOUSE in the HOME PARK, equally neat from outside and with the stalls divided off by wooden arcades with Tuscan columns (cf. Royal Mews below, p. 85). The house itself is chiefly 1817–18.

House and stables lie to the N of Charles II's canal, and it is advisable to walk along it to the W in order to obtain the Versaillean impression of the approach to the palace. The three main avenues in the Home Park may go back to Charles's plan or may be part of the new plan of William III, the centre-piece of which was the creation of the FOUNTAIN GARDEN. In its essence it still remains. *Wise* and *London* filled in the W end of Charles's canal, planted the three avenues of dwarf yew-trees which are now the feature in this part of the gardens that gives them most individuality, made the Broad Walk which runs along the E front of the palace and much further W and S (and can now boast one of England's most gorgeous herbaceous borders), and closed the Fountain Garden against the rougher Home Park outside by *Tijou's* masterly gates (now mostly at the S end of the Privy Garden). In the SW

51

corner of the Home Park was the BOWLING GREEN, with four corner pavilions. One of them remains, with C19 additions.

Following the Broad Walk to the S the entrance to the FLOWER GARDENS is reached. Their position, open to the S as against that of Wilderness and Tiltyard to the N, stands to reason. Of Henry VIII's PRIVY GARDEN nothing but some walling survives. The moat and the large number of heraldic beasts have long disappeared. At the S end of the Privy Garden are displayed ten out of the twelve magnificent GATES wrought by *Tijou* for the Fountain Garden, and for which he was paid the colossal sum of £2,160. They are perhaps the most spectacular individual piece of craftsmanship at Hampton Court, though of a skill so excessive as to hurt the feelings of any Ruskinian or Morrisite. In fact, however, there is a deliberate contrast between the broad luxuriant curves of the centre-pieces with lush three-dimensionally curling leaves and garlands and the plain sensible uprights in between.

The little KNOT GARDEN facing the Elizabethan corner of the S front of the palace is an imitation of Tudor gardening laid out in 1924. The SUNK GARDEN belongs in its general plan to the time of William III, but in its present appearance is an excellent example of that mixture of formal layout and informal, cottagey planting which one connects with Miss Jekyll and Sir Edwin Lutyens. S of the Sunk Garden stands the BANQUETING HOUSE. These small banqueting houses or plaisances are a typical piece of Tudor garden furnishing, but this one was only built *c*. 1700. Wren gave it its battlements, with the same (surprisingly early) feeling for the necessity of some harmony between a new building and a large and important set of pre-existing old ones which he had shown when completing Tom Tower in Oxford.

The tour of the gardens comes to a dead end here. The Orangery and the Vinery have already been mentioned (*see* p. 76). Visitors now retrace their steps to the E front of the palace and continue their tour of the gardens by

following the Broad Walk to the N. Behind the N corner of
Wren's façade appear the walls and roofs of the E range of
Chapel Court (*see* p. 74), and then a Tudor passage leading to the TENNIS COURT which was built by Henry
VIII in 1529, but has now a series of close-set large C18
windows which makes it as light looking as any sports
building of the present day. At the far N end of the Broad
Walk stands FLOWER POT GATE, one of the entrances to
the palace grounds from Hampton Court Road. It dates
from 1699 and has putti with baskets of fruit and flowers
by *Nost*. To the W of the N parts of Broad Walk lies the
WILDERNESS, a set piece in French late C17 gardens. Its
present landscaping is, of course, later; but the MAZE remains of the original layout. It is of hornbeams. Immediately N of the Maze is LION GATE, the chief N entrance
to the palace and the place in which Wren planned to have
his grand entrance from the Bushey Park avenue. As it is,
the Lion Gate is something of an anti-climax after the
scale of Bushey Park. The stonework bears Queen Anne's
monogram, the ironwork George I's.

The end of the tour of Hampton Court are the TILTYARD
GARDENS. It is here that in Henry VIII's time tourna-
ments were held. Spectators sat on towers placed at intervals along the high brick walls. Only one of them remains. The tiltyard became a kitchen garden under
William III, and an ornamental garden in 1924. From the
S exit of the Tiltyard Gardens the Outer Green Court is
reached, and from there turning W Hampton Green.

HAMPTON GREEN. An exceptionally fine group of houses
lies on its S side, close to the E end and turning S towards
HAMPTON COURT BRIDGE (rebuilt in 1933 in brick and
Portland stone to *Sir Edwin Lutyens's* designs). These
houses are all Crown property and were built mostly in
the time of William and Mary and Anne for people close
to the Court. Not one of them is outstanding, but as an
informal group they are well worth studying. The early
C19 MITRE HOTEL makes a stately start, then PALACE
GATE HOUSE and THE GREEN, OLD COURT HOUSE
(leased in 1708 to *Wren* and remodelled by him and again

c. 1730: note the enormous tulip-tree in the garden),
COURT COTTAGE and FARADAY HOUSE, with a late
C18 curved bay. After that the BEARSTED MEMORIAL
HOSPITAL, built apparently early in the C19 and the
largest private house on the S side of the Green: eleven
bays.

The ROYAL MEWS consists of a magnificent barn dated 1570
with two rows of small round-headed windows in the refaced front wall and a king-post roof (the building is now
divided into two storeys), and a square block of somewhat
earlier date. This is built around a courtyard. Most of the
detail is renewed, but the Tuscan arcade opening out into
the stalls remains inside the NW range. On the N side of
the Green stands the most ambitious of the houses sub-
ordinate to the palace: HAMPTON COURT HOUSE, now
a home for old ladies. A nine-bay front with low curved
galleries leading to square little wings. Mansard roof with
central dome. Probably mid C18, much altered, and never
very distinctive in its architecture. In the garden a grotto
with plenty of ammonites. – Further E PRESTBURY
HOUSE, early C18; CRAVEN HOUSE, *temp.* George III;
and so on to HAMPTON COURT ROAD. In it on the r.
several tea-houses with verandahs, some of them as fanciful as if they stood at New Orleans; on the l. facing them
WILDERNESS HOUSE, a noble plain five-bay house of
c. 1700. Its neighbour is the KING'S ARMS, with two
symmetrical curved bays, early C19. Walking on towards
Hampton Wick one passes IVY HOUSE between Lion
Gate and Flower Pot Gate (*see* Hampton Court: Gardens),
then GLYCINE HOUSE, with old iron rails and gate,
PARK HOUSE, Late Georgian, SUNDIAL COTTAGE,
half-timbered, probably C17, and LANCASTER HOUSE
of *c.* 1700. The latter is in Hampton Wick parish.

HAMPTON WICK

PARISH CHURCH ST JOHN THE BAPTIST, 1829–30, by
Lapidge (cf. Hampton Church). The usual rather starved
yellow stock brick building of the period with lancet windows, W turret, and galleries on three sides.

HOME PARK HOUSE, close to the Hampton Wick entrance to the Home Park, early C18, of good proportions. Along the road to Hampton Court more old houses, so close to the palace that they are noted under Hampton Court.

HANWELL

The remains of the village are a great surprise, a little triangular green and a curved lane with plenty of old and some highly original houses leading to the church. The s end to the prospect is the old Brent viaduct of the Great Western Railway, a fitting if austere backcloth and a perfect screen from the other side, where the Uxbridge Road carries the main western traffic.

PARISH CHURCH ST MARY. Not an old building. By *G. G. Scott*, 1841, one of his earliest churches, flint with London stock dressings and a broader spire; in the detail still something of the thinness and prim rectangularity of the Commissioners' style. The interior also is still somewhat timid. Tall octagonal piers, and an odd small clerestory with quatrefoil windows. – PLATE. Good late C18 collection (Chalices, Patens, and Flagon of 1781). – MONUMENT to Margaret Emma Orde by *P. M. van Gelder* (the sculptor of Adam's Montagu Monument at Warkton), 1806, modest but quite original: a plain slim urn against a back plate flanked by fluted demi-columns with unorthodox bases and caps, and supporting a kind of gable with convex sides; a touch of Chinese in the Grecian chastity of the rest.

ST THOMAS, Boston Road, by *Edward Maufe*, 1934. The street runs along the E side which displays a Crucifixion by *Eric Gill* against and below the round E window, and the tall square NE tower with a green copper cap. All other windows are narrow lancets, the one in the centre of the W side being the largest. The church has a brick exterior, but inside the concrete is showing in the walls and the cross-vaults without transverse arches or ribs (an effect of poverty doubtless not intentional).

CUCKOO SCHOOLS, E of Greenford Avenue, 1864. Big and
self-possessed with its tall tower, and highly incongruous
amid the little streets and crescents of the good between-
the-two-world-wars council housing.

CHURCH ROAD. By the little Green: CROSSWAY, and
next is to the N HANWELL PARK, now Golf Club House,
indifferent Georgian. Then to the W SPRING COTTAGE,
MADGE HILL, THE SPRING (is it early C19 or altered
about 1910?), the HERMITAGE (a peach of an early C19   62a
Gothick thatched cottage with two pointed windows and
an ogee-arched door, all on a minute scale), and REC-
TORY COTTAGE.

HANWORTH

The monuments of Hanworth are few and too scattered to
be taken in as related to each other.

PARISH CHURCH ST GEORGE, a dull *Teulon* design of
1865, lacking even in those obtrusive qualities which make
many of his churches at least very noticeable (Ealing). Of
the medieval church nothing remains but two late C15
pieces of stained glass, angels, surrounded by early C17
quarries with flowers. (A Royal coat of arms from the
same window, dated 1625, is now in the Rectory.) James
Wyatt replaced the original church by a small one of his
in 1812. The present nave seems largely his, but it is so
overlaid by Teulon's design that no impression of its real
character (it had a little polygonal bell turret) can be obtained. – PLATE. Chalice and Paten, 1632; Paten, 1780;
Flagon, 1882.

The original HANWORTH HOUSE was a shooting box of
Henry VIII, 'his chief place of pleasure', as Camden says.
After his death it belonged to Katherine Parr. Of that
period the stables give a vague reminder. Only parts of the
walls and two large fireplaces at the back are Tudor. The
house itself, known as Tudor Court, is *c.* 1850–60 and of
no merit. In front are two late C18 garden structures opposite each other, each in its pediment with a terracotta
medallion so exactly like those made in 1521 by *Giovanni*

da Majano for Hampton Court that they must belong together.

HANWORTH PARK. The estate is now largely an aerodrome. In its middle still surrounded by trees stands the house, now the Hanworth Club Hotel, built after a fire in 1797, with a delightful façade and a large Italianate mid-C19 addition with a tower in the W. The S side is of two storeys with a one-storeyed Greek Doric four-column portico, and four bays l. and four bays r. of it. These as well as the whole upper floor have cast-iron verandahs of graceful forms. Above the upper verandah appears in the centre instead of a pediment a barge-boarded gable of low pitch. ·

HANWORTH HOUSE. The house now known under that name is in Main Street much further S. Its centre is *c.* 1700, with an C18 addition on the W and a modern one on the E.

ORIEL SCHOOL, Hounslow Road, by *W. T. Curtis* and *Burchett*, 1936. A typical example of progressive Middlesex C.C. architecture of the date.

HAREFIELD

Coming from London it is only at Harefield close to the border between Middlesex, Herts, and Bucks that one reaches the open country and can forget about the outer dormitory ring of the metropolis.

PARISH CHURCH ST MARY. It lies right in the fields, at the foot of the hill which the village climbs up—an irregular picturesque little building with aisles the same height as the nave and three distinct roofs. The N aisle and the low NW tower are battlemented. The building material is mainly flint rubble with stone dressings, but part of the tower is refaced with brick, and the S aisle has delightful flint and stone chequerwork. The interior is a pleasant mixture of many periods. The C14 dominates with the typical quatrefoil S nave piers with four slim intermediate shafts, the pointed arches with S-shaped chamfers and the curvilinear tracery of the S aisle

windows. But the w wall of the nave is supposed to
incorporate Norman masonry, and the chancel dates back
to the C13: see a blocked lancet window in the N wall.
Tower, N aisle, and N chancel chapel are early C16. The
nave roof is barrel-shaped and plastered; so is the chancel
roof, but with pretty early Gothic Revival panelling. The
detail of the chancel arch seems to belong to the same
style.

The prevailing impression in the church is one of happy
crowding: BOX PEWS, a Gothic Revival GALLERY in the
w part of the N aisle, a SCREEN of c. 1500 (much restored)
separating N aisle from N chancel chapel, plenty of other
furnishings, and more funeral monuments than any other
church of similar size anywhere near London.

The chancel especially is as cram-full of curious objects
as the rooms of the Soane Museum. The REREDOS with
sumptuous acanthus scroll and ribbonwork carving and
two elegant kneeling angels on top looking up towards two
COMMANDMENT BOARDS of frosted glass, the equally
sumptuous ALTAR RAILS and the CHAIRS are said to   17
come from a Flemish monastery. In style they are as close
to French work as they are alien in England. – The Georgian PULPIT is an intricately combined affair with reading-
desk and pew for the parish clerk, four little cages of
different size, shape, and height. – a good late C17 CHEST
of hutch type is in the Vestry. – Of ancient GLASS there
are only a few C16 pieces of little importance in the E
window of the N aisle. – PLATE. Chalice and Paten, 1561;
Chalice, c. 1629; Flagon and Paten, 1720.

MONUMENTS. They must be taken topographically.
Two large monuments jog against the reredos, four-square
and solid in comparison with its courtly grandeur. On the
r. is the most stately of all the Harefield monuments, that
of Alice Spencer, Countess of Derby † 1636, a four-poster   24
tomb with the Countess lying on a tomb-chest in whose
w wall three kneeling daughters are set in niches. The four
columns with thick looped-up curtains of stone support a
baldacchino with crests at the corners. The renewed colouring is somewhat gaudy, and the whole of a robust naïvety,

surprising if really by the hand of *Maximilian Colt* (Mrs
Esdaile) who carved the monument to Queen Elizabeth
at Westminster Abbey. The second husband of the
Countess was Lord Chancellor Egerton whose daughter
was the mother of Lady Julian Newdigate, and it is the
Newdigate family whose members are commemorated in
most of the other Harefield monuments. A famous carver
of a later generation, *Grinling Gibbons,* showed his more
up-to-date version of the Countess of Derby motif in his
monument to the left of the altar, dedicated to Mary, wife
of Sir Richard Newdigate † 1692, and Sir Richard himself.
Here again a reclining figure and a canopy with curtains.
But now all is white, the Lady lies in a comfortable position half sitting up; she displays a simple loose Roman
robe and no emotion whatever. – The s wall of the chancel
has a recessed tomb-chest of *c.* 1500 with against the back
of the niche the kneeling little brass effigies of John Newdigate † 1545 and his wife with thirteen children. Above
this in the wall are three large identical niches with three
white urns of very similar shape. The middle one is to
Elizabeth the mother of Sir Roger Newdigate (founder of
the Newdigate Prize) † 1765, signed *R. H.* (Mrs Esdaile:
Richard Hayward), that on the l. is to Sophia his first wife
† 1774, evidently by the same hand, that to the r. to
Hester, his second wife † 1800 (by *J. Bacon Jun.*). The
left urn has a reclining allegorical figure and the genius of
death on top, and says: Fungar Inani Munere!. The middle
one has Faith, Hope, and Charity, and Religion on top
and says: ΤΩΝ ΑΓΑΘΩΝ Η ΜΝΗΜΗ ΑΕΙΘΑΛΗΣ. The
right one has Religion kneeling and an angel above and
says: ΜΑΚΑΡΙΟΙ ΟΙ ΠΕΝΘΟΥΝΤΕΣ. The slender dark
niches, the chaste whiteness of the urns, and the classical
imagery are in the strangest contrast to the massiveness
of the preceding monuments of the Baroque. – Above the
niches mostly restored pieces of c15 to c17 armour,
especially notable the c15 salade. – Against the N wall of
the chancel several individually less important wall monuments, for example Sarah Newdigate † 1695 (with two
seated cherubs l. and r. of an urn, in spite of its indifferent

quality by *Grinling Gibbons*), Richard Newdigate † 1727, with a bust (according to Mrs Esdaile by *Rysbrack*) on top, Edward Newdigate † 1734, with a profile portrait in relief in an oval medallion (Mrs Esdaile: *Rysbrack*?), and Charles Parker † 1795 (son-in-law of a Newdigate), with an allegorical scene by *J. Bacon Jun.*

In the N chancel chapel monument to Sir Robert and Sir Francis Ashby † 1617 and 1623, the usual affair with the principal figures kneeling opposite each other, their children in relief below, and with columns with looped-up curtains on l. and r. The Ashbys of Breakspears were after the Newdigates the chief landowners in and around Harefield. In the same chapel various brasses: William Ashby and his wife who died 1537, George Ashby † 1514 and wife, both palimpsest. A tablet shows reproductions of the fragments of late C14 and C15 figures on the back of the Ashby brasses.

In the nave against a spandrel on the N side William Ashby † 1760, an excellent portrait bust above a grey oval inscription tablet with white ash branches around, ascribed by Mrs Esdaile to *Sir Robert Taylor*, the architect-sculptor.

In the S aisle against the S wall the small brass to Editha, wife of William Newdigate † 1444, the earliest Newdigate effigy and the earliest monument in the church altogether. Also a tomb-chest of *c.* 1500 similar to the one in the chancel. Yet another with brasses of John Newdigate † 1528, his wife † 1544, and seventeen children, against the E wall. In the SE corner epitaph to Sir John Newdigate † 1610, and his wife, the same usual type as the Ashby monument in the N chapel, but a little earlier in style in that it has pilasters instead of columns and a round-headed niche instead of the curtain arrangement and the out-curving entablature of the other. By *W. White*. In the NE corner Sir Richard Newdigate † 1678, and his wife † 1685, signed by (*William*) *Stanton*. Against the W wall a pretty if somewhat sentimental urn with broken lily carved on; it is the monument to Diana Ball † 1765.

On the floor several black marble slabs, for example to Abraham and John Stanyon, by *William Stanton*.

Against the outer N wall the tablet to Robert Mossendew, gamekeeper to the Ashby family † 1744, with a primitive relief and the following inscription:

> In frost and snow thro' Hail & rain
> He scour'd the woods & trudg'd the plain
> The steady pointer, Leads the way,
> Stands at the scent then springs the prey
> The timorous birds from stubble rise
> With pinions stretch'd divide the skys
> The scatter'd lead pursues the sight,
> And death in Thunder stops their flight.
> His spaniel of true English kind
> Who's gratitude reflam'd his mind
> This servant in an honest way
> In all his actions copy'd Tray.

In the churchyard an unusual number of wooden 'bedhead' tombstones.

The manor house of the Newdigates stood S of the church. It was razed to the ground early in the C19. The manor house of the Ashbys, BREAKSPEAR, still stands on the road to Ruislip. The centre is late C17 brickwork, with a shell-hooded door on the N side concealing a hall and a dining-room of the C16 and early C17. Close by is a delightful C17 DOVECOTE, square with pyramidal roof. The walls are brick with diaper work of vitrified headers. No purist can object to the luxuriant growth of creepers. A third manor house was MOOR HALL, ½ m. S of Harefield church. It belonged in the Middle Ages to the Order of St John of Jerusalem; a CHAPEL of the early C13 is the only surviving feature. It is only 34½ by 18 ft and has flint rubble walls with stone dressings, lancet windows, and indications of the original division into two storeys.

The centre of Harefield Village is the spacious Green with the KING'S ARMS, a half-timbered inn chiefly of the C17, on one side. HAREFIELD HOUSE of the early C19 stands slightly to the S. Opposite it is the VICARAGE of the

grossly picturesque Gothic type of *c*. 1860 which is dis-
cussed more fully under Harrow. The two buildings start
a main street down the hill with quite a number of pretty
cottages, and towards the end the ALMSHOUSES, built
by the Countess of Derby (whose monument is in the
church) in 1600. They are of brick on an H-shaped plan,
with straight-gabled roofs and groups of diagonal chimney-stacks. N of the Green there is now (on the site of
Harefield Park) the HAREFIELD COUNTY HOSPITAL, a
large complex of soundly designed buildings completed in
1937 (by *W. T. Curtis*). Further out CRIPPS FARM COT-
TAGE with its barns, one of the best of the twenty-five
Harefield farms mentioned in the Royal Commission
volume on Middlesex. To the NE is a characteristic classical BAPTIST CHAPEL of 1834.

By the SE corner of the parish close to the Ickenham border
lies BRACKENBURY FARM with its moat complete on
three sides and a good weatherboarded C16 barn. Half a
mile SE, on the road from Uxbridge to Harefield, is the
charming early C19 lodge to HAREFIELD PLACE, a
dainty thatched *cottage orné*. The house itself is indifferent
early C19.

(In addition the MTCP lists: CROWS NEST FARM, Breakspear Road, C16–C17 with interesting brick detail;
WHITE HORSE INN, C18 brick; MANOR COURT, between church and Harefield House, partly C16, partly late
C17.)

HARLINGTON

S of the village is open country, though the Great West Road
is near, N is the railway and much new housing. The church
is on the W side of the village lane, on the other side are a
few farms with good buildings and barns (DAWLEY
MANOR, CHURCH FARM).

PARISH CHURCH SS PETER AND PAUL. Flint rubble
with much ironstone, a fine colour harmony especially as
seen with the old yew-trees to the N and S. The tower of
c. 1500 has a turret, a battlemented parapet, and a cupola

on the turret (cf. West Drayton, Harmondsworth, Uxbridge). The pretty s porch is *c.* 1500, reconstructed. The
nave is Norman and possesses the best Norman doorway
in the county, with four orders, the outer with battlement
motif on jambs and voussoirs, the second and third with
colonnettes (shaft-rings, zigzag decoration between, and
fluted capitals). The second voussoirs have beakhead
ornament, the third zigzag. The fourth order is plain. The
interior is not impressive; chancel of the C14 (with recess
in the s wall); N arcade and N aisle new. The trussed-
rafter roof may be as old as C14. – FONT. C12, square
bowl with round-headed blank arcades. – STAINED
GLASS. E window by *Kempe*, 1873. – OAK BRACKET, s
wall, beautifully carved with mid-C14 foliage. – PLATE.
Chalice, Paten, and Flagon of 1672, Dish of 1734, Paten
of 1775. – MONUMENTS. John Monemouthe † 1419,
rector; brass demi-figure; cf. Hayes, Stanwell, Greenford, Harrow, Against the same N wall of the chancel a
recess with a four-centred arched top and an elaborate
straight canopy (cf. South Mimms, Norwood, etc.). In
the recess were the small brasses of Gregory Lovell †
1545 and wife (now against s wall of chancel). There is
also a smaller recess in the larger, proving the use of the
monument as an Easter Sepulchre. In niches in the N and
s walls are the recumbent effigies on tomb-chests of Henrietta Fane, Countess of Salis † 1856, and of the Count de
Salis † 1836, by *R. C. Lucas* (whose fame is connected with
the dispute over the so-called Leonardo da Vinci Flora at
the Berlin Museum, restored or made by Lucas). In the
nave Sir John Benett, Lord Ossulstone † 1686, and his
two wives, with three outstandingly good portrait busts.
The Royal Commission dates the monument 1694–5.

HARMONDSWORTH

The village lies in yet undisturbed peace surrounded on all
sides by arterial and sub-arterial roads. Its first claim to re-
membrance is its tithe-barn, but the doorway of the church
also ranks amongst the chief monuments of Middlesex.

PARISH CHURCH ST MARY. Its distinguishing exterior
feature is the little open cupola on the top of a tower the 7
upper parts of which are of brick and contrast with the
flintwork of the lower part and the rest of the church.
The tower is on the SW, twice as wide as the S aisle which
is, in its S wall and arcade, C12. The doorway is next to that
of Harlington the most elaborate piece of Norman decoration in the county: of three orders, the inner with rosettes
and knots of square shapes running uninterrupted through
jambs and voussoirs, the middle one with plain shafts and
primitive beakheads in the voussoirs, and the outer again
with uninterrupted zigzag. It is reset in the C12 wall. The
arcade inside has cylindrical piers and scalloped capitals. 3
The arches are pointed and have hood-moulds. They
cannot be earlier than the early C13, that is their erection
must have come after that of the more completely preserved Norman arcades at Laleham. The N arcade opposite has wider spacing of the piers which are also C13.
The hood mould of the arch is the same as at Stanwell.
The N chapel was added in the C14, and the chancel removed in the C15. SEDILIA and PISCINA, both with
cinquefoiled heads belong to that date. The interior with
no clerestory is not specially impressive, though the roofs
of N chapel (hammerbeam) and nave are preserved and,
what is more, a good many of the low BOX PEWS of
c.1500 with slender buttresses. The FONT is absolutely
unadorned, octagonal of Purbeck marble and on round
shafts: c. 1200.
TITHE BARN. The Manor went from the King to William 34
of Wykeham in 1391, and he made it part of the endow-
ment of Winchester College. The barn probably belongs
to this period in the history of the manor. It is 190 ft long,
36 ft wide, and 36 ft tall. It is aisled and has for the nave
span tie-beams on curved braces supporting king-posts.
The main posts are 15 by 14-inch timbers. There are
three E entrances and three floored bays behind them.
The only two noteworthy houses lie opposite each other on
a narrow lane S of the Green and the church: THE
GRANGE is of 1675 and has the five bays, two storeys, and

hipped roof over a modillion cornice that belong to the date. But the windows are not evenly spaced, the door has no adornment, and the original staircase has rather heavy turned balusters. – HARMONDSWORTH HALL is indifferent red brick, C18.

(THE LODGE, early C19, and SUN HOUSE, timber-framed and re-fronted, are in the centre of the village; CENTRE HOUSE, timber-framed, C16, is at the W end; SIPSON HOUSE, late C18, in Sipson Road, Sipson Green. MTCP.)
LONDON AIRPORT (*q.v.*).

HARROW-ON-THE-HILL

Harrow means three things : an urban district, a town, and a school. As for the urban district, its population in 1949 was 222,000, and it includes Hatch End, Pinner, Stanmore, and Wealdstone, which are treated separately. On South Harrow (Roxeth) and North Harrow notes appear at the end of the account of town and school. There is between town and school, in the case of Harrow, no such separation as, say, between Godalming and Charterhouse. They have instead grown into each other, until in the end the school has sucked so much of its life-blood out of the town that we can now only with difficulty reconstruct the pre-school or even pre-Victorian appearance of Harrow-on-the-Hill, eminently attractive as it must have been. It enjoys all the advantages of a situation up a sudden eminence in a relatively flat landscape. The High Street runs up the gentlest ascent and comes close to the church whose spire is seen between the tree tops from the street as prominently as from the surrounding country on the N, E, and W. Much open country is still left around Harrow Hill, chiefly thanks to the school or indeed the various schools.

In the following pages the parish church will, as usual, be described first; for the rest it may be advisable to follow the course most likely (and advisable) for visitors, namely from Harrow-on-the-Hill station southwards.

PARISH CHURCH ST MARY. Externally the best thing is the general view with the rough-cast tower and its tall handsomely scaled, octagonal lead spire. In detail restorations have taken away most of the original character. The lower parts of the tower are Norman : the small windows N and S with enormous splays inside, and the modest W portal of two orders with an undecorated tympanum of flint resting on a very slightly segmental lintel. Nave and chancel are C13, the chancel with lancet windows, the nave of five bays with a plain double-chamfered pointed arcade on low round piers. The transepts seem to be a little later. Clerestory and roof belong to the C15. The roof is flat-pitched with cambered tie-beams on curved braces. The braces spring from wallposts carved with figures of apostles under canopies, and the wallposts in their turn rest on coarse grimacing head corbels. – FONT. C12, round bowl with ornament developed from scalloped Norman capitals; the shaft with spiral fluting. – PULPIT. Handsome oak of c. 1675 (though given to the church in 1708) supported on six scrolled brackets like the legs of contemporary tables. – STAINED GLASS. In the chancel lancet windows by *Kempe* and *Towers*; in the E window, by *Comper* 1908, individual figures, hardly any red, chiefly white and blue. – PLATE. Chalice and Paten of 1568, Chalice of 1638 (compare the stems!), Flagon of 1633. – BRASSES. An excellent series in the chancel floor, especially a small knight in armour of c. 1370 (E. Flambard?); John Flambard, late C14, also in armour; and John Byrkhed † 1468, priest with saints on the orphreys; head and most of the architectural canopy missing. The small brass of John Lyon, founder of Harrow School † 1592, and his wife, is against a pier of the N arcade. Other MONUMENTS. Right above the Lyon brass is *Flaxman's* Memorial to Lyon, 1815. The theme is that of the teacher instructing boys, the interpretation tender and intimate, similar to that of Flaxman's more famous Warton Monument in Winchester Cathedral. The Lyon Monument has a gothicizing top and the gentle classicist relief goes well with its gentle curves (as well as classicism and romanticism go in Blake's drawings). – James Edwards, collector and bookseller † 1816 ('to his skilful research and liberal

spirit of enterprise his country is indebted for the rarest
specimens biblical and classical of the typographic arts'),
relief above inscription with portrait medallion, Capo di
Monte vase, and books; by *Turnerelli*. Edwards owned
the Bedford Missal. In his will he stipulated that his
coffin should be made out of his library shelves. J. H.
North † 1831, with allegorical figure weeping over an urn;
by *Hopper*. – Joseph Drury † 1835, 'ludomagister' of
Harrow School, with two boys standing respectfully by
his bust; by the younger *Westmacott*. No older monuments of importance. That to W. Gerard † 1607, and his
wife, with two figures kneeling opposite each other in profile survives in fragments (N transept).

SCHOOL AND TOWN. The High Street must once have
wound up its way right to the church and Grove House.
The school was nothing but one small building. Only
c. 1800 did it begin to expand. We can divide its growth
into two phases. First it took over the larger existing
houses, such as Grove House and The Park, etc., and
converted them, then in the forties and chiefly from the
fifties to the seventies it built its own boarding houses. It
is they and the 'public buildings' of the school, mostly
put up between the sixties and the nineties, which give
Harrow its character now, a formidably mid-Victorian
character of hearty and confident gloom. Starting from the
N the first school houses form a perfect introduction to
this specific character of Harrow. Walking along Peterborough Road and the Grove toward the centre of the
school there are NORTHWICK LODGE (no longer a
school house), the older part of ELMFIELD, and especially THE GROVE higher up the hill (town houses of
varying size, dating chiefly from 1830 to 1850 and taken
over for school purposes). Thus we reach the first boarding houses built as such. They are characterized by their
towering height quite out of keeping with the tradition of
the town, by their purple brick with bands or diapers in
vitrified blue brick or yellow brick or both, the E.E. detail with nothing fanciful, their picturesque asymmetrical
compositions, and their porches or bay windows of

timber. THE GARLANDS, 1863, by *C. F. Hayward*, brother of a housemaster, shows this overwhelmingly assertive Public School style at its most concentrated; THE KNOLL, oldest part on the l., 1867 (also by *Hayward*), in a somewhat more playful mood. Its later parts connect it with HILLSIDE of 1870. All these are in Peterborough Road. In the Grove are ELMFIELD, whose taller addition of 1892 introduces us to the Late-Victorian Harrow style (of Norman Shaw derivation as so much of secular architecture was at that time all over England). GROVE HILL and THE FOSS of 1854 and 1859 are quieter than the Garlands, also brick with Tudor diaper and stepped gables; RENDALLS of 1853 has not even such ornamental gables. Its windows are straight too, with hood-moulds. It is an honest utilitarian structure, interesting for the date. Then, before reaching the 'public buildings', a diversion to the left should be made, down the hill. At the corner of Peterborough Road is the OLD MUSIC SCHOOL of 1873, as small as a wayside chapel; at the foot of the lane is the NEW MUSIC SCHOOL, by *E. S. Prior*, 1891, a remarkable contrast in size illustrating the growth of the school within a generation. The building is not one of Prior's most interesting, and its best view (from the E) not the one usually seen. Between the two music schools are from E to W the tall BUTLER MUSEUM, Shavian in style, by *Basil Champneys*, 1886, then the low small Harrow-Gothic LABORATORIES by *Hayward*, 1874, then the NEW SCIENCE SCHOOLS, small, in the Hampstead Garden Suburb style (1922, 1934), and finally round the corner towards Chapel and Library the NEW SCHOOLS, by *F. Barnes*, 1855 (N wing 1924).

Thus the FORUM SCHOLASTICUM is reached: a picturesque group strung up along the High Street, interesting, more thanks to the effects of the hillside than to especially high merits of the buildings individually. Harrow has never been fortunate in its architectural efforts. It has engaged some of the most distinguished architects: *Sir George Gilbert Scott* for Chapel and Vaughan Library (on the right), *Burges* and then fifty years later *Sir Herbert Baker* for Speech Room and War Memorial Building (on the right). The CHAPEL, 1854–7, is of flint with stone dressings, exhibiting to the street a front with two large different gables. Inside is a nave with a wide S and a narrower N aisle, tall round piers and open timber roofs. The transepts were added 1902–3. Around most walls run thick blank arcades of E.E. design with memorial tablets. The Vaughan Memorial is by *Onslow Ford*, the reredos by *Sir A. Blomfield*. The glass is chiefly of 1857–61; in the chancel by *Wailes*, 'improved' by *A. K. Nicholson*, who did also the W windows with the exception of one over the inner entrance which is by *Hardman*. The N aisle windows are by *Clayton & Bell*, those in the S aisle by *A. Lusson* of Paris. The VAUGHAN LIBRARY, 1861–3, is red brick with those patterns of vitrified blue and yellow brick which were to become so typical of Victorian Harrow and seem to appear here for the first time. A path paved with encaustic tiles leads to the centrally placed entrance in a deep porch with polished pink and grey marble columns and naturalistically carved capitals. Inside is a bay window (with a splendid view) in line with the entrance. The stained glass is by *J. C. Bell* (1883, 1885).

The SPEECH ROOM was designed in 1872. It has a straight front to the street with windows with plate tracery between two low corner towers. (Against one of them now stands a statue of Queen Elizabeth, given in 1925, and coming from Ashridge Park.) The back, however, is semicircular, which has the oddest results in the interior. The architect adopted the Greek theatre plan for good functional reasons, but being thoroughly mid-Victorian in his outlook was impervious to the jarring discord between the plan and his Gothic detail. Note the change in size of the black E.E. piers on the platform side and those of the semicircle, also the conflict in the ceiling. The stained glass behind the platform is by *J. C. Bell*. The older part of the ART SCHOOL on the r. of the Speech Room is by *W. C. Marshall*, 1896. On the l. is the WAR MEMORIAL building begun in 1921 which is much more civilized and smoother than Speech Room or Library. It takes its style from the surrounding buildings, leaves out all trimmings, and adds some Baroque detail. The terrace with its spectacular stairs has been much attacked but is likely to become one of the key effects of Harrow. Inside all is bare stone domes and distinguished-looking dark woodwork, the very style which would appeal to wealth and nobility about 1930. The panelling of the Alexander Fitch Room is Elizabethan.

The OLD SCHOOL is now reached by means of Sir Herbert 45b Baker's approaches. It is a picturesque little building with its two projecting wings with Tudor bay windows, a stone porch lying far back between them, and a little cupola on top. What most visitors do not realize is that this charm belongs to 1820. The old school building itself dates from 1611 (that is forty years after the foundation of the school). It is now the W wing of what is called the Old School (one room with oak panelling of c. 1700 and a large fireplace in the middle of the long outer wall). At the N end is the Headmaster's hooded throne, at the E end an armchair and a little table for the other master. The children sat on low narrow forms arranged choirstall-wise. The bay window was inserted when the building was enlarged to *C. R. Cockerell's* designs in 1820. Then also the stepped gables were added, the porch, the cupola, and the whole E wing. So by 1820 this was all that Harrow needed in the way of classrooms. As for living accommodation this was provided by the use of existing houses: the former Druries already in the C18, then the Moretons in 1806, the Grove in 1820, the Park in 1831, etc.

Standing on the steps of the Old Schools the HEAD-MASTER'S HOUSE is on the left, the DRURIES on the right flanking the entrance to what is left of the town in its own right. The Druries dates from 1864, by *Hayward*, again in his characteristic robust style: purple brick with blue headers, and a composition as if it were a spa hotel at Harrogate or some such place. The Headmaster's House is of 1840–5 and interestingly plain and sound, with straight-headed windows with hood-moulds, a stucco porch, and Jacobean gables. The lighter brickwork and style are like Rendall's. But attached to it and forming at the same time the beginning of the High Street is another Harrovian Gothic turreted structure of Hayward style. Its date is 1866.

So the town street starts with a delightful variety of small houses of which the very first, Nos 3–7, next to that of 1866, are typical: cool elegant Regency, then projecting tile-hung gables, then plain c18 brick. The MORETONS follow, Georgian private houses mainly rebuilt 1826. THE FLAMBARDS, late c18, THE PARK, 1795 to after 1803, at that time Lord Northwick's Harrow house, with a Venetian window at the street end and the relief of a lion above, and opposite BRADBY'S, 1848, brick, of five bays with a Tuscan porch. The Square is disappointing, with a *Hayward* PUBLIC HALL and the KING'S HEAD showing nothing of its early record (established 1533). Of old Harrow the net of streets survives: CROWN STREET with rows of cottages to the w and parallel with High Street, and other streets straight or curved leading down the hill to the w. Along the High Street and its continuations LONDON ROAD and SUDBURY HILL are good specimens of wealthy private houses from the heavy square three-bay house of Georgian tradition to pretty early Gothic Revival villas (Park Cottage) and early castellated or crowstep-gabled Tudor villas (Woodside, The Gerards) to 'architect-designed' residences of later decades (Manor Lodge, 1884, with plenty of terracotta in a style reminiscent of the Loire Châteaux; The Orchard, 1900, by *A. Mitchell*, slate-hung, etc.) and to genteel flats of *c.* 1930. Of school buildings there are down here only WESTACRES, a serviceable plain brick house of 1908, the former SANATORIUM, tucked away down Mount Park Avenue, by *Hayward*, 1864, now dank, deserted, and overgrown, an ideal subject for a John Piper. The OLD GYMNASIUM is between West Street and the Old School— *Hayward* of 1864–7 at his least acceptable for such a purpose. The NEW SANATORIUM is lower down still in a large Late Georgian house converted in 1929. Other large

private houses of similar and later date are on the slopes of
the hill (BYRON HOUSE, Byron Hill, etc.).

A few buildings around the foot of the hill must be mentioned: ROXETH FARM, Lower Road, on the E, one of the
none too rare survivals of complete farms to the NW of
London; HARROW AND WEALDSTONE STATION, 1912,
by *G. Horsley*, Neo-Georgian brick with stone dressings,
brick quoins, pediment, and tower, not a very satisfactory
composition; SOUTH HARROW L.T. STATION, by
Charles Holden, 1935, a little mannered compared with the
excellency of the 1932–3 stations (perhaps in an attempt
to create greater variety); ROXBOURNE SCHOOL, Tor-
bay Road, by *W. T. Curtis & Burchett*, 1937, a typical
example of progressive Middlesex C.C. architecture of
the date.

ST ALBAN, Church Drive, North Harrow, 1936, by *A. W.
Kenyon*. Brick with a fine, square tower, one of the best of
its style in England; the rest of the composition not without reminiscences of the Early Christian style; simple
white interior with tunnel vault and narrow aisles; the fit-
ments, especially the light fittings, appear now a little
dated in the modernistic, Swedish way. To be regarded as
lasting monuments of that particular phase in England,
they are not well enough made. The two curved ambones
are an interesting idea, unfortunately much cheapened
since by the frequent adoption of the same curved effect
for shop counters and bars.

HARROW WEALD

For Grims Dyke *see* separate entry.

PARISH CHURCH ALL SAINTS, Uxbridge Road, 1890, by
Butterfield, with a semi-detached S tower a little E of the
W end; a good typical later Butterfield interior, and glass.

Very little exists now to remind one of the past villages of the
Harrow Weald area (a few cottages in THE REDDING,
Wealdwood Road), but much of the past woods can still
be traced in the extensive grounds of the many large
private houses. Few of these date back beyond 1850. The

most important of them is BENTLEY PRIORY, originally an early C18 house but added to considerably by *Sir John Soane* from 1788 onwards. The exterior is now wholly Victorianized, and the Italianate tower makes it look even more convincingly 1850ish, but inside the entrance hall, a staircase, the circular 'tribune' for displaying works of *virtù*, and the billiard room (former dining-room) remain.[1] HARROW WEALD LODGE, Uxbridge Road, now Harrow Urban District Council, has a core of C18 pedimented brick, much altered. THE KILN, S end of Common Road, also C18 brick, altered, with an old kiln standing in front of the house; WOODLANDS, S end of Clamp Hill, now also belonging to the District Council, whitewashed, with many polygonal bay windows. For the mid-Victorian style in its wealthiest domestic forms Harrow Weald is invaluable. The connoisseur can study a whole range of characteristic houses of the third quarter of the C19. In order of style Victorian Italianate is represented by THE HALL, Brookshill; Victorian Gothic by HILL-SIDE, Brookshill (by *Roumieu*), of the gloomy dark diapered brick kind so frequent amongst Harrow School buildings; by Harrow Weald Park, now THE MANOR, Brookshill, 1870, very ambitious and extensive with battlements and pinnacles, all of stone; and by THE CEDARS, E end of Uxbridge Road. The Italian and Gothic Revivals were followed by what the time itself called the Domestic Revival, that is a free adaptation of Tudor forms with picturesque many-gabled compositions and the warm and rich effects of much ornamental tile-hanging and half-timbering. Harrow Weald possesses a gem of
62b that style: *Norman Shaw's* GRIMS DYKE, 1872, originally built for a popular R.A. genre painter, Goodall, and later the home of W. S. Gilbert (of Gilbert and Sullivan). The house is in the Wealdwood Road. In its garden a fountain, with river gods, originally erected in Soho Square *c.* 1700. Minor and more derivative examples, but all as large and varied as Grims Dyke, are HANWORTH HOUSE, Uxbridge Road (Lord Jellicoe's house,

1. Information kindly supplied by Miss Dorothy Stroud.

now also Harrow District Council), and PRIORY CLOSE, Common Road, by *Waterhouse*, 1890. OLD BARN just s of Priory Road shows the survival of this strongly Victorian style into the post-First-World-War years. Finally at the w end of the borough, s and sw of The Cedars, is a recent estate of two-storeyed prefabricated houses. They are of the B.I.S. (Brit. Iron and Steel Federation) type and designed by *Frederick Gibberd*, an example how aesthetically good emergency construction can be, if texture, colour, and those details which are unaffected by shortages of materials are handled with taste. The upper floor is faced with corrugated-steel sheets painted in dark colours. The graceful porch has slim tubular steel shafts.

BELMONT SCHOOL, Fisher Road, by *W. T. Curtis & Burchett*, 1935. A typical example of progressive Middlesex C.C. architecture of the date.

HATTON

The CHAPEL is in a converted C16–C17 farmhouse. The HOUSE formerly known as Temple Hatton is now St Anthony's (Crusade of Rescue) and so considerably added to that its original C18 features tend to disappear.

HAYES

Hayes is now chiefly factories and working-class houses (population with Harlington 66,000 in 1949). But the old village centre is surprisingly well preserved in the middle of this recent development. After having left the railway station one passes through a new shopping centre and along a large estate of council houses and reaches at the corner of Freemans Lane a group of cottages. Behind them, a little further N, is the Church and the Manor House. The church is approached by a C16 Lych Gate.

PARISH CHURCH ST MARY. A church with much inside that is unusual. Externally it is a flint rubble building with a late C13 chancel with lancet windows in the N walls, a C15 N aisle and W tower, and an early C16 S aisle and picturesque open timber S porch. In the chancel the   8b

C13 SEDILIA (with moulded capitals) and PISCINA are preserved. In the nave the N arcade has low octagonal piers and simple double-chamfered arches. The S arcade has octagonal piers and four-centred arches of typical early C16 form. There is no clerestory. All original roofs are preserved (though the church was restored by *Sir G. G. Scott* in 1873): in the chancel wagon-shaped with close-set rafters, in the nave boarded and panelled, in the aisles flat-pitched with chamfered tie-beams and curved braces. – FONT. Round bowl of *c.* 1200 with very coarse lobed leaves along simple scrolls. – WALL PAINTING. Large, against the N wall: St Christopher carrying the Child Christ as he wades through a stream swarming with serpents and wondrous fishes (with a mermaid of the type usual in misericords amongst them). On the bank sits a little boy angling. The banks extend upwards along the painting as though perspective were still an unknown science. Yet the painting can hardly be earlier than 1500. – PLATE. Interesting Chalice and Paten of 1623 (French or Spanish?); Almsdish, 1693.

MONUMENTS. Brass to Robert Lance in chancel, small demi-figure of priest, *c.* 1370, the earliest brass in the county. The same type was later repeated at Stanwell, Harlington, etc. – Walter Green † 1456, tomb-chest with traceried panels and brass effigy on lid. – Thomas Higate and wife † 1576, tomb-chest with brass figures on lid. – Sir Edward Fenner † 1612, standing wall monument with Sir Edward stiffly lying on his side, his head propped up on his elbow. The effigy is placed between columns and at the top are two small (much better) allegorical figures and an arch. In the tympanum an inscription in a broad scrolled strapwork cartouche. – Edward Fenner † 1615, simple epitaph with frontal demi-figure in shell niche between pilasters. The gentleman in armour lays a long hand with long fingers on his helmet which lies in front of him. Very noble, very self-conscious, and very typical of the ideals of Mannerism.

(HAYES COURT, Church Road, opposite the church. Dove-cote, octagonal, early C18. MTCP.)

HENDON

For Edgware, Golders Green, Hampstead Garden Suburb, Mill Hill *see* separate entries.

The growth of Hendon is chiefly connected with the Edgware Extension of the L.T. Northern Line. This was opened in 1926. The population of Hendon itself was 16,000 in 1921, 44,000 in 1931; of the whole borough 40,000 in 1911, 116,000 in 1931, and 158,000 in 1949. That means that some clusters or groups of village houses remain, but that most housing and the chief public buildings are pre-modern C20.

PARISH CHURCH ST MARY, Church End, that is the old NW end of Hendon. A rewarding building, much more so than the exterior with its little C15 W tower of ragstone and its cemented walls would make one expect. The interior is two churches in one, a C13 nave, chancel, and N aisle, with an early C16 N chapel, and a second, larger nave replacing the old S aisle, but with its own spacious S aisle. This addition, obviously the work of a sensitive as well as bold architect, is *Temple Moore's* of 1914–15, one of the rare cases in which a neo-Gothic architect, by respecting old work and adding frankly new work to it, has considerably enriched the original effect. The old arcades are low, on low octagonal piers, the new ones high, allowing the S aisle the same height as the new nave and keeping the old clerestory openings as windows from one nave into the other. Of old details the E end of the old chancel should be examined with the remains of wall arcading on foliated C13 capitals. The chancel arch was renewed in 1827.

Furnishing and ornaments are also of unusual variety and good quality. – FONT. Heavy square bowl on short 14a shafts; each side has eight intersected arcades on short columns with block capitals. Of the Norman fonts of Middlesex this is the most successful. – PAINTING. S aisle, Flight into Egypt, *Bassano* – School. – STAINED GLASS. N chapel, 1887, Faith, Hope, Charity, in semi-Pre-Raphaelite figures. – PLATE. Chalice and Paten of 1607, Paten of late C17, Flagon of 1730, two Chalices,

Patens and Cruets of 1890, designed by *Bodley*. – MONU-
MENTS. In the N chapel a tiny brass to John Downer,
1515; a magnificent large black marble slab on a low tomb-
chest to Sir Jeremy Whichcot, 1677, with nothing but bold
lettering, a large coat of arms, and a border; the standing
wall monument to Sir William Rawlinson, 1703, with
semi-reclining life-size figure; and the epitaph to Bishop
Fowler of Gloucester, 1714, with a long inscription between Corinthian pilasters and weepy cherubs perched
left and right (cf. Smythe Monument, Cranford). Against
the chancel arch are the monuments to Sir Charles Col-
more † 1795, by *Flaxman* (rather a commercial product
with small standing figures of Faith and Hope) and to
Giles Earle †1811, by *J. Smith* (with seated figures of
Faith and Hope).

ST JOHN, Algernon Road, an early *Temple Moore*, 1895. Plain
but sound and genuine. Inside a noble simple mahogany
PULPIT of *c.* 1760 (from St Michael Bassishaw in the City)
and an elegant FONT, small cup on a bulbous baluster,
and wooden REREDOS (from an unrecorded City church).

TOWN HALL, by *Watson*, 1900; PUBLIC LIBRARY, by
T. M. Wilson, 1929; TECHNICAL COLLEGE, by *H. W.
Burchett*, 1937. These three are typical examples of official
architecture in brick with stone dressings, the earlier still
quite jolly, the two later ones genteelly Neo-Georgian or
Neo-Palladian. They are saved, however, by the fact that
they lie close to each other along The Burroughs instead
of scattered as in most suburbs.

DANIEL ALMSHOUSES, Church Road, opposite Church
End, 1686, but much restored in the C19. Two-storeyed
centre with gable, little gabled corner pavilions, and one-
storeyed tenements between.

The only surviving cluster of houses older than a hundred
years is at the S end of THE BURROUGHS, by Watford
Way, chiefly cottages, but one dignified early C18 house
with a back of brick and rubbed brick.

Just W of the church are the GREYHOUND INN, originally
the Church House, and CHURCH END FARM with three
gables and a fine grouped chimney stack.

Of individual houses nothing need be said about ST PETER'S
OUVROIR, Brent Street (where Norden, the Antiquary,
and Woolner, the sculptor, lived; built before 1750), and
of CLATTERHOUSE FARM, Claremont Road (originally
the sub-manor of Clitherows). But HENDON HALL (or 54
Hendon Place, now a private hotel) possesses the most
important individual piece of architecture in the borough:
a portico, four brick columns with intermittent rustication and on them the richest of Corinthian capitals, entablature, and pediment. The capitals and pediment are
said to have come from Canons originally (*see* Stanmore).
From there, at the sale of the property, they are supposed
to have gone to Wanstead. The Hendon portico was then
transferred from there and added to the C18 house which
Garrick owned from 1756 to 1779. Of this the front door
is visible behind the portico, and a back porch. Most of
the house appears now in a form given it about 1850, in
nice harmony with the previous elements. Further additions were made much more recently. On top of the
hill, opposite Hendon Hall (Manor Hall Avenue), an
OBELISK erected by Garrick as a Shakespeare memorial.
At the foot Melpomene, Terpsichore, Thalia, and Shakespeare, all four now headless.

WATLING ESTATE, on the Edgware border. An L.C.C.
estate of 4,000 houses laid out in 1926 by the County
Council architect, *C. Topham Forrest*. It takes advantage
of the principles developed in the garden cities and garden
suburbs and applies them successfully to the scale of
lower price houses. The vistas in the undulating streets
with the many old trees preserved are excellent. Just N of
the estate in Dean Lane, Upper Hale.

JOHN KEBLE MEMORIAL CHURCH, by *D. F. Martin-
Smith*, 1937. One of the most interesting of the few
London churches in the idiom of the C20, stock brick
with a stepped-up front, a square tower and a concrete
lantern, rather in a French taste. Inside a plain square
main room, with a W gallery and a ceiling with a diagonal
trellis coffering.

HENDON AERODROME. Established as early as 1910. In

those days Hendon was the centre of flying training and air racing. The aerodrome was also the terminus of the first official air mail service in the United Kingdom (1911, Hendon–Windsor, to mark the Coronation of George V).

HESTON

The Borough of Heston and Isleworth (population in 1949 108,000) includes Cranford, Hounslow, Isleworth, and Osterley, which are dealt with separately.

No atmosphere, mostly built between the two wars. The church, more interesting inside than outside, stands forlorn and all on its own.

PARISH CHURCH ST LEONARD. Only the late C15 w tower is old, and that also must have been much restored when *Bellamy* rebuilt the rest of the church in 1866. The charming w porch and Lych Gate (with a trestle construction) were reconstructed from old materials. The w door, however, is genuine late C15 and impressive. The interior has a gem of a FONT COVER of *c.* 1500, octagonal, oak, of cupola shape with a finial at the top and flowing blind tracery in the panels. Unfortunately this piece too is much restored. – PLATE. Tazza (with engraving of Feast of Cana) and Paten of *c.* 1685, Flagon of 1698, Chalice and Paten of 1741. – MONUMENTS. Brass to M. Bownall † 1581, and wife, with woman in bed with baby, an angel and figure of Christ above. – W. Cary † 1757, by *Will. Atkinson*: tablet without figures. – Robert Child of Osterley Park † 1782, an excellent composition signed by *Robert Adam* and *P. M. van Gelder* (the two also worked together at Warkton). Above a very Grecian sarcophagus in relief stands a chaste urn against the usual pyramid or obelisk. Two putti play around the urn, and farther out are two exquisitely designed candelabra.

HILLINGDON

See also Swakeleys.

Hillingdon consists of the two parishes of w and e Hillingdon.

WEST HILLINGDON is now completely absorbed in Uxbridge. Uxbridge High Street continues to the S into Hillingdon, and a few of the C17 and C18 houses still stand. The PARISH CHURCH ST ANDREW lies further E on the London Road. It is by *Sir G. G. Scott*, and one of his stodgier efforts in the Early Gothic style (1865). Further N in Park Road is PARK LODGE (Business College) with nice C17 brick stables.

EAST HILLINGDON must once have had an attractive centre. Its church is quite stately and good houses were close by. Now an A-road cuts right across and has brought rows of shops with it.

PARISH CHURCH ST JOHN THE BAPTIST, of flint and surprisingly of a piece in its appearance, considering that nave and aisles are C14 and the W tower 1629. In 1847–8 *Sir G. G. Scott* restored the church and added transepts and E parts (not very effectively). There is one remarkable fragment in the church older than the rest, the C13 chancel arch with stiff-leaf capitals (the best of the date in Middlesex) on short shafts which in their turn rest on head-corbels. The N one is original : a grimacing face with tongue sticking out. The nave receives much light from the large W window in the tower. The arcades have octagonal piers with capitals and arch mouldings typical of their date. The C15 N aisle roof has its main timbers supported by corbels with stone busts (cf. Stanwell). No furnishings of importance but some PLATE (two Chalices and Patens, 1636, 1637; Flagon, 1686) and several remarkable MONUMENTS. The large brass to Lord Strange, 19a erected 1509, in the N aisle is the most ambitious medieval brass in the county. Lord and Lady Strange and a small daughter between them are represented under tall gables with incurving sides. Other brasses in chancel (1529), nave (1579), and S aisle (1599). The best later monuments are in the chancel : Sir Edward Carr † 1657, and Henry 25 Pagett, Earl of Uxbridge † 1743. The Carr Monument is 30 an up-to-date variation of the old-established theme of the kneelers facing each other. Not only are the costumes later than one usually finds on tombs of this type, but the idea of having the children stand in front of the prayer desk between the parents, ready to walk out of the monument towards us, heralds the conception of a new age. The perversely steep broken gable on top against which two allegorical figures can sit as on stiff chairs also shows a spirit of innovation not quite certain yet of where to turn. – The Uxbridge Monument opposite is infinitely more accomplished, and consequently less gritty. The effigy in Roman garb is semi-reclining on a tomb-chest, head and hands splendidly modelled. The altar background has urns standing in front of the flanking columns, a straight pediment on top, and the customary grey pyramid in relief rising behind the figure and between the columns. – In the nave Thomas Lane ('having acquired a fortune by constant application' † 1795), by *John Bacon*, a seated allegorical figure holding a medallion with profile portrait. – Several more C17 and later epitaphs and tablets.

Opposite the church on the w at the entrance to the Harlington Road the RED LION INN and THE COTTAGE (C16 with gabled front); on the N THE CEDARS, with an excellent symmetrical s front of late C16 date. The centre is a gabled porch, l. and r. of it are two larger gables. The building is brick, all windows are C18. Of the same period the iron garden s gate. The two remaining big houses, Hillingdon House and Hillingdon Court, C18 and early C19, are of no particular architectural merit. Of the outlying farmhouses the best is KIMBOLTON, Yiewsley Road, by Chapel Lane, brick and pretty well completely of the C16.

HORNSEY

For the Highgate parts of Hornsey, that is the triangle between the borough boundary and the w side of Archway Road and Aylmer Road, see the volume of this series dealing with the County of London.

The five or six villages and hamlets forming the nuclei of the present Borough of Hornsey (population in 1950 *c.* 98,000)

have so completely become part of London that hardly any
trace of their former separate existence can now be discovered. Hornsey Village itself lies in the NE corner of the
borough, Muswell Hill farther W, and Crouch End SW;
Stroud Green is SE of Crouch End.

PARISH CHURCH ST MARY. The medieval church has
disappeared except for the W tower of three stages, with
diagonal buttresses and battlements (top part modern).
The new church was begun farther E in 1888, to designs
of *James Brooks*, large but with none of the interest which
Brooks's best churches (Battersea Lavender Hill, Gospel
Oak, etc.) rouse. The W front was added recently by *Sir
Charles Nicholson*, but the tower is not built yet. The
point one remembers about Hornsey is the contrast between the competent somewhat mechanical Victorian
church and the old tower in the overgrown well wooded
churchyard. – PLATE. Two Flagons, 1624; Chalice, 1634;
Paten, 1700. – MONUMENTS. John Skevington, c. 1520,
brass in three tiny parts, inscription above and below and
a baby in swaddling clothes between (chancel, N wall). –
Gge. Rey and two wives, late C16, large incised slab with   19b
minutely drawn costume, very handsome in a Hillyard
way, though coarser (tower). – Richard Candish, 1601, a
four-foot plain little obelisk (nave, N wall). – Francis
Musters † 1680 at the age of fifteen, a charming kneeling   28a
figure in clerical garb with cherubs holding a crown above
his head. Under a strongly projecting pediment. – Lewis
Atterbury † 1731, and his granddaughter Penelope
Sweetapple, nothing but a Corinthian column with a
shield on top. – Samuel Rogers, author of the *Pleasures of
Memory* † 1855, simple classical memorial with medallion
portrait by *Behnes*.

ST AUGUSTINE, Archway Road, by *J. D. Sedding*, 1885. The
W front, 1916, by *J. H. Gibbins*. An original interior with
a big wide nave, very low arcades and aisles, and a very
tall clerestory with wide blank arcading and narrow single
lancet windows inserted. Some of the decoration by *H.
Wilson*, c. 1895.

M.—7

CHRIST CHURCH, Crouch End Hill, 1862, by *A. Blomfield*. The early Blomfield red-and-black brick arches inside have recently been whitewashed out of recognition.

ST GEORGE, Priory Road, Hornsey, damaged in the Second World War. In it is the octagonal C16 FONT from the old Hornsey Church.

HOLY INNOCENTS, Tottenham Lane, 1877, by *A. Blomfield*, still in his early, less refined but more masculine style (*see* above).

HOLY TRINITY, Stapleton Hall Road, Stroud Green, 1878–85, by the younger *Ferrey*, 'not without a certain dignified spaciousness inside' (GB).

PRESBYTERIAN CHURCH, Muswell Hill Road, 1903, by *G. and R. P. Baines*. Blatant contrast of flint with brick dressings, a merry little spirelet on the NW tower and a little turret on the crossing.

HORNSEY TOWN HALL, Crouch End, 1934–5, by *R. H. Uren*. Brick, freely grouped blocks with a tall square tower. A pleasant planned forecourt between the Town Hall and the busy Broadway, with two plain municipal office buildings on l. and r.

Of old houses very little is left, hardly one street with more than one or two, and none outstanding anywhere. Examples: EAGLE COURT opposite Hornsey Church; STAPLETON HALL in Stapleton Hill Road, Stroud Green; No 132 TOTTENHAM LANE. The approaches to Muswell Hill (Fortis Green Road, Muswell Hill itself and Colney Hatch Lane) retain something of a leafy character.

HOUNSLOW

Nobody can say that the High Street at Hounslow possesses much character, but it may be worth recording that in Treaty Street to its S an attempt has been made early in this century to provide something like a Civic Centre, with the COUNCIL HOUSE on one side and the PUBLIC LIBRARY and PUBLIC BATHS on the other. Both are by *Nowell Parr* and of 1905. The OLD TOWN HALL is of 1857, in the High Street, of three bays only, Italian High Renaissance.

PARISH CHURCH HOLY TRINITY, 1828 (chancel 1856).
A comparatively large specimen of the Commissioners'
style, yellow brick, no spire, a narrow bleak front and
lancet windows, oddly with Perp tracery. Roofless at the
time of writing. Inside some handsome early C18 PLATE
and one small but interesting MONUMENT, two small
kneeling figures opposite each other in a moulded frame,
with a broken pediment. The date is *c.* 1540, that is very
early for this type which became so popular later. The
quality is remarkably good.

The famous old powder mills have alas been pulled down,
and the large BARRACKS at the end of Barrack Road show
little of the original building of 1793. Mostly *c.* 1860.

(The MTCP also lists Nos 86 (late C17), 180 (early C18), and
the Nag's Head (C18) in the High Street, and The Lawn
in Lampton Road (early C19).)

ICKENHAM

The centre of the village is the Green which has lost much
of its character since its s side has been taken by a new shopping arcade and the street crossing it from s to N has become
a B-road.

PARISH CHURCH ST GILES. The usual small aisleless
Middlesex village church of the same type as Perivale,
Greenford, etc. The date is C14. It was enlarged early in
the C16 by a N aisle as wide and nearly as long as the rest
of the church. The roofs are old (chancel probably before
1400, nave C15, W aisle Elizabethan), yet the spatial impression is not very happy. The most interesting parts of
the building are the rustic timber-framed s porch, the
pretty little timber bell-turret and the mid C17 vestry
with arched recesses in N, W, and s walls. Their windows
are modern. The COMMUNION TABLE is early C17, the
FONT a good oak-carved octagonal piece of late C17 date.
PLATE. Flagon, 1682; Chalice, 1782. Otherwise no furnishings require mention. But the church has BRASSES of
the 1580s to members of the Say family, and at least two
later MONUMENTS of interest. Robert Clayton † 1665, a   26b

recumbent marble infant in swaddling clothes, no doubt torn out of its original context, but in this accidental loneliness all the more pathetic, and J. G. Clarke (of the family who then owned Swakeleys), who died in his twenty-fifth year in 1820. *Thomas Banks* is the sculptor of the fine relief of the youth seated and reading.

BUSHEY ROAD SCHOOL, by *W. T. Curtis & Burchett*, 1937. A typical example of progressive Middlesex C.C. architecture of the date.

ISLEWORTH

The village is a compact growth between the Twickenham Road and the Thames with the church at its N end, close to the grounds of Syon House, and the market place at its S end.

PARISH CHURCH ALL SAINTS. The W tower is C15, of Kentish rag with diagonal buttresses and crenellated top. The stair-turret is lower than the top. The body of the church was, save for the outer walls, destroyed in the Second World War. It was of 1705. The EPITAPH to Sir Orlando Gee † 1705, by *Bird*, survives; frontal demi-figure with elaborate wig, holding a scroll and addressing us as from a pulpit; flanking columns with twisted lower part.

ST FRANCIS, by *E. C. Shearman*, 1933–5, with its apse to the Great West Road, a large brick structure without steeple, the inside very wide and tall with extremely narrow aisles.

The prettiest view of the village is from the river with the church and the trees of the churchyard, the trees by Syon House on the r., and an informal little square on the l., on which lie the LONDON APPRENTICE Inn and a few nice Georgian houses (NOS 59 and 61 CHURCH STREET).

Also in Church Street, REYNOLDS HOUSE, *c.* 1700; off it towards the Twickenham Road in Mill Plat are INGRAM'S ALMSHOUSES, 1664, a simple row, one-storeyed and with their big pediments rather Dutch-looking. Higher up Mill Plat DUNDEE HOUSE, Georgian. (Also GROSVENOR

HOUSE, late C18. MTCP.) In the village itself not much of note. In the market a commodious little former SCHOOL HOUSE, Neo-Gothic of 1845 with a little turret and opposite a sound sturdy INN of *c.* 1840.

Larger residences with their gardens surround the village. On the S: GORDON HOUSE, Richmond Road, Early Victorian Italianate; on the W: GRUNDY HOUSE, Twickenham Road, excellent, *c.* 1700, brick, five bays, stone windows with aprons below and segmental tops; the taller wings are later; so is the upper part of the centre. Further W by Worton Road the neglected remains of two Georgian residences: WORTON COURT and WORTON MANOR. In better state but not specially interesting WORTON HALL (London Film Productions); S of Grundy House in the Twickenham Road, VAN GOGH HOUSE, No. 158–60, *c.* 1700, of five bays, a fine example of its date; van Gogh taught here in a prep school in 1876. (The GEORGE INN, Twickenham Road, is early C18. Nos. 116–22 a terrace of C18 houses. MTCP.)

On the N lies Syon House and the London Road. Coming from Brentford No. 52 LONDON ROAD on the left is Early Georgian. On the right after having passed the entrance screen to Syon House follows a handsome minor Georgian group consisting of the COACH AND HORSES, then PARK COTTAGES, then SYON LODGE with delicate detail (according to the MTCP transferred from Foley House) and a good iron gate. (SYON PARK HOUSE, where Shelley went to school, is early C18. MTCP.)

SYON HOUSE. In 1431 a Brigittine convent, founded by Henry V in 1415, was moved to Isleworth and rebuilt on the site of the present house. Building was still going on in 1468. The claustral plan of the house no doubt carries on the cloister of the convent, though it must be assumed that the composition of the C15 was not as symmetrical as it is now. In the SW part of the house adjoining the cloister two undercrofts are preserved of typical plain C15 rib-vaulting. After the Dissolution the convent was given to the Duke of Somerset in 1546 and after his execution to John Dudley, Earl of Northumberland.

To the mid C16 belongs the general appearance of the house to-day, a square block of about 100 by 100 ft with square corner turrets. The exterior was entirely refaced about 1825 and appears now to be wholly C19. Of the Somerset-Dudley period are also the stables to the NW and an outbuilding to the N of the house (both much altered). In 1604 the house passed to the Percys, Earls of Northumberland. Some wood panelling of Late Gothic style in a room on the first floor has Percy badges and must have been brought in from elsewhere. The two lodges W of the house seem to be early C17 but are re-faced. The main contribution of the Percys is the outer arcade of eleven bays on the E side, plainly and competently Italian in style and traditionally connected with repairs which *Inigo Jones* did for Syon House some time after 1632. This E front of Syon House is topped by the Northumberland Lion (of lead) taken to Isleworth from the former Northumberland House, Strand.

In the C18 the property went to Sir Hugh Smithson, afterwards 1st Duke of Northumberland. He commissioned *Robert Adam* in 1761 to carry out extensive alterations entirely in the antique style. Adam in his *Works* calls him 'a person of extensive knowledge and correct taste'. Adam's plans were at first much more ambitious than what was ultimately executed. He intended to fill the courtyard completely by a circular saloon and insert between this and the E front an oval two-arm staircase with two oval rooms on l. and r. As it is only the following rooms were remodelled: ENTRANCE HALL, centre of the W side, nearly a 'double cube'; apse at the N end to hold a copy of the Apollo Belvedere, the idol of C18 artists and dilettanti; at the S end a tunnel-vaulted recess with curved steps up to the neighbouring rooms. The recess is separated from the hall by a screen consisting of two Roman Doric columns supporting a thin entablature. There is no wall above it so that hall and recess are, in a manner eminently characteristic of Adam, divided and yet one. The walls are decorated with aedicules with wooden columns, Roman Doric in the centre, but on the

sides with Late Roman spiral fluting of the kind Adam
had met in Italy and Spalato. The steps on the s side lead
to the square ANTEROOM with a polished scagliola floor
and twelve columns of Verde Antico with gilt Ionic
capitals, and entablatures (gold on blue) jutting forward
over each of them to support small pieces of antique
statuary. The walls are pale green, the doors mahogany
and gilt (a luxurious, even heavy impression after the
whiteness of the Hall). In the Anteroom a seated statue of
the 6th Duchess by the American sculptor *Connelly*, a
pupil of Hiram Powers, and a melodramatic transparency
of Belshazzar's Feast by *John Martin*. The DINING
ROOM follows E of the Anteroom, long and somewhat
narrow with two screened-off apses at its E and W ends.
The mantelpiece is exceedingly rich. On either side of it
are three niches for Roman figures. After the white and
gold of this room the large WITHDRAWING ROOM is
strong in colour again, a warm red, with Spitalfields silk
wall hangings, a coved ceiling painted by *Angelica Kauff-
mann* with small figures, and a glorious carpet, dated 1769
on the border. The furniture is of the Regency period,
from Northumberland House. The door at the E end
opens into the Library or GREAT GALLERY, 136 ft long
all along the E front, and only 14 ft wide. *Adam* overcame
these difficult proportions by keeping the room low, sub-
dividing the walls into many parts, and by a decoration of
'great variety and amusement', as he says of it. The
colour scheme is predominantly mauve and pale green.
From the point of view of correct Classical Revival the
detail is most objectionable, but it has much charm and
lightness. Motifs of Roman '*grottesche*' and of Spalato,
but also of the Renaissance, are used with Rococo freedom.
The contrast to the tiny round and square BOUDOIRS in
the NE and SE turrets should be appreciated specially.
From the centre of the round one hangs a gilt bird cage
with a clock. The square one has painted panels with trees
and birds in imitation of Chinese silks.

Along the London Road is the SCREEN, that is the entrance arch supporting a Northumberland Lion outlined

against the sky, and on either side five bays, with lower columns and straight entablature. It is a most delicate, spirited composition, the apogee of Adam's taste in transparency, of a 'filigree' character which Horace Walpole saw clearly enough when he passed the gateway while it was being built in 1773, but which he strongly disliked.

On the river front is an elegant BOAT HOUSE, with a curved centre with Ionic columns; recently attributed to *Capability Brown* (D. Stroud). There is a rather melancholy terrace with weeping willow alongside it. In the grounds also a large glasshouse of Kew type by *Fowler*.

KINGSBURY

PARISH CHURCH HOLY INNOCENTS, Kingsbury Road, Kingsbury Green, by *Butterfield*, 1883–4, decidedly a minor work, with only a small polygonal W turret; stock brick with coloured patterns; the interior plastered with occasional tile effects, a timber chancel screen with tiled reredos, 'quaint and characteristic, though ugly enough' (GR). – PLATE. Chalice and Paten of 1704.

PARISH CHURCH ST ANDREW, Church Lane, Kingsbury: two churches in one churchyard, the old one very small, the new one all the prouder and in fact of more historic associations than the old building. The latter is sometimes supposed to incorporate pre-Conquest work. The W corners are similar to long-and-short work, but only similar, and the walls are more probably Norman than Saxon. Were they Saxon, they would be the only stone remains in Middlesex of so early a period. Inside the aisleless church is a LECTERN consisting of an angel in Greek peplum brought from a City church demolished about 1880. It is C17. There is also a BRASS showing the small figures of John Shepard † 1520, his two wives, and below his eighteen children.

The new church originally stood in Wells Street, W1, and was re-erected at Kingsbury in 1933. It was a famous monument of Early Victorian Anglo-Catholicism, built in 1847 by *S. W. Dawkes* and *Hamilton*. Its Perp front with NW tower and spire is big and earnest (and the spire succeeds in giving Kingsbury a genuine, not suburban look, when seen above the trees of the churchyard from across the Welsh Harp). The interior is also spacious, with five tall Perp arches, clerestory, and side aisles. There is nothing left of the thinness of the Commissioners' style; solid, knowledgeable, and a little stodgy, the church is one of the first to deserve the description Neo-Gothic and not Gothick (earlier, e.g. than Christ Church, Ealing). The interior arrangements were, moreover, on the original site an ingenious adaptation to awkward conditions. All the same, *The Ecclesiologist* objected to it, because it was Perp Eastlake still, in his *Gothic Revival* of 1872, calls 'the selection of so late a type of Gothic a mistake.' However, Benjamin Webb, co-founder of the Cambridge Camden Society and Editor of *The Ecclesiologist*, became vicar in 1862 and remained in charge until 1885. He called in several of the leading artists and architects of the Anglo-Catholic movement to improve the interior. *Street* did the metal chancel screen and the very original metal pulpit. The sumptuous reredos was also designed by him (sculpture by *Redfern*). To *Burges* is due the heavy litany desk and the monument to Webb's predecessor, John Murray † 1862, a cusped niche in the S wall with the recumbent effigy of the vicar. The font cover was done by *Pearson*, the lectern by *Butterfield* for Murray. The E window with Hardman glass, designed by *Pugin*, also belongs to Murray's time, the other windows are mostly by *Clayton & Bell* (especially charming in their chaste design and reticent colouring the NW and SW windows, 1868, 1877). Across the W end runs a wooden gallery with painted panels by *Alfred Bell* all along the parapet. The church possesses a missal designed by the architect *Birch*.

At the SW corner of Church Lane is BLACKBIRD FARM, half-timbered, probably of the C17 with a contemporary barn.

In KINGSBURY ROAD, a good recent factory by *Brian O'Rorke*.

LALEHAM

The village makes no use of the Thames, in contrast to most Middlesex villages in similar positions. From the river Laleham is no more than 'enormous willows and queer suggestions of old houses on the banks' (William Morris).

PARISH CHURCH ALL SAINTS. Outside the building appears C19 with the exception of the W tower and the N chancel (Lucan) chapel. The chapel is Early Tudor brick, diapered, and with four moulded brick three-light windows. The tower is an odd specimen of heavy-handed Early Georgian, all brick, with very broad quoins ending in capitals and a stone-dressed Venetian window on the W front. There is a heavy parapet on top and on this a horrid recent turret. The tower is dated 1732. Inside, the church
2 has Norman arcades on the N as well as S side of the nave. The only other Norman arcade in the County is at Harmondsworth. Laleham has demi-columns against the W wall and then three columns on each side (but the nave was originally longer towards the E). The S arcade is now blocked, as the S aisle was pulled down at an unknown date. The capitals are scalloped, the arches are single-chamfered, except in the NE arches where early C16 brick replaces them. In the S wall higher up are some reset bits from a former Norman doorway. Against the W wall of the N aisle a large PAINTING of Christ on the sea with Peter by *G. H. Harlow*, probably *c.* 1810–15. Against the S wall of the chancel wall monuments to George Perrott † 1780, by *W. Tyler*, and to Henrietta Hartwell † 1818, by *Chantrey*, both minor.

Close to the church CHURCH FARM, a late C17 cottage. Farther S and nearer the river a triangular Green on whose W side MUNCASTER HOUSE, *c.* 1700, with a large Victorian addition, THE COVERTS, *c.* 1700. THE THATCHED COTTAGE, a sweet little affair of Blaise Hamlet type with a thatched verandah with rude tree trunks, probably early C19. The drive to the S leads to LALEHAM HOUSE, now The Abbey, shortly after 1805, compact, with a Greek Doric porch and altogether very progressive for its date.

LITTLETON

The first impression is the contrast between the vast bare embankment of the reservoir to the N and the vast bare sheds of the London Film Company to the W on the one hand, and the small group of church, rectory, manor farm and manor house on the other.

PARISH CHURCH ST MARY MAGDALENE. The church is 9 a study in brick, although the C13 nave and chancel were originally ragstone and flint rubble. But the early C16 added a brick W tower, heightened early in the C18, a S porch, and a brick clerestory to the nave. There is also a N chapel, dated 1705, and, of c. 1730, a further N extension of this. The C19 refaced the S aisle and its buttresses. Thus looking from NE all seems brick, dominated by the mauve of the old parts of the tower and the russet of the top. The clerestory is light red, the porch again mauve, the N chapel of 1705 has a chequerboard pattern with vitrified headers and a double-curved gable for the part of 1705 and a straight one for the later part. The interior is as delightful as the exterior, a very short nave of only two bays and a low chancel separated from it by a screen. The S pier is round and thick, c. 1200, the N pier octagonal and later C13. The arches are double-chamfered, as is the chancel arch. The chancel has original deep-splayed N windows. Those in the S wall are copies. The walls of the chancel and the spandrels of the nave are rubble unplastered. An effective contrast in the nave is the brick clerestory. The church has a wealth of less usual furnishings, a late medieval LOCKER in the S aisle S wall; a complete set of (restored) PEWS of about the same date; CHOIR STALLS 16 (also restored) with cusped ogee arches and panelling in the spandrels, C15, said to come from Winchester; a very much and fancifully restored ROOD SCREEN of c. 1500; ALTAR RAILS of sumptuous Flemish or French Baroque of c. 1700 and an early C18 PULPIT with a curious narrow high window into the SE angle between nave and chancel to give it sufficient light. On the N wall under the tower an Italian Trecento PAINTING of six panels with six saints. – PLATE. Chalice and Paten, 1632; four Patens, 1677; Paten, 1680; Chalice, 1712; Flagon, 1726.

MANOR HOUSE, a picturesque group of buildings dating from the C15 to the C19.

RECTORY, the typical five-bay house of *c.* 1700 with hipped roof.

LONDON AIRPORT (HEATHROW)

Size approximately $4\frac{1}{2}$ square miles. Ultimately to be 7 square miles. The final runway pattern is under construction at the time of writing: a dual parallel system of six runways varying in length from 5,800 to 9,500 ft and in width from 250 to 300 ft. The hexagonal terminal area in the centre as yet undeveloped so that no architectural features can be pointed out. Architect for the future buildings: *Frederick Gibberd*.

LONGFORD

At the W end of the village a little BRIDGE with cast-iron parapets, marked W.R. 1834. In the High Street several half-timbered cottages, especially good the two-gabled C16 one opposite the White Horse Inn. Also some later brick houses, especially Longford Close and Weekly House (early C18).

MILL HILL

The sudden NW spread of London between the two world wars stopped short of Mill Hill. It is firmly connected with the suburban Boroughs of Hendon and Finchley now, but on its N lies still the open country. Nearly all buildings of architectural interest are strung up along the Ridgeway and up to Highwood Hill.

PARISH CHURCH ST PAUL, 1829–36, a typical cheap church of its date in the Commissioners' style, cement-rendered with lancet windows and the plainest of turrets on the W and E angles. In the E window a Deposition of Christ in PAINTED GLASS, C18, copied from an Italian painting.

MILL HILL SCHOOL, founded specially for sons of Non-conformist parents in 1807. The main buildings are by *Sir W. Tite*, 1825-7. The centre of the long main block is a giant portico of six unfluted Ionic columns, rather heavy, and overlooking the grounds towards London. Farther W is the Chapel, by *Basil Champneys*, 1898, and the very pretty group of Tuck Shop, Winterstoke Library (1907), and Murray Scriptorium, picturesque, with a tall, low-starting roof and turret in the style at that moment just coming over to England from Richardson's and Stanley White's America (the whole group by *Collcutt* of the Savoy Hotel and the Imperial Institute).

NICOLL ALMSHOUSES, Milespit Hill: truly minimum, of 1696, one-storeyed, with a long roof starting immediately above the tops of the little doors.

COTTAGES. By the Nicoll Almshouses, that is the corner of Milespit Hill and Ridgeway, was the centre of Mill Hill Village. Quite a number of cottages, weatherboarded and otherwise, survive N and S of the Almshouses. A few more will be found facing the school, then by the corner of Hammers Lane, of Laurence Street, and then at the top of Highwood Hill, where it meets Marsh Lane (for example, the RISING SUN INN, late C17 brick).

HOUSES. Nothing of outstanding value, but a good deal still of dignity and pleasantness. Following the Ridgeway from E to W LITTLEBERRIES, now the Convent of St Vincent de Paul, a late C17 nucleus with one finely decorated room, a temple at the foot of the garden, and a large chapel by *Tasker*, 1887 (a spacious interior with aisles as high as the nave and a transept of two bays at the E end); BELMONT, now the Mill Hill Prep School, Georgian, much altered, with a pretty early C19 Gothic cottage or hermitage in the garden; ST MARY'S ABBEY, also built around a late Georgian private house. Then up Highwood Hill to HIGHWOOD HOUSE, stuccoed front with semicircular Ionic porch, neglected; HENDON PARK, also stuccoed, of less character and just as neglected; HIGHWOOD LODGE, an exceptionally pretty early C19 cottage with barge-boarded gables and the lower parts heavily castellated.

s of the Ridgeway in Laurence Street is St Joseph's College, by *Goldie*, 1866–71, with additions; unattractive in spite of its tower with a gilt statue of Joseph and its prominent position. s of this the Linen and Woollen Drapers Cottage Homes, two pretty garden-villagey groups of cottages, the earlier one by *George Hornblower*, 1898.

Much farther se, not far from Watford Way and the Hendon Aerodrome, is Copthall, whose grounds are playing fields. The house was built in 1624 but its Jacobean gables and ornaments are almost entirely C19.

(In addition, the MTCP lists Church House, Ridgeway, late C18, and Featherstone House, Wise Lane, *c.* 1700 but refronted C18).

NORTHOLT

Parish Church St Mary. A modest village church lying back from a green which still keeps some of its character amid new suburban houses and fast-traffic roads. The nave of flint and ironstone rubble is only 44 by 25 ft. The chancel is brick and smaller still. The date of the nave is *c.* 1300 (see the N and s windows). Its simple roof like that of the chancel and the chancel altogether seems to be *c.* 1500. Across the w end of the nave is a wooden gallery on Tuscan columns, erected, it is said, in 1703. – Font. Octagonal, with simply decorated panels of late C14 character. The cover is of 1624. – Painting above altar: Adoration of the Magi, seems Flemish or Dutch C18. – Royal arms: Stuart, late C17, above chancel arch. – Plate. Chalice of 1702 and Paten. – Monuments. Brass to H. Rowdell, 1452, in armour; to John Gyfforde † 1560, and wife with twelve children (palimpsest of C15 brasses); to T. Bures † 1610, with kneeling figure of vicar.

NORTHWOOD

Parish Church Holy Trinity. By *Teulon*, 1854, in his least ostentatious mood, with additions of 1894 and 1930. Inside a *Burne Jones* window (Grosvenor Memorial, 1886).

PRESBYTERIAN CHURCH, Hallowell Road, by *Rowntree*, 1914, pleasant Neo-Georgian brick.

MOUNT VERNON HOSPITAL CHAPEL, by *F. L. Wheeler*, 1904. A strikingly complete example of progressive church design, well placed on a hill. The exterior has Voysey's excessively battered buttresses with on the s side large broad windows filling the whole width of the wall between them. An original little w tower and all details (also in the woodwork inside) of frank Art Nouveau licence.

NORWOOD

PARISH CHURCH ST MARY. The fact that the s, w, and e walls are of the C12 to C13 can be evident only to the student. The exterior was refaced rather gaudily with black flint and multi-coloured bricks in 1864; the tower is later still. A C13 lancet window can still be seen in the chancel s wall and one in the nave w wall. The chancel and nave roofs are C15. – FONT. Plain octagonal C15. – PLATE. Flagon, Chalice, and Patens of 1708. – MONUMENTS. Cheesman Monument, *c.* 1530–40, almost identical with Kirton, Edmonton: niche with Perp panelled jambs and four-centred voussoirs above tomb-chest with elaborate quatrefoil decoration. Above the niche a suspended HELM of *c.* 1600 with vizor and a cross-hilted sword. – John Merrick † 1749, standing wall monument with life-size semi-reclining figure on sarcophagus with straight tapering sides; the whole against an obelisk background: whom by? – J. Robins of Regent Street, 1831, very unpretentious with little sarcophagus in relief above an inscription tablet, but generous branches of weeping-willow hanging down to the l. and r. – Two or three nice C18 epitaphs.

FREE SCHOOL, Tenterlow Lane, N of the church, 1767. A pretty example of what small village schools still were like in the C18.

The village green is unusually large, but around it nearly all older houses have gone. THE GRANGE, C18 double house, may be noted.

OSTERLEY

ST MARY, 1856, by *J. Taylor Jun.* Not without the grit so typical of its date.

L.T. OSTERLEY STATION, by *S. A. Heaps* and *Charles Holden*, 1934. A little mannered with its tower, compared with such somewhat earlier designs as those of the Cockfosters Extension of the Piccadilly Line.

TRAINING COLLEGE, originally International College, 1867, by *John Norton* and *Massey*. Yellow and red brick, large symmetrical Gothic structure. A series of portrait medallions on the ground floor; their choice could not be more characteristic: Montesquieu, Goethe, Dante, Homer, Aristotle, Cicero.

GILLETTE FACTORY, Great West Road, by *Sir Banister Fletcher* (author of the indispensable historical compilation of architectural history). Of a very incongruous, timidly modernistic grandeur.

OSTERLEY PARK

56 Of Sir Thomas Gresham's house of *c.* 1575 only some masonry of the W wing and the major part of the four corner towers survive. It was evidently similar to Somerset's Syon House close by. Child, the banker, bought it in 1711. He seems to have refaced Gresham's towers and also altered the interior of the STABLES, NE of the house, which are in their exterior (except for the cupola and details) still of Tudor appearance. The stable boxes are separated from the gangway by early C18 arcades.

In 1761 Robert Child asked *Robert Adam* to decorate the house. The final plans must be of 1763. Work went on in two stages. The unforgettable feature of Osterley Park, the PORTICO, belongs to the first, that is the sixties. The detail may be due to Wood's recent publication of the Temple of Bel at Palmyra (Lees-Milne), but the basic idea is wholly Adam's, the idea of using the motif of the antique temple façade in so utterly unantique a manner. Greek and Roman front porticoes are always placed against solid walls, the columns standing out like the figures of a frieze in high relief. Robert Adam with his delight in transparency opens the whole centre of the E front by a double portico at the head of a wide staircase, thus boldly connecting outer space and inner courtyard space. The effect with the slim unfluted Ionic columns is as delicate and celestial and as chastely theatrical as any opera Gluck might have composed in these very same years.

The rooms at Osterley Park are throughout lower than at Syon House owing to the fact that the main floor and the whole inner courtyard are raised on a half-basement. This comparative lowness is especially marked in the ENTRANCE HALL of c. 1766–73, all white with two segment-headed coffered apses and a general scheme of decoration still markedly more structural and less filigree than in the later rooms. Yet the use of the more elegant segmental arch instead of the grander and fuller semicircular arch of the Burlingtonians is already clear indication of Adam's new *finesse*. The LONG GALLERY seems to have been virtually left alone by Adam. The restrained decoration looks c. 1720, that is the years after Sir Thomas Child had acquired the estate. It has an outer door from the w, also in the style of 1720. This is reached by a curved double staircase with typical Adam iron balustrade, and underneath it Adam has built a grotto on a plan copying in miniature that of the interior of the Mausoleum of Diocletian's palace at Spalato which Adam had investigated and made known to the English dilettanti in his folio of 1763. The DINING ROOM is remarkable chiefly for its exquisite furniture designed by Adam in 1767. The large landscapes are by *Zucchi*, the stucco is white and in the ceiling has grapes and ribbons unusually Rococo. The STAIRCASE has the original lamps and iron balustrade. The ceiling has a painting of the Apotheosis of William of Orange by *Rubens*. The LIBRARY, with architectural bookcases also still in Adam's earlier and more structural manner, is again white. The ceiling decoration of the same *finesse* as in Entrance Hall and Dining Room.

In the SE wing the DRAWING ROOM is also part of the earlier work. It is warmer in tone than the Hall and the Library, which is as it should be. It keeps its original Adam carpet. The three next rooms are later, 1775–7, and at once recognizable as such by their excessive thinness of decorative motifs. This is especially evident in the ETRUS-CAN ROOM, adorned with motifs familiar from Pompeian wall paintings. Adam did five such Etruscan Rooms (of which four in London), but this is the only one which remains. The chairs are designed by him too, as is the spectacular State Bed in the BED CHAMBER and the furniture and carpet in the TAPESTRY ROOM. The tapestries are French, designed by *Boucher*. They give a luxuriance to this room quite different from the daintiness of Adam's ceiling ornament.

In the grounds is a serpentine lake S of the house and two CONSERVATORIES NW of it. Both were designed by Adam in 1780. One has an eight-column low Tuscan portico, the other a semicircular front with three Venetian French windows, if they can be called that. The BRIDGE is in ruins, which suits its Piranesian cyclopic rustication. The ENTRANCE LODGE of 1777 is altered.

PERIVALE

Perivale is reached from the Western Avenue by turning off into a country lane just opposite the HOOVER FACTORY, by *Wallis, Gilbert, & Partners*, 1932–8, perhaps the most offensive of the modernistic atrocities along this road of typical by-pass factories. Perivale church and rectory, almost completely hidden behind trees, form the most unexpected and gratifying contrast.

6   PARISH CHURCH. Its distinguishing feature is its C16 weatherboarded little W tower, very unusual in Middlesex (cf., however, Greenford, a mile farther W). The body of the church is essentially C13, less than 50 ft long, aisleless, and with a C15 roof in the nave. The chancel has a low side window in its S wall and a C15 roof with a central king-post with four-way struts (cf. Greenford). – FONT.

Plain octagonal C15 with handsome cover of 1665, a pine-cone finial on four volutes. – PLATE. Ornate, enamelled French C19 Chalice. – MONUMENTS. A tiny brass in the nave floor to Henry Millet † 1505, and his two wives, with their sixteen children. – Lane Harrison † 1740, by *Thos. Ady*: putto holding a shield, placed against a pyramid. – Ellen Nicholas † 1815, by *R. Westmacott*: fine inter-laced group of young woman on couch, supported by an angel, against a plain pointed backplate.

PINNER

Still a compact little country town, though surrounded and overlaid by recent building in the 'outer-suburban' style. Up the HIGH STREET with several pretty half-timbered houses (especially No 4 with the modern date 1580, a tea-room opposite, and the Queen's Head and its neighbour) and Georgian brick houses one approaches the church. The vista is remarkably successful in an intimate way. On the left horse-chestnut trees screen off CHURCH FARM, a long, low building of C18 and C17 date with weatherboarded barns behind. In the centre is the grey church tower and *Sir Ernest George's* tile-hung COCOA TREE TAVERN (now Conserva-tive Club; 1878) added to a plain Georgian brick house. On the right the leafy Church Lane meanders away.

PARISH CHURCH ST JOHN THE BAPTIST. As the battle-mented W tower of flint and freestone dressings with its diagonal buttresses is of the C15, the first impression is of one more of the all-round typical minor Middlesex churches. In fact the body of the church is early C14 (con-secrated 1321), and the plan and some lower parts of the NE wall may well go back to the C13. The church has a nave of four bays, aisles, narrow transepts, and a long chancel, lower than the nave. Vestry and S choir chapel were added in the C19. To *Pearson's* restoration in 1880 is due the roof with gabled dormers, excellent inside as well as outside. The walls are flint with ironstone quoins. The arcade is of low octagonal piers with plain double-chamfered pointed arches. The same double-chamfering appears in the chancel arch. The original windows are lancets without any enrichment, or (aisles) with pointed cinquefoiled heads. The E window of five lights was inserted in the C15. – ALTAR RAILS. Plain, C17, with alternately plain and twisted balusters. – MONUMENTS. Only that to Sir Christopher Clitherow deserves notice, who lived in a 'corrupt, seditious, wicked age' and died in the year 1685. The epitaph has no portrait. The central motif is an urn with festoons hanging down from it. It stands on a sarcophagus and is flanked by Ionic columns with a pediment (an early occurrence of the urn-type of monument, so popular about 1800). In the churchyard stands the obelisk which *John Claudius Loudon* of encyclopaedia writing and gardenesque gardening fame, erected to his parents in 1843. It has an arch cut in on each side at the foot, and higher up two ends of sarcophagi sticking out incongruously.

E of the church in Church Lane is PINNER HOUSE, dated 1721, with a five-bay brick front a little more ambitious than the accepted standard. The centre bay has a pediment and giant pilasters with sunk panels decorated with a criss-cross at top centre and foot. The capitals are nothing but bulging cushions. Further E Church Lane meets Nower Hill (NOWER HILL HOUSE, by *Cecil Brewer*, 1906, is a good example of its date, all white, with sensitively designed woodwork detail) and Moss Lane. All this part of Pinner has still the character of well wooded countryside outside the town. Victorian and post-Victorian houses have large enough grounds not to disturb its character. Up Moss Lane to the N a cluster of farms is reached going back to Tudor days. TUDOR COTTAGE is one of the most picturesque half-timbered farmhouses in the county. EAST END FARM has simple exposed timber-framing. EAST HOUSE has Georgian refronting. N of this hamlet suburban development interferes, and nothing of note is to be found until at the corner of Paines Lane MOSS COTTAGE is reached with an irregular weather-boarded front and some Jacobean details inside.

Of the large buildings farther away, by far the most interesting is HEADSTONE MANOR inside the Recreation Ground. It formed part of the Archbishop's manor of Harrow. Its brick-banked moat remains, and inside the brick-fronted house much of late C16 and C17 timber. At the E end is the so-called chapel, perhaps part of the original hall. High up on the W it has a small two-light window with horned leaded panes. S of the moat is the barn of c. 1600 with ten bays, a queen-post roof and attached to it outside lower originally open timber arcades with shaped brackets for pushing farm carts in, one for each arcade. The barn is now used for concerts and theatricals.

COMMERCIAL TRAVELLERS' SCHOOL at Hatch End, by the railway, tall and bulky, with Franco-Flemish gables and dormers and many additions. The original building was opened in 1853 (*Lane & Ordish*), the wings are of 1868 (*Knightley*). Chapel by *H. O. Creswell*, 1904.

PINNER PARK SCHOOL, Headstone Lane (1935) and CANNON LANE SCHOOL (1937), two of many brick schools soundly designed for the Middlesex C.C. by *W. T. Curtis & Burchett*.

Close to it on the E is WOODHALL TOWERS, 1864, known locally as Tooke's Folly, a glum and imposing tower built with excessively thick walls of brick in all available colours. Most of the rooms of this proud residence are in the tower. But there are also lower parts with French *tourelles* and spirelets. The house was built by Mr Tooke who lived himself at PINNER HILL (now Golf Club House), which has insignificant Victorian additions to a Georgian brick house still visible on the E side. PINNER HOUSE, Church Lane, *see* above. – PINNER PLACE, behind Marsh Lane, by West End Avenue, a sound five-bay Georgian brick mansion, is now derelict.

POTTERS BAR

The urban district includes Bentley Heath, Dyrham Park, South Mimms, and Wrotham Hall (*qq.v.*). Potters Bar consists of two parts, the old to the S along a main SW–NE street, and the new, essentially suburban, farther N, by the railway station, with the main street parallel to the old.

St John. An example of 'pleasing decay': Norman Revival, 1835, by *Blore*. Built of roughcast stone blocks, the proportion of windows to wall and of the windows themselves as in the Gothic Commissioners' churches, but round-headed. An asymmetrical front with a short SW tower. Disused.

War Memorial, 1920, by *C. F. A. Voysey*, corner of Causeway and Hatfield Road, free Gothic shaft with cross, standing on a base with shafts ending in finials; inscriptions in interesting lettering.

Oakmere, Early Victorian, still fairly classical mansion in well-kept grounds.

Houses. If anybody wishes to know what *Sir Banister Fletcher* was like as an architect in his early years, he can look at The Gables, corner of Darkes Lane and The Avenue, with three tile-hung gables and little white oriels, the design exhibited in 1909, and at Seldown, 23 The Avenue.

POYLE

Along the straggling main street of the village a few cottages, half-timbered or of brick, for example The Hollies and a house 60 yds further N.

PRESTON

Lyon's Farm, a good group, the main cottage of five bays, early C18. The out-houses are old too.

RUISLIP

The urban district (with Northwood) had a population of 66,000 in 1949. The village with its church, almshouses, and moated farm is now so closely surrounded on all sides by suburban developments that the small and fairly completely preserved nucleus of old building comes as a surprise from whatever direction it is approached.

PARISH CHURCH ST MARTIN, a sizable building (over 100 ft long) of flint rubble with stone dressings. The parapeted C15 tower stands in the SW corner, added to a nave of C13 date. The S arcade has alternating round and octagonal piers and pointed arches of one square and one chamfered order. The N arcade is a little later; cf. the double-chamfered arches. The chancel arch belongs to the same period, but the chancel (with its fine roof) and the S aisle were rebuilt in the C15, and the N aisle and S chancel chapel somewhat later still. The nave has traces of WALL PAINTINGS of c. 1500 from the life of a saint. More wall paintings (St Michael) at E end of N aisle. – In the chancel are some C14 slipware TILES with leaf, fleur-de-lys, and heraldic designs. – FONT. C12, flat square bowl with foliage design in the spandrels of the top. – PULPIT. Hexagonal, Jacobean, with restrained chiefly abstract ornamentation (studding, faceted blocks, etc.) – DOORS. N, N to chancel, N aisle rood loft, all of C16. – CHESTS in naves and N aisle, oak, iron-bound, hutch-type, early C16. – BREAD CUPBOARD in N aisle, 1697, with four shelves, decorated pilasters, large decorated bracket, and segmental pediment. – PLATE. Very fine Chalice of 1595 with Paten, two Flagons of 1725. – MONUMENTS. Ralph Hawtrey † 1638, and his wife † 1647, by *John* and *Matthias Christmas*: epitaph with two busts in oval niches. It should be compared with the Barkham Monument at Tottenham (1644) to appreciate the difference between conservative and progressive work at that moment. The Hawtrey Monument has nothing yet of Carolean courtly ease and self-conscious elegance. – Thomas Bright † 1674, with mourning putti l. and r. of an aedicule with inscription.

The churchyard is screened from the streets on the W and N by rows of cottages of C16 and C17. The effect is one of seclusion, especially since the street façade of the cottages hardly reveals the fine half-timbered work preserved at the backs: Nos 1–3 High Street, also Nos 5–7, but especially Nos 9–15, with a projecting upper floor and the close timber framing of c. 1500. A picturesque inn, the OLD

SWAN, with a s range of *c*. 1500, lies opposite Nos 9–15. To the N of the church are ten half-timbered ALMS-HOUSES.

N of this group of village houses lies the MANOR FARM, on the site of the motte-and-bailey castle of Ernulf de Hesdin. The outer enclosure of earthworks contains 350 acres. The river Pinn runs through it. To the s of the river the inner enclosure with mound and ditch. The MANOR FARM lies in the old bailey; it has the narrow timber framing of *c*. 1500, with C18 and C19 additions on E and NW. It is now publicly owned and well looked after. Of the BARNS one is used as a library. It is weatherboarded and has an excellent roof of *c*. 1600. The manor was given by Hesdin in 1096 to Bec Abbey in Normandy and later became a cell of Ogbourne Priory (Wilts) which belonged to Bec.

In Bury Street a few more old houses deserve notice: the OLD HOUSE and the PLOUGH INN (with remains in exterior and interior essentially *c*. 1500 or earlier).

The parish is richer in good farmhouses than any other in the county. The Royal Commission volume on Middlesex lists more than fifty.

LADY BANKES SCHOOL, Dawlish Drive, by *W. T. Curtis & Burchett*, 1936. A typical example of the progressive style of Middlesex C.C. schools of the thirties.

BOURNE SECONDARY MODERN SCHOOL, Southbourne Gardens, by *H. V. Lobb*. Also Middlesex C.C. and equally characteristic of its later date: 1946–7.

A rather *outré* modern house may also be mentioned: in PARK AVENUE, by *Connell, Ward & Lucas*, 1935.

SHEPPERTON

The view of the little square at Shepperton towards SE, if one places oneself so that the dolled-up inn in the N and the filling station are concealed, is one of the most perfect village pictures Middlesex has to offer.

PARISH CHURCH ST NICHOLAS. Its most characteristic feature is its oblong brick W tower of 1710, crowned by five battlements on the W and E, and only four on the N and s. The church behind is of flint rubble and dates from 1614. Evidently much old material was used in the reconstruction. The plan is unusual, with substantial transepts, so that to the length of about 65 ft corresponds a width of about 48. The church is aisleless, but has a wooden gallery of early C19 date across its w end and another, on thin iron columns, across the w side of the N transept, of rude and homely workmanship. The box pews, also early C19, are completely preserved. The roof is ceiled and whitewashed. No monuments of importance. – PLATE. Of 1822, 1848, and 1869.

RECTORY to the N of the church, lying back too far to play its part in contributing to the village square. An exquisite front of c. 1700, seven bays and two one-bay slightly projecting wings, coved cornice, and hipped roof. The exterior does not reveal the fact that inside is a spacious hall of c. 1500 with moulded beams (the hall of Grocyn's rectory when he held the living of Shepperton from 1504 to 1513).

The village square has a delightful row of houses opposite the church on the s side, chiefly the KING'S HEAD and WARREN LODGE. The village street leading to the N out of the square is also uncommonly complete in its cottages (with nothing yet to jar at all). It ends with TOY COTTAGE on the l. and the wall of the MANOR HOUSE on the r. This can be seen only from the river, a friendly stuccoed five-bay front of c. 1830 with verandah.

At Shepperton Green on the road to Littleton, WHITE COTTAGE, a particularly attractive brick and timber-frame cottage.

SOUTHALL

For Norwood *see* separate entry.

No coherent picture of older times survives. The High Street has lost its character. The PARISH CHURCH OF ST JOHN was nothing but an inexpensive London stock brick chapel of 1838 with the usual lancet windows, its successor of 1901 is of no importance. In Lancaster Road is the church of St George, consecrated 1908, by *Sir A Blomfield*. (The splendid organ made *c.* 1704 by *Griffin* comes from St George's, Botolph Lane, in the City.) The few surviving farms (Dormers Wells Farm, mainly *c.* 1700) deserve no special description. Off North Road is Grove House, with five bays, segment-headed windows, and a hooded porch evidently early C18, but also nothing particularly remarkable. Yet Southall should be visited by any architectural Middlesex traveller, because of its Manor House.

Southall Manor House (now Borough Health Department), a complex building. The street front is with the rooms behind of 1587, except for the projecting l. (NW) wing which is C18. But the rest of the N front is again of the earlier building period. The house is timber-framed with close-set standards. The composition of the original street front is irregular yet no doubt far from haphazard. The designer must have deliberately used the greatest variety of heights, widths, and depths for his various gabled bays: from l. to r. first a wide bay with a large gable, a slight projection on the first floor, and one pedimented oriel on the ground floor and a second on the first; then a polygonal bay window projecting a little further and with a smaller and lower gable; then the porch, still further advancing and with a gable of the same dimension as the previous one; finally the r. bay with a bay window identical with the other but farther away from the porch so that a semblance of symmetry between porch and bays is avoided. Also the bay window is not like the other crowned by a small gable but has a strongly projecting large one, as high as the one on the l. The entrance hall has a contemporary fireplace.

St Bernard's Hospital (Hanwell Asylum), Uxbridge Road. A vast complex of buildings, begun 1831. The heavy classical gatehouse probably of that date. Chapel, 1881.

(Almshouses, Norwood Road, red brick, 1814. MTCP.)

SOUTHGATE

The borough (population *c.* 75,000 in 1950) is now mostly built over, but there remains some open country in the N parts and uncommonly many public parks and recreation and sports grounds. Village character can still be found on Winchmore Hill and to a lesser degree by Southgate Green. Palmers Green, farther s, is wholly London.

PARISH CHURCH CHRIST CHURCH, Waterfall Road, 1863, by *Sir George G. Scott.* Built by the side of the old churchyard and the remains of the old church (still in a seemingly rural spot). The remarkable features are the *Morris and Co.* windows: that on the w of the s aisle designed by *Rossetti,* fine and delicate, 1865; in the N aisle Christian virtues by *Burne Jones,* 1865, 1866, 1885, 1898, riper and more luxurious. – PLATE. Two Plates of *c.* 1700, Tankard of 1738, and Christening Cup (?) of late C18.

ST JOHN, Green Lanes and Hoppers Road, 1904–9, by *John Oldrid Scott.* A rich exterior with a big crossing tower and two round E turrets with leaden spirelets. Plenty of flint rubble and flint panelling is used. Flamboyant Dec. E window.

ST MICHAEL-AT-BOWES, Palmerston Road, 1874, by *Sir George G. Scott.*

ST PAUL, Church Hill, Winchmore Hill, 1828. A cheap church of the Commissioners' type, aisleless, of yellow brick, with a thin wooden w gallery and a flat ceiling.

FRIENDS MEETING HOUSE, Church Hill, Winchmore Hill, 1790. A plain front of door and two windows with a pediment. Inside just one rectangular room with the honest old benches. Burial ground on the w.

L.T. STATIONS. Three of *Charles Holden's* most excellent designs are in the borough. The skill in varying a fairly fixed number of elements is wholly admirable. SOUTH-GATE has a circular ticket hall with a playful little lantern and is surrounded by a shopping arcade. ARNOS GROVE has also a circular ticket hall but one of greater repose and dignity. The canopy on the ground floor is square in contrast to the curve above. OAKWOOD (by *C. H. James* and *Charles Holden*) is rectangular and yet essentially different from, for example, Sudbury Town. All 1932–3.

DE BOHUN SCHOOL, Green Road, 1936, by *W. T. Curtis & Burchett*. An example of the progressive style of Middlesex C.C. schools of the thirties.

SKINNERS' ALMSHOUSES, Green Lanes and Fox Lane, Palmers Green, a pretty composition of 1895 by *W. Campbell Jones*. Two wings, with wooden arcading in front, steep tall tiled roofs, and a central half-timbered gable with a copper-covered cupola behind. In niches in the gateposts two small figures of an old man and old woman in poor clothes, *c.* 1700.

SOUTHGATE VILLAGE. Of Southgate Village the Green still exists, a bare large triangle of grass with old shops in the E, but C 20 middle-class houses and flats intruding from N and W. Two good houses of Early Georgian date remain on the N side: ESSEX HOUSE and ARNOSIDE, a total of six bays, with the two porches side by side in the middle. Original iron railings and gates. Some more Georgian bits in the High Street and Blagdens Lane. More important than these remains of the village itself are the surviving larger houses surrounding the village centre: Arnos Grove and (closer to Palmers Green) Broomfield House in the S, Southgate House in the N, Grovelands in the E, and Enfield Old Park on Bush Hill in the NE.

BROOMFIELD HOUSE, Broomfield Park, apparently C17. A curious rectangular block of a shape typical of the Restoration and after, but half-timbered. The entrance hall with the staircase lies in the centre of the building. Its w door leads on to a loggia with two wooden Tuscan columns. This faces a wide monumental avenue of trees. The walls and ceiling are decorated by paintings ascribed to *Sir James Thornhill*. A lead cistern outside bears the date 1736.

ARNOS GROVE, Cannon Hill, now an administrative centre of the Electricity Board (Northmet). The company has added big N and S wings, but between these the house still stands which Mr James Colebrooke built in 1719 (a stone with this date in the hall floor). The building is of red brick with rubbed brick dressings, seven bays wide, two and a half storeys high. A pediment of three bays width and a little cupola behind it emphasize the centre. The garden side was the same as the entrance side. A handsome example of a common type. The E porch is modern, the shallow W apse was added c. 1788. At that time the main room to the W was redecorated in an exquisite Adam style. Two columns screen the apse from the rooms. The architect of these alterations was *Sir Robert Taylor*. The staircase hall has still original wall and ceiling paintings, dark and baroque. They are signed by *Lanscroon*, 1723. The NW corner rooms have good decoration of the same period, especially a fireplace of Kent style with a face of the sun as the central motif.

ENFIELD OLD PARK (Bush Hill Golf Club), Bush Hill. Early C18 with additions of 1838 and later. To the S of the house part of a C18 garden well with sculptured decoration has been excavated. On the gable of a cottage a little farther S are three small carved figures of C15 (angel, male and female saint), reported to come from a chapel on the estate. On the stables, C18 with cupola, are two carved corbel heads, also of C15.

SOUTHGATE HOUSE, High Street, now a school, Late Georgian.

GROVELANDS, The Bourne, originally called Southgate 60 Grove, now a hospital. Built by *John Nash* for Mr Walker Gray; design exhibited at the Academy in 1797. Small, only a villa, but most impressive. The garden front has a recessed loggia with four giant Ionic columns and only one window each side of it. The sides have a projecting centre with coupled Ionic giant columns left and right of the door and again only one window each side of it. The windows have arched tops with tympana with the fanwise fluting so popular with Adam and his followers. There is a low upper floor and a weighty attic with horizontal oval windows above the Ionic entablature. The whole is cement-rendered and looks over extensive grounds with a serpentine lake landscaped no doubt by *Humphry Repton*.

WINCHMORE HILL VILLAGE. The top of Winchmore
Hill is still comparatively rural and nicely wooded.
Weatherboarded cottages survive in Wade's Hill, Hop-
per's Road, and Church Hill. Early C18 houses: DEVON
HOUSE, Church Hill, and ROWANTREE HOUSE, The
Green, with its neighbour (c. 1720). Early C19 houses in
the same streets and in Vicars Moor Lane.

SOUTH MIMMS

PARISH CHURCH ST GILES. Chancel (C13), w tower (C14),
and nave (C15) of flint, N aisle (early C16) of brick, refaced
by *G. E. Street*, who also added the S porch. The church
was in existence in 1136. The tower has diagonal buttresses, battlemented parapet, and a stair-turret higher
than the parapet in the SE corner. The nave is of modest
dimensions with octagonal piers and octagonal concave
capitals. The arches are four-centred. A staircase to the
former rood loft is preserved in the S wall. The N chancel
chapel is separated from the N aisle and the chancel by
wooden screens (early C16) of fifteen and ten bays. Each
bay ends in a steep gable with slightly concave sides. The
w door has a richly cusped ogee arch. Aisle and chancel
have simple contemporary roofs. The chancel chapel is a
chantry endowed by Henry Frowyk in 1527. He probably
also financed the building of the aisle. The Frowyk family
were successful City merchants. In the aisle windows are
fragments of GLASS, two of them dated 1526, showing
groups of kneeling figures in blue, mauve, amber, and a
little green; no red. – DOOR in w tower, nail-studded, C15.
– CHEST in nave, of elementary hutch-type, may be as old
as C13: anyway the earliest piece of furniture in the
county. – FONT. Four short C13 shafts support an absolutely plain, big, square bowl. – PLATE. C17 Set re-cast
by *Keith's* in 1890. – MONUMENTS. The chief pride of
South Mimms church are its Frowyk tombs: the brass to
Thomas Frowyk † 1448, his wife and nineteen children
in the w tower, and the two splendid canopied monuments in the chancel and the N chancel chapel. The latter

is earlier in its style and supposed to represent Henry 20
Frowyk the Younger, who died before his father, Henry 21
the Elder, probably buried in the chancel monument.
Both have tomb-chests with quatrefoil panels, corner
posts with shaft-rings, and canopies with four-centred
arches. But whereas the tomb in the aisle chapel is purely
Perp, the probably only slightly later one in the chancel
has a Renaissance top cornice and corner posts developing
in their upper parts into bulbous, leaf-covered Renaissance balusters (a remarkable example of the gusto with
which craftsmen at some distance from the Court threw
themselves into the new Italian fashion). The tomb looks
as though it might be of *c.* 1540. – In the churchyard
Cavendish-Bentinck Mausoleum, *c.* 1900, by *Weir-
Schultz*, a cool, correct Doric temple *in artis*.

CHRIST CHURCH: *see* under Barnet in the Hertfordshire
  volume of this series.

EARTHWORK, 1 m. N of the parish church, W of the road
  to Hatfield, motte-and-bailey castle of over two acres
  area. The motte is circular, the bailey kidney-shaped;
  state of preservation poor.

CLARE HALL (now a sanatorium). Into the street wall and
  gate a few fragments are built in, said to come from *Wren's*
  St Antholin in the City of London.

STAINES

The development of the last twenty or thirty years which
raised the population of Staines from 6,000 in 1901 to 21,000
in 1931 and 39,000 in 1949 has fortunately by-passed the
church and its neighbourhood completely. To an exceptional
degree this area has preserved its character of a hundred
years ago.

PARISH CHURCH ST MARY. The pleasant peace of the
  neighbourhood makes up for the few attractions of the
  church. Its W tower is its most interesting feature: brick
  and in its two lower storeys dating from 1631. These have
  plain buttresses and segment-headed windows on the
  upper storey. The top storey, also brick, belongs to 1828,

when the whole rest of the church was reconstructed by
J. B. Watson, a poor job, though spacious, with yellow
stock brick walls and lancet windows, and inside a gallery with leafy iron balustrade on three sides. – PLATE.
Paten of 1798 and Set of 1842. – No monuments of
importance.

ST PETER, Laleham Road, prosperous brick building with
steeple towards the Thames, 1893–4, by *G. H. Fellowes
Prynne*.

CONGREGATIONAL CHURCH, Thames Street, *c.* 1830,
stuccoed with Ionic W loggia.

DUMCROFT (now an Approved School) to the NE of the
church is of 1631, but so much altered and added to
that little original material survives outside. Are the three
curved and scrolled gables genuine? The interior possesses
one room with old panelling and a fine fireplace with marquetry landscapes.

LONDON STONE, W of the church, in the recreation ground
by the river. It is a poorly preserved stone, probably postmedieval, on a pedestal of 1781, marking the former W
limit of the jurisdiction of the City of London over the
Thames.

CHURCH STREET leads from the church into the town, a
well preserved Georgian street towards its W end.

HIGH STREET. Although several houses of C17 and C18
remain, there is no common character any longer except
that of 1920–40. Of the old houses the best are the BLUE
ANCHOR, quite a stately inn of *c.* 1700 with red and vitrified bricks in a chequerboard pattern, and Nos 32–6 also
of *c.* 1700.

CLARENCE STREET, between High Street and the bridge,
is a good example of a market town development of the
latest Georgian phase, dateable by its name to the time of
George IV. It leads to the BRIDGE, of three noble stone
arches, 1829–32, by the great *Rennie* of Waterloo Bridge
fame.

GARAGE, 49 London Road, by *C. H. C. Kirby*, 1934. A
good, early example of the Modern Movement in English
architecture.

STANMORE

The two parishes of Little and Great Stanmore stretch in a
NW direction parallel to the W border of Edgware. Their
character is similar, in so far as both have a completely
'outer suburban' S, just like, say, Edgware, and an almost
completely rural N. For the purposes of this book they can
be treated as one. Their main attractions are Great Stanmore Church with Stanmore Hill and the surrounding
houses, and Canons with St Lawrence, Whitchurch. There
is a good reason to discuss the latter below, under
Canons.

PARISH CHURCH ST JOHN THE EVANGELIST, two
churches in one churchyard. The old one was consecrated
in 1632 by Archbishop Laud. Although provided with a
battlemented tower it must have been every inch as
rational and matter-of-fact as what the Victorians called
the 'red brick boxes' of the C18. Yet overgrown and open
to the sky it is now truly picturesque (one of the best ruins
in the county). In the nave stands a mid-Victorian Gothic
Mausoleum to the Hollond family of Stanmore Hall. The
date is 1866.

The new church was begun in 1849 and designed by
Clutton, 'extraordinarily good and solid for its date . . .
better than Scott' (Goodhart-Rendel). It contains much
of the furnishings of the old church, especially the FONT
with the Wolstenholme crest, by *N. Stone, c.* 1632, some
C17 PLATE (Flagon, 1616; two Patens, 1632, 1637; and
Paten, 1709), and the following MONUMENTS: John Burnell † 1605, and family, the usual type of epitaph with
the two principal figures kneeling opposite each other,
and the children kneeling small, in relief, below, flanking columns and a top with two obelisks and a crest with
strapwork. – Sir John Wolstenholme † 1639, excellent
bearded marble figure, asleep: a typical *Nicholas Stone*
and part of a larger monument. – John Wolstenholme
† 1669, a stout four-poster with substantial drapery and
columns with capitals as elementary as if they were of the
C10: all of stone. The effigy of John Wolstenholme is

M.—8

recumbent, that of his wife semi-reclining and looking pensively at him. A babe and little girl are lying behind her back, rather incongruously: surely a case of wrong re-assembly. However that may be, the whole monument is a belated follower of the Harefield type (Countess of Derby). – John Dalton, by *Bacon*, 1791, a good if con-servative work with a life-size mourning woman bent over an urn with portrait medallion: no trace yet of the Gre-cian taste. – Elizabeth Dalton † 1812, a slim draped 'Grecian' urn with portrait medallion. – 1st Earl of Aber-deen, by *Boehm*, 1875, recumbent. – Plenty of minor C18 and C19 tablets in the tower.

A number of houses worth noting are close to the church: the RECTORY of 1721 with additions, the TITHE BARN and OLD CHURCH HOUSE, and the astonishingly elaborate sham MANOR HOUSE, built in 1901 with genuine half-timbering, old roofing tiles, an old oak porch, old glass, etc.

The main development of the village was along the present Broadway (No 33, Georgian brick), Church Road (Regent House, with charming early C18 door), and up Stanmore Hill. Here there are still on the left many cottages, first of brick, then by the corner of Green Lane a weatherboarded group, then some larger Georgian houses (Mill House, Rookery). On the right are houses in their grounds: the DOWER HOUSE, picturesque elaborately irregular mid-C19 brick with gables, chimney-stacks, etc., then STAN-MORE HALL, a Victorian castle with a nucleus of 1847, rest 1890. Much redecoration by *Morris and Co.* in the nineties. Ragstone and free-stone, in the Tudor style with tower and gables. A little NE of Stanmore Hall is WAR-REN HOUSE, elaborate Early Jacobean Revival with a rich porte-cochère.

CANONS AND ST LAWRENCE CHURCH. James Brydges, son of the 8th Lord Chandos of Sudeley, was made Earl of Carnarvon in 1714 and Duke of Chandos in 1719. From 1707 to 1712 he was Marlborough's Paymaster-General of Forces abroad and amassed a fabulous fortune. He in-herited the Canons Estate (so called because originally belonging to the Priory of St Bartholomew-the-Great) through his first wife and erected a mansion on it in 1713–25. He was not an easy client, and architects changed several times. *Talman* (of Chatsworth) was the first, then *John James*, to whom the essence of the design of the house itself is probably due, and *Gibbs* (1716–19), and after him *John Price*. The building was a square block of freestone, two-storeyed with a lower attic storey above the cornice and statues on the parapet. On its s side it had a giant attached Ionic portico. It was all extremely lavish, 'the most magnificent' house in England, said Defoe, with *Bellucci* paintings on the ceilings of hall and staircase, plasterwork by *Bagutti* (Defoe calls them: Paulacci and Pergotti), long straight radiating avenues in the park (laid out by *A. Blackwell*), an equestrian statue of George I and a standing figure of George II. Handel was the Duke's *Kapellmeister* from 1717 to 1719. Pope's neat comments on Timon's Villa in the Epistle to Lord Burlington of 1731 are familiar and no doubt suggested by Chandos even if not meant to apply only to him. Pope's doubts proved justified. The estate was broken up almost immediately after the princely owner's death. A sale took place, and much of value was removed. The staircase went to Chesterfield House in London and from there to the Odeon Cinema at Broadstairs, where it was blitzed out of existence. Altar, pulpit, and font of the private chapel can be seen at Fawley Church, Oxon, the organ at Holy Trinity, Gosport, Hants, iron railings at New College, Oxford, and the Hampstead parish church, London, and the statue of George II in Golden Square, London. Some parts of the great portico are said to have been bought by Earl Tylney for Wanstead (cf. Hendon Hall).

In place of Chandos's palace a worthy cabinet-maker, Hallet, built, partly with the materials from Canons, a villa for himself which still survives, though enlarged, and heightened in its effect by *C. E. Mallows* in 1910. Since then the North London Collegiate School for Girls has taken it over and made extensive utilitarian brick additions to it at its back.

Parish Church St Lawrence, Little Stanmore (or Whitchurch), Whitchurch Lane. Of the medieval church only the plain W tower remains. It is brick, cemented, and of the early C16. The rest of the church was rebuilt by Chandos in 1715, very much in the style of a private chapel, and dedicated in 1720. It has an unassuming exterior with undecorated arched windows and broad Tuscan corner pilasters. The interior is all the more surprising : unaisled and with a chancel, or rather retro-choir, appearing in a stage fashion between two tall columns of dark wood and above a low reredos of wood (now in the anteroom to the Mausoleum and replaced by a Neo-Gothic one). The whole room is painted from vaulted top to bottom with virtues, evangelists, biblical scenes, and figured architecture by *Laguerre*. Only the glass of mid-C19 date is objectionable in these surroundings. Of the large more colourful paintings to the r. and l. of the altar and to the r. and l. of the (renewed) *Gerard Smith* organ in the retro-choir the Nativity and Pietà are according to Vertue by *Bellucci*, the other two by *Laguerre*. At the W end of the church is a wooden gallery with the Duke's box in the centre. It is emphasized by a canopy with a *Bellucci* copy of Raphael's Transfiguration. The contemporary ironwork and the box pews should also be noted.

So there is plenty to see in the church, but while the E end in its original form with the vista through the columns must have been highly effective in the sense of the international Baroque, especially as concealed side light gives radiance to the retro-choir, the church itself is Baroque only in its intentions. The glow which one would expect from such lavish decoration is absent. The climate is English and moderate. So long as this country remained faithful to its own Baroque, the Baroque of Greenwich and Blenheim, success was assured. Where it strove to emulate the Berninis and Asams it failed.

Chandos gave a set of silver-gilt PLATE to the church in 1716. It consists of two large Chalices, two Patens, Tankard, and Almsdish.

Attached to the church in the N is the Chandos Mausoleum, a smaller room also completely painted with feigned columns, niches, etc., and a figured dome. The monument 28b to the Duke stands against the E wall. It is impressive though sculpturally by no means up to the standard of Rysbrack and Roubiliac. It is *Andrew Carpentier's 'chef d'œuvre'*. The recent attribution to *Grinling Gibbons* is stylistically very improbable. The Duke stands in the middle, in Roman costume and bewigged, his two wives kneel like virtues to the l. and r. 'veiled and devout' (Mrs Esdaile). Plain pilasters separate the three figures. They carry urns, and between the urns is a kind of canopy in relief, the whole of a grand and noble restraint. Against the S wall are two more monuments to members of the family: Mary, wife of the first Marquess of Carnarvon † 1738 (a black sarcophagus against a pyramid in relief in an altar surround; no figures), and Margaret, Marchioness of Carnarvon † 1760 (a colossal plain classical sarcophagus with S-curved fluting at the end).

N of the churchyard are the plain LAKE ALMSHOUSES, founded 1693; farther W in Abercorn Road a new SCHOOL, one of the many put up in the 1930s by the County Council in a sensible modern idiom (by *Curtis & Burchett*).

STANWELL

PARISH CHURCH ST MARY. Its chief attraction is its tower as it appears from the Green: first stage C13 flint rubble as the rest of the church, second stage flint and chequer C14, third stage smaller flint, late C14, spire shingled. The short nave has a C13 S arcade with piers alternating between circular and octagonal. The chamfered arches have hood moulds (cf. Harmondsworth). The E window of the S aisle and the N and S windows of the chancel are early C14, the chancel E window is a little later. The clerestory and roof are of the C15; the chancel roof of trussed-rafter type may even belong to the same date as the elaborate blank wall arcading on the S side of the chancel and the sedilia in which every curve is ogee.

The old roof of the C14 S aisle has gone but the figured corbels (a Queen, two Kings, a Bishop, a Knight, a man, a woman, a pilgrim) remain. The N aisle is 1863. – PILLAR PISCINA, C13, and PISCINA with credence and aumbry recently discovered. – PLATE. Flagon, 1688; Chalice, 1799; Almsdish, 1800; Paten, 1806; Communion Plate, 1817. – MONUMENTS. Brass in chancel to Richard de Thorp † 1408, demi-figure praying, of the same type as Robert Lance at Hayes. – Lord and Lady Knyvett † 1622, by *Nicholas Stone*: standing wall monument with more than life-size white marble figures kneeling opposite each other; flanking black columns with crumpled alabaster curtains tied to them, broken segmental pediment with achievement. On the base inscription and thick hanging garlands.

LORD KNYVETT'S FREE SCHOOL, 1624, unattractively situated, but of architectural importance. As against the original Harrow School and the Enfield Grammar School, the schoolhouse proper and the masters' lodgings are here combined into one composition of two three-bay halves. Each half has a central door with a heavy flat plastered surround and a pediment and two windows. On the school side they are tall and renewed, on the living-house side they are in two storeys with unmoulded surrounds and original. The building is of brick with a pitched roof. The village centre is a triangular Green with at its S end the church, in the SE a few mellow Georgian houses (chiefly one of the early C18 with seven bays and two storeys). To the N at the beginning of the road to Heathrow two good half-timbered cottages. Towards Stanwell Moor lies STANWELL PLACE in its grounds, a plain cement-rendered Late Georgian house. At Stanwell Moor THE CROFT with a C17 core and an unadorned Georgian brick front.

SUDBURY

SUDBURY COURT, in Sudbury Court Road, preserves something of the country lane character, since the new arterial road bypasses it. The house itself may have a C17 core, but has been much altered.

L.T. STATIONS. Sudbury Town and Sudbury Hill, 1932, 64
the earliest which *Charles Holden* built in the style that
was then adopted on the Cockfosters extension of the
Piccadilly Line and elsewhere. Outstanding examples of
how satisfying purely by careful detailing and good proportions such unpretentious buildings can be. Note the
variations in the canopies and the fenestration.

SUNBURY

Up to Hampton the Thamesside has for centuries been a
villeggiatura of London. W of Hampton it is less closely
attached to the town. River villages such as Sunbury have
still an occasional bigger house, but nothing like the
continuous Georgian or pre-Georgian row of well-to-do
houses as on the river front of Chiswick, Twickenham, or
Hampton.

PARISH CHURCH ST MARY. Of the modest church designed by one *Wright*, Clerk of the Works at Hampton
Court, and built in 1752, only the walls of W tower and
nave remain, without distinguishing features. In 1856
Teulon descended upon this guileless building and recast
it vigorously. The effects of his steamroller sensitivity
are here particularly revolting: a heavy chancel with
round-headed windows, multi-coloured brick decoration
everywhere, even, to add 'interest', to the tower. A gloomy
depressing interior with iron-ornamented gallery. –
PLATE. Chalice of 1662, Flagons of 1670 and 1746, Pie
Dish of 1752.

ST SAVIOUR, Upper Sunbury, 1911–12 by *J. S. Alder*. –
PLATE. Chalice acquired from a private collection and
attributed to the German C14.

SUNBURY COURT (Salvation Army Youth Centre) is the
large mansion of Sunbury, now cut off from the Thames
by a road and small houses. It was originally of seven bays
with straight passages leading to outer pavilions. The
centre survives, the passages are altered. The centre has
Ionic pilasters, and pediment (a glaring red brick with

stone dressings is used). The date is *c.* 1770. In the Saloon
Arcadian wall paintings by *Elias Martin,* the Swedish
painter who lived in England from 1768 to 1780. Between
Sunbury Court and the church a few more good houses:
DARBY HOUSE, late Georgian; then in French Street
IVY HOUSE, early C18, and another later house S of it; in
Thames Street more villagey cottages and also ORCHARD
HOUSE, *c.* 1700, with good iron gate; in Church Street
and Green Street: HOLLY COTTAGE, CHURCH VILLA,
and farther N HAWKE HOUSE, of 1703. S of the church
also a few nice buildings.

The whole neighbourhood of Sunbury, also E and N of
Kempton Park, stands under the sign of the METRO-
POLITAN WATER BOARD. The large buildings were
originally put up by five different companies before the
M.W.B. was founded in 1902. They range from the
typical official Italianate of 1853–5, with towers and chimneys, to sound plain modern brick and a monstrous big
affair on the Hanworth–Sunbury Common road (1927–9),
which with its pompous symmetry and its lack of windows
looks like an expensive war memorial.

SWAKELEYS

46a Swakeleys (now Foreign Office Sports Association) was
built between 1629 and 1638 by Sir Edmund Wright. Its
exterior belongs with small exceptions to these dates. It is
of brick with stone or plaster dressings. The plan is H-
shaped with identical bay windows at the ends of the four
projections. The porch is in the middle of the W side, a
subsidiary door in the middle of the E side. Both these recessed centre parts of the elevation are oddly bitty with
small and crowded windows. The wings are broader in
treatment: large windows of four or six lights with mullions and transomes, pediments above them, though not
immediately above as a true classicist would have put
them, but separated from them by the main entablatures
of ground floor and first floor. Plenty of curved gables
crown the lively composition. The gables also have top

pediments, a typical feature of *c.* 1630. Compared with
Inigo Jones designs Swakeleys appears conservative, but
it should never be forgotten that before 1640 or 1650
Jones stood virtually alone in pleading for a pure Italian
style. Where then do such Middlesex houses as Boston
Manor, Brentford, and Forty Hall, Enfield, belong? The
very fact of Swakeleys being dated so securely can perhaps be taken as confirmation for the view set out on
pages 17, 29, and 53 that the classical details of both these
houses should be attributed to the mid C17. Inside there
is still much panelling in many rooms, though most of it
is restored and renewed. The porch has still Jacobean-
looking strapwork ornament, whereas the Saloon possesses a plaster ceiling of pure Inigo Jones character, one
of the finest in the county. It could well be of *c.* 1635,
considering the date, say, of the Queen's House at Greenwich, but would in that case indicate a more advanced
decorator (closer to the Court) than the architect of
Swakeleys was. Perhaps it is more likely that the ceiling
of the Saloon was re-done about 1660, when the classical
screen in the hall was put up. The bust of Charles I in its
pediment is so inappropriate in size and position that it
is no doubt a later addition. The staircase has paintings of
somewhat later date, poor work attributed to *Streater*
(Borenius). N of the house are extensive much altered
C17 STABLES and a square DOVECOTE of the second
half of the C17.

Amongst the not many surrounding farms there is one at
least of highest appeal: MANOR FARM with an exceedingly varied E view; half-timbered, early C16, with original
windows, and two contemporary gabled brick wings. Part
of the moat also remains.

(SWAKELEYS FARM, Warren Road. Dated 1709, plus additions. MTCP.)

TEDDINGTON

The architectural pleasures of Teddington are considerably
fewer than those of the villages preceding and following it
along the Thames. What remains in one's mind of a suburb

now as much built over as Twickenham farther N is the historically more than aesthetically impressive contrast between the two churches of St Mary and St Alban standing side by side in Ferry Road. There could be no more poignant memento of the natural and intimate role of the church in the village of the C16, C17, C18, and its ambitious yet so much less convincing role in our time.

PARISH CHAPEL ST MARY. A tiny brick building with a N aisle whose brickwork (diaper pattern of dark vitrified headers) betrays its early Tudor date (windows C19). The rest (except for the C19 chancel) dates from 1753–4, a miniature copy of John James's design at Twickenham with one of those sweet battlemented towers of which provincial Georgian church-builders were so fond, and a N front with round-headed windows and even a pediment. The interior is curious, with its Gothic piers of 1877 (or 1893?) and its three parallel plastered pointed tunnel vaults. Good GLASS in three S aisle windows, of 1870 and 1880. – PLATE. Two Almsdishes of 1765, the rest C19. – BRASS to John Goodyere † 1506, and wife. – MONUMENTS to Sir Orlando Bridgman † 1674, and to W. T. Stratton † 1814, the latter with a kneeling woman under an altar overhung by a branch of weeping willow is by *Sir Richard Westmacott*.

PARISH CHURCH ST ALBAN, 1889 (consecrated 1896), by *W. Niven*. Incomplete in the W. Yet, as it is, its size is bewildering: aisles and ambulatory, chancel of three vaulted bays, and unvaulted nave of five, all of ashlar stone, very high, very correct, and rather cold.

SS PETER AND PAUL, 1863–73, by *Street*. Disappointing. Yellow and red brick; no steeple.

At the E end of the HIGH STREET a pretty terrace of three brick cottages of 1759, a few more scattered farther W. At the W end ELMFIELD, a dignified C18 house of five bays with a Greek Doric porch added later.

In and around PARK ROAD towards the entrance of Bushey Park more good houses, especially THE ELMS of *c.* 1700, OLD MANOR COTTAGE, and FRITHVILLE. Also pleasant Regency villas.

TOTTENHAM

Tottenham (population in 1949, 130,000) lies along the High Road which is part of the Roman Ermine Street. No break is noticeable between Stoke Newington in the s and Edmonton in the N. The manor of Tottenham, however, lay much farther w, halfway to Wood Green, close to White Hart Lane, and the village church is not far s of the former manor house grounds. It forms, with the Vicarage and Bruce Castle and its park, a deliciously rural oasis in a borough otherwise virtually all suburbia, Victorian, and post-Victorian.

PARISH CHURCH ALL HALLOWS, Church Lane. The w tower is early C14, of four stages, the fourth being C18 brickwork with battlements. The storeys below are flint with stone corners. The s aisle was widened late C15. It is of Kentish rag, with a contemporary s porch of brick with dark brick diapering and stone dressings. The N aisle and the E parts are C19. The point one remembers about the exterior is the contrast of textures between flint, rag, and rubble as seen from the SW or the vicarage front garden. The interior is disappointing, in spite of good individual features. The general impression is of C19, because of the E parts and the upper parts of the nave. In the nave only the six piers (octagonal and rather low) are of C14 (later than the tower). – GLASS. W window N aisle, three lights with three large seated Evangelists above three small seated Prophets : French late C16. – COMMUNION TABLE, C17, in N transept. – MONUMENTS. Richard Canteler and wife, also Sir Ferdinando Heyborne and wife (née Canteler) † 1602, 1623, 1618, 1615. The two couples kneel opposite each other in profile, each with a praying-desk between ; each couple in front of a flat arched niche. The three short piers of the niches are hidden by three obelisks (a less usual motif); inscriptions below on the base. – Sir John Melton and wife † 1640: the couple kneels in the same way, flanking Corinthian columns, broken segmental pediment : a conservative work for its date, as appears clearly by comparison with the monument to Mary Barkham and her husband Sir Robert Barkham † 1644, by *Edw. Marshall*. Here the stiffness of the earlier monuments is replaced by courtly ease and dignity. Frontal demi-figures; below along the base small kneeling figures in relief of four children with two babies lying in front of them; the decoration also with the fuller and rounder forms of the Inigo Jones period. Very advanced in style.

ST BARTHOLOMEW, Craven Park Road, 1904, by *Caroë*. Smallish, low, red brick, standing back a little, typical of its architect.

HOLY TRINITY, The Green, 1828–30, by *Savage*. Typical of its date: a plain yellow brick building with aisles, the nave and chancel slightly projecting to w and E. The same plain little turrets on the aisle and nave corners in w and E. All windows lancets—all rather thin and bare, with no excesses of feeling.

HIGH CROSS, High Road. So much restored that neither the brick core of *c.* 1600 nor the early Gothicist stucco trimmings appear.

44b BRUCE CASTLE, S of the church, in its own grounds, a late Elizabethan manor house of the typical E-shape, with late C17 additions and alterations. As the Elizabethan stone work is very renewed and the windows have C18 sash, the impression is not very pure. The wings have semi-octagonal fronts, the central porch, projecting as far as the wings, has been remodelled in 1684 and provided with a square tower and a cupola. The balustrades on top of the porch and around the tower top and the little cupola are what now characterizes the S façade. The N façade is plain early C18 brick, the w wing still later Georgian. Quite separate to the w stands a circular brick tower of 21 ft diameter decorated with blank pointed arcades; a fine military-looking object of C16 date and no known purpose.

PRIORY, now Vicarage. A good Early Georgian front hides a house built in 1620 for Joseph Fenton, a barber surgeon in the City of London. An excellent plaster ceiling still in the dining-room, and minor contemporary details in other rooms. Of the Early Georgian remodelling the staircase with twisted balusters is one witness; the sumptuous fireplace of the dining-room another. The gate is also contemporary, but comes from the old Vicarage.

The HIGH ROAD still has plenty of late C17 and C18 bits, but they are scattered and do not merge into a picture anywhere. They can only serve to remind one of the ribbon of houses that stretched along here, passing the Green and by-passing the church. The best examples of pre-Georgian and Georgian brick architecture, though never outstanding, are Nos 583 and 585 (Lane House), 658–74, a modest not at all uniform group, 683–5 and BAPTIST CHAPEL (c. 1830 Doric), 790–802, a complete group dated 1691 on a sundial at No. 790 (MTCP), 808–10, 879–81, and so to BROOK HOUSE which is essentially of c. 1700.

(The MTCP also lists 13–16 BRUCE GROVE, early C19 part of a group of sixteen houses, and 1–10 PROSPECT PLACE, two-storeyed, semi-detached cottages of 1822.)

Of farms in the Lea Valley of which there must once have been quite a number the only survival is ASPLIN'S FARM, just E of Northumberland Park railway station, a modest neglected front of c. 1750 with early C17 parts behind.

C20 architecture is chiefly represented by the WHITE HART LANE ESTATE, a large L.C.C. enterprise begun in 1911 to W. E. Riley's designs and continued from 1921 onwards to the designs of G. Topham Forrest. It is all small houses of a friendly kind, very influential on municipal building on the Continent and in America. The difference between the earlier and the later parts (s and N of Risley Lane) is noteworthy too. – A good factory in the modern style, D. Gestetner, Fawley Road, by Tecton, 1936.

TWICKENHAM

For Hampton, Hampton Court, Hampton Wick, Tedington, and Whitton, all included in the borough, whose population in 1949 was 108,000, see separate entries.

What matters at Twickenham is the church and the streets close to the church. Beyond this minute nucleus the rash of

suburban shopping parades and suburban houses has spread
in the late C19 and chiefly in the last forty or fifty years.
Large or otherwise important properties near the centre
were in the C18 towards NE Orleans House, Marble Hill,
Cambridge House, and so on. To the S lay Pope's villa and
Horace Walpole's Strawberry Hill. This and Marble Hill
happily survive. Of the others only small fragments or
nothing is left.

10b PARISH CHURCH ST MARY. The W tower is three-
storeyed, of Kentish rag, with diagonal buttresses and a
stair-turret reaching up higher than the battlemented top
of the tower. The body of the church was redesigned by
John James and rebuilt 1714–15. James was one of the sur-
veyors to Queen Anne's Fifty New Churches, and author
and translator of several books on the theory of architecture. His chief work in London is St George's, Hanover
Square. The Twickenham church has a plan wisely em-
phasizing the N and S sides, that is the sides visible from
village and river. The nave has five bays, the chancel projects. Bays two to four also project (one can hardly say
transeptwise, because the projecting part is wider than the
rest). They have big pediments on broad, robust brick
Tuscan pilasters, with something of the vigour of Vanbrugh and Hawksmoor. The rubbed and gauged brickwork is superb. The E end has a circular window and a
straight segmental pediment. The whole obviously an
architect's not a local mason's work. The interior with
wooden galleries (altered) on N and S, not taking notice of
the exterior projections, is disappointing, especially as it
is unattractively painted. It has, however, the original
wooden REREDOS and metal ALTAR RAILS. A C17 COM-
MUNION TABLE is in the vestry. – PLATE. Paten of 1661,
Dish of 1692.

The connections of the church with Pope are familiar.
Here is the monument to his parents and himself, the
tablet (outer wall of chancel) to Mary Beach, his nurse,
also put up by him (in a Gibbsian frame of intermittent
rustication). A larger monument to Pope was erected by
Bishop Warburton, a plain broad obelisk in relief with

portrait medallion, very restrained, by *Prince Hoare* (N gallery). Other noteworthy MONUMENTS: Francis Poulton and wife † 1642, two frontal demi-figures, their hands crossed on a skull. The whole top part of the monument has disappeared. – M. Haure, top of N stairs, a flaming urn in the round, ascribed by Mrs Esdaile to *Bushnell*. – Sir W. Humble † 1705 (Esdaile: *Bird*). – Nath. Piggot † 1737 (Esdaile: *Scheemakers*). – Chaloner Ogle, signed by *Rysbrack*, 1751, with a putto amid trophies against a short obelisk (N gallery). – Gge. and Anne Gostling, signed *John Bacon, Jun.*, 1800, with a mourning figure seated in front of a tall pedestal supporting an urn. Good and genuine, not at all mawkish. – Lady Mary Wildman † 1825, draped urn by *R. Westmacott*.

HOLY TRINITY, Twickenham Green, 1839–41, by *Basevi*, with a W tower imitating crisply and thinly in yellow brick the local C15 tower type. Inside slim tall piers without capitals supporting four-centred arches. Aisles with lean-to roofs, no clerestory. The chaste somewhat brittle character of the Gothic Revival of the Commissioners' Churches. Instructive contrast to the vulgar and thick chancel and transepts added by *Dolman*, 1863.

ST STEPHEN, Cambridge Park, begun 1874. By *Lockwood & Mawson*.

The charm of Twickenham village is all in the short stretch between church and Lebanon Park, white Georgian houses of any height, shape of doorway and porch, and position of bay window. The river is unembanked here (hence the plots of garden between street and water) and appears narrow with the leafy Eel Pie Island opposite. Off Riverside lies SYON ROW, an orderly terrace of twelve houses, 1721, with varied doorways, ranging from the leaf-scroll decoration of *c.* 1700 to the Gibbs type with intermittent rustication.

In the remaining village streets one has to look specially for bits of weatherboarding and old brickwork. On the fringe of the village is:

YORK HOUSE (Municipal Offices), *c.* 1700, H-shaped with 52b only slight projections; plain and dignified, brick with quoins on a cemented, rusticated ground floor; hipped roof. The only decorative element is the N door with a steep broken pediment of S-curves ending in thick scrolls.

ORLEANS HOUSE, built for James Johnstone, Queen Anne's Secretary of State for Scotland. Louis Philippe lived here 1800–14 and 1815–17. The house was pulled down in 1927. Its main surviving feature is the Octagon by *Gibbs*, 1730. Exterior with the typical Gibbs windows and rubbed brick pilasters. Inside splendid plaster work, figures on the pediments of fireplace and doors, and busts in round niches higher up, all by *Artari* and *Bagutti*.

MARBLE HILL, built *c.* 1720 by George II for his mistress, Henrietta Howard. Later the residence of Mrs Fitz-herbert. The design is ascribed to *Roger* or *Robert Morris* or *Lord Pembroke*. It is uninspired, five bays, with lower wings. Ionic giant pilasters for the centre on the N side, and nothing noteworthy otherwise. The gardens were laid out by *Bridgman*, and there is correspondence between him and Pope on them (1724). Along the W side of the gardens runs:

MONTPELIER ROW, 1720, one of the best examples near London of well-mannered, well-proportioned terrace de-velopment. No doubt by the same masons as Syon Row (cf. above). 1–15 survive, then some Victorian inter-lopers, then again houses of 1720 ending in Montpelier House and SOUTH END HOUSE, the latter with a very pretty Early Gothic Revival addition in the SW. All the houses are of yellow brick with rubbed red brick dress-ings, absolutely flat except for the doors. These also with-out porches or even pilasters. The various motifs of the surrounds are a good study in 1720 detail.

CAMBRIDGE HOUSE has gone, so have FORTESCUE HOUSE in the W and RADNOR HOUSE in the S. Of Rad-nor House only a little Rococo Gothic summer house has escaped the bombs of the Second World War. The house itself was very early Gothic Revival (cf. Strawberry Hill below). A little N of Radnor House, in Crossdeep, lies the house called CROSSDEEP, a very fine example of the un-pretentious C18 residence, five bays, two and a half storeys, the door with an entablature curved up in the middle, a typical motif of *c.* 1720–40. The windows of charming plain Gothic wood-detail. Good iron gate.

POPE'S VILLA, also in Crossdeep, now a convent school. The villa has been replaced by a neo-Tudor house by *Kendall.* Pope's establishment possessed one of the earliest picturesque gardens ever laid out. Pope was busy on it as early as 1718. It was very miniature and fragmentary. The Grotto, that is the subway under the road, is the only remaining feature, lined with minerals which his friends had given to Pope. It is curious to think that Pope considered this job 'natural', as against the stiff artificiality of the Dutch and French gardens traditions; to us it seems highly artificial.

STRAWBERRY HILL. This is by far the most important and rewarding of the monuments of Twickenham, preserved in excellent state, owing to the care and appreciation of St Mary's Roman Catholic Training College which it now houses. It was of all early Gothic Revival buildings of Britain the most influential and appears still as charming and convincing now as it must have been when it was new. 57

Horace Walpole was thirty when he bought 'a little plaything house' close to the river in 1747 (letter of 8 June 1747). He redecorated it and altered it a little in 1748, but only in September 1749 he mentions his 'future battlements'. So the idea of converting the cottage into a Gothic castle seems to belong to that year. After that he never looked back. He consulted a few friends and a number of folios of engravings of medieval work and started on addition after addition, until by 1776 the house was complete. The only later work is the office wing by *Wyatt* of 1790, the Waldegrave ballroom of the 1860s between these and the house and the new wings needed for the College. Horace Walpole could indeed be proud of his castle, a place equally suited to writing *The Castle of Otranto* and the catty letters which poured forth from it in such unparalleled numbers, a place, that is, both amusing and awful, both Rococo and romantic. The actual designing was at first done by *John Chute* of The Vyne, Hampshire,

Walpole's friend, and *Richard Bentley*, son of the great philologist, and then, after 1761, for a while by *Thomas Pitt*, later Lord Camelford. Later still designs were provided by *James Essex* (whose best known works are at Cambridge).

The Gothic style for domestic purposes was not as absolutely new in 1750 as is often presumed, and as it seemed to those from Germany and France who were aware of what the Prime Minister's son did, but not of what had been done before. Even if one forgets about Vanbrugh's appreciation of the virile Middle Ages and about Hawksmoor's fantastic towers of All Souls College, Oxford, there remain such things as Gibbs's Gothic Temple at Stowe (which Walpole called 'pure and beautiful and venerable', 4 Aug. 1753), Sanderson Miller's Gothic titbits (which Walpole scorned), Batty Langley's naïve efforts at a Gothic columnar order, at Twickenham itself Radnor House, engraved with its Gothic front as early as 1754 and probably built in the thirties, and (also not far from Twickenham) Kent's Gothic doorway and windows of 1732 at Hampton Court (*see* p. 71). Of Kent Walpole says that he never knew 'how to enter into the true Gothic taste' (Sept. 1753). What then did he mean by the true Gothic taste? If one looks up his letters, one finds a very odd, illogical mixture of meanings. 'The charming venerable Gothic' is what he calls it (25 July 48). Other words of description for genuine or imitation Gothic buildings are 'pretty', 'neat', and so on. 'Venerable barbarism' also occurs (27 April 53). His enthusiasm for Gothic forms and Gothic gloom is undoubted, though he liked to conceal it and playfully to pretend only to be 'grave about trifles' (6 Oct. 53). But he was grave, at least in one way: he insisted on many details about the house being accurate copies of existing and published Gothic work.

That attitude was new and became two generations later the attitude of a more archaeologically minded epoch. In Walpole there is still vacillation between tracery as an alternative to Chinese fretwork and as a motif belonging to a venerable past age. Still, even where he copied he copied in a spirit very different from that of the C19. For he did not mind in the least whether a tomb became a fire-place or a bookcase. Accuracy mattered, but any feeling for a work of the C13 or C14 as an organic whole not to be separated from its genuine setting was still absent. Even with its exact copies here and there the whole of Strawberry Hill remains make-believe, and it is that very ambiguity of it that makes it so much more attractive than the heavy-handed exactness of C19 period imitation. Walpole was as far from Ruskin's or Morris's ideals of purity as Roubiliac with the naturalistic rocks of his tombs or Robert Adam with his use of artificial stone or the sham bridge in the grounds of Ken Wood. In fact Essex designed a sham bridge for Strawberry Hill in 1792, and the garden gates were made of lithodipra in the sixties.

Looking at Strawberry Hill from the river one sees the original toy-house in front with its bay window and one window to the l. The battlements are the first medievaliz-ing alteration. The room to the r. of the bay window was added in 1754, the bay facing s and one room w of it in 1753–4. The windows in this early part are still exactly as fanciful and unarchaeological as Gothic work by Kent. The long gallery wing with its buttresses, uniform in con-trast to the variety of the older group, is of 1763, while the rooms behind it sticking out in a rather untidy way to the N were added in 1759 (Holbein Chamber with 59a Little Cloister below), 1763 (quatrefoil Cabinet now called Tribune), and 1772 (Great Bed Chamber). The round w tower is of 1761–71 and the Beauchamp turret N of it of 1776. To build a house on this scale completely asym-metrically was perhaps Walpole's most important single innovation. It was an application to house design of the principles established for picturesque gardening in the 1720s (see Chiswick, p. 34). That application seems to belong entirely to Walpole, and he probably knew it when he wrote as early as 25 Feb. 1750: 'I am almost as fond of the Sharawaggi, or Chinese want of symmetry, in build-ings, as in grounds or gardens.' The grouping of the whole in the final state in which it appears, for instance in engravings of 1784, is indeed most felicitous, neither over-crowded with fancy detail nor uniform as classical Georgian architecture of 1750 or 1760 deliberately was. Compared with it Wyatt's office wing of 1790 separated from the house by the competent and ornate mid-Victorian ballroom (whose architect oddly enough seems unrecorded) is competent but dull, similar to so much college work done about 1800. The teaching wings of St Mary's College are fortunately screened by trees so that from many viewpoints Walpole's *bijou* can still be appreciated very much in its pristine form.

Only the gardens are no longer what they were. *Riant* as Walpole wanted them (27 April 53) they may still be, but the rustic cottage, the sham bridge, the shell bench have all gone, and the CHAPEL IN THE WOOD is in sad decay (but will be restored by the College). It is a small building, 8 ft wide, built to make a nice show of Walpole's stained glass and to house a C13 shrine which he had brought from Rome. The exterior is inspired by the Audley Tomb at Salisbury; the interior has pretty blue and gold fan vaulting and blue and yellow tiles.

The house itself is entered from the N, along a passage skirting the Little Cloister. In the LOBBY Virgilia, a white marble relief, 1871, by *Woolner*, who once had been a pre-Raphaelite. On the ground floor the low old cottage parlour still clearly visible.

The STAIRCASE HALL with its two thin spindly piers and originally a 'paper painted in perspective to represent Gothic fretwork' is perhaps the most purely Walpolian work now preserved. The Chippendale Gothic staircase balustrade itself, the little Tudor-like supporters on the newel posts, and above all the lantern with its yellow glass; Walpole himself wavered in his descriptions of the staircase between 'the most venerable gloom . . . that ever was since the days of Abelard' and 'so pretty and so small that I am inclined to wrap it up and send it you in my letter' (letters of March and June 1753). Staircase and Library were built in 1753–4. The LIBRARY has elaborate brown and gold Gothic bookcases copied from the side doors to the screen of Old St Paul's. The multiplication of the motif and its translation into wood, needless to say, alter their character completely. The chimneypiece imitates John of Eltham's tomb in Westminster Abbey. Walpole and his friends knew these works from Hollar, Dart, and similar engravings. The ceiling is inspired by c16 plasterwork, but the central rosette is of course a classical c17–c18 idea. Whereas the staircase is *Bentley's* design, the Library is by *Chute*; Bentley's suggestions were rejected by Walpole. The other rooms in the front block, the first to be remodelled, are of minor interest. They have Gothic fireplaces (for example in the Little Parlour on the ground floor from Bishop Ruthall's tomb in Westminster Abbey) but not much else to be remarked on. The next room decorated in a more ambitious vein is the HOLBEIN CHAMBER above the Little Cloister. It dates from 1759 and is divided by a screen with fantastic Gothic detail—as original as anything invented by Rococo decorators on the Continent. The gates to the choir at Rouen were Bentley's source of inspiration here. The chimneypiece is copied from Archbishop Wareham's tomb at Canterbury. The ceiling is again of Tudor plaster character.

The GALLERY, designed by *Thomas Pitt* after Walpole's final quarrel with Bentley and completed with the Cloister below in 1763, reveals more than anything in the house how close the spirit of that gothicizing of 1760 is to the Rococo on the one hand and to Robert Adam's classicizing on the other. Looking at this gilt fretwork, at the ever-changing reflections in the bits of mirror glass in the niches and the small panels of the plaster fan vault, it seems difficult to understand why Walpole should have been so disgusted with Adam's 'gingerbread and sippets of embroidery'. But then Walpole's judgment was always easily swayed by personal animosity, rancour, or gossip. All is glitter and *gaité* in the Gallery (no venerable gloom, no pedantic copistry). Yet the big door does indeed come from the N door at St Albans, and the vault from the aisles of Henry VII Chapel in Westminster Abbey.

The GREAT BED CHAMBER of 1772 N of the Gallery has a fireplace from the tomb of Bishop Dudley at Westminster Abbey, the BEAUCLERC ROOM in the thick tower from no less a monument than Edward the Confessor's Shrine, however 'improved by Mr Adam' (with whom Walpole was not yet cross in 1766). The ceiling pattern is inspired by the rose window tracery of Old St Paul's. Finally in 1763 the CHAPEL (or Tribune or Cabinet) was built, also N of the Gallery. It is mostly of *Chute's* design, of quatrefoil shape and with the most entertaining of Rococo-Gothic vaults, said to be derived from the York Chapter House. This however must be taken with several pinches of salt, not only because one would look in vain there for the star of yellow glass which terminates Walpole's vault, but also because of the intricate flowing traceries. The walls were originally covered with bric-à-brac, a collector's cabinet with eighteen cameos let into its front, paintings, statuettes, vases, and so on. The whole Strawberry Hill collection was sold in 1842, when the house belonged to the Waldegraves. They added the BALLROOM S of the Round Tower: excellent and not at all pedestrian Neo-Gothic of the sixties.

CARPENTERS' ALMSHOUSES, Hampton Road, 1842, by *Pocock*, a homely yellow-brick range with an arcaded front of pointed arches and a separate wavily barge-boarded gable for each little dwelling. Two large cedar trees in front.

HEATHAM HOUSE, Whitton Road, by the river Crane, Georgian brick, altered.

NEVILLE HOUSE, 137 London Road, nice early C18.

SANDYCOMBE LODGE, Sandycombe Road, a symmetrical cottage with central gable and lower wings with prettily rounded corners. The house which *Turner* the painter designed for himself in 1812 and built as his own 'architect, contractor, surveyor, foreman, and clerk of the works'.

TWYFORD

TWYFORD ABBEY, 1807–9, by *P. Atkinson* (now Alexian Brothers). Cement-rendered and castellated (the type which appears so often in contemporary books on the seats of the gentry) : two buildings, mansion and to the l. stables, now connected by modern additions. The SE part is older but also gothicized at the front.

PARISH CHURCH ST MARY, no more than a chapel in the grounds (now just outside the grounds) of the house. The front is of 1806 and the rest does not look older. The chief interest of the church lies in the two Moyle MONUMENTS : Robert † 1638, erected 1657, and Walter † 1660. They are both epitaphs with a bust in an oval niche, pilasters on r. and l., an inscription tablet below and a pediment above, yet the older has still the restraint of the Commonwealth, the later in costume, pediment, and all details goes Baroque.

GUINNESS BREWERY. Opposite the old buildings of Twyford, across the railway, that is in Willesden, lies this big brick group of factory buildings, a good design by *Sir Giles G. Scott*, 1936.

UXBRIDGE

See also Harefield.

Uxbridge (population in 1949, 54,000) to the end of the C18 was one of the most important market towns of Middlesex, close enough to London to serve the city and too far to be swallowed by it. It had excellent road connections with London, and after 1770 the Grand Junction Canal as well. The centre of the town is more effectively marked than in most places of the size of Uxbridge. The new L.T. STATION of 1938 (not one of the best efforts of that otherwise so eminently enlightened body) stands in axis with the MARKET HOUSE, a stately building of 1789 with a central lantern and a ground floor originally as entirely open as any Le Corbusier design. The supports are Tuscan columns. The ground floor was used for pitching corn and as a meeting-place for farmers and dealers, the upper floor for storing grain and also for the charity school.

PARISH CHURCH ST MARGARET, nestling behind the Market House and forming with it an irregular triangle from which the High Street runs N and S and Windsor Street W. The church was originally a chapel-of-ease to Hillingdon but grew in importance with the development of the town. Its prosperity is marked chiefly by the addition of an incongruously large S aisle (late C15 with new windows) by the Guild of St Mary and St Margaret. Looked at from the S the aisle appears nearly as high as the tower. Nave and N aisle are early C15, the N tower, not in axis with the rest of the building, C14. The latter was rebuilt c. 1820 and provided with its pretty cupola (cf. Harmondsworth and Hillingdon in the neighbourhood). The building is of flint rubble with stone dressings. The interior is not especially impressive, except for the roofs. They are all old, and that of the S aisle of hammerbeam type is one of the best in Middlesex. The church is poor in old furnishings. The FONT is late C15 with quatrefoiled panels (cf. Brentford). – PLATE. Chalice of 1686 or 1696, two Patens of 1720, Paten of 1726. – Of MONUMENTS the most remarkable by far is that to Leonora Bennet † 1638, an altar tomb with the effigy stiffly semi-reclining on the tomb-chest the middle of which has a round recess with prison bars behind which the artist has displayed a generous charnel-house still-life. One bony hand grips the bars.

ST JOHN, St John's Road, Uxbridge, just on the Bucks border is of 1838 (by *Henry Atkinson*), the Early English stock brick Commissioners' type.

METHODIST CHURCH, New Windsor Street, 1847 : exactly the same type as St John's, not a usual ideal for the Methodists to follow.

CONGREGATIONAL CHURCH, The Lynch, plain Neo-Greek stucco front of 1845–50.

FRIENDS' MEETING HOUSE, Belmont Road and York Road, a plain honest London stock brick cube of 1817.

The High Street and Windsor Street contain plenty of old houses, both timber-framed and Georgian or pre-Georgian brick, but very few individually noteworthy. As a street WINDSOR STREET has at present more character, since the High Street is rapidly changing into a c20 shopping street. The best single buildings are the RED HOUSE, No 113 High Street, early c18, and the so-called TREATY HOUSE at the N end of the High Street. It has a probably Jacobean curved gable towards the street, but its N and S sides are early c16. In the S two bay windows with brick-shaped mullions and transomes, the N side a picturesque view with straight gables, diagonal chimney stacks, and a turret (the irregularity chiefly due to the fact that the building was originally much more extensive on the N). The main S porch is late c18. In the S the High Street runs without any break into West Hillingdon (q.v.).

WEALDSTONE

PARISH CHURCH HOLY TRINITY, 1881, by *Roumieu & Aitchison*.

R.C. CHURCH ST JOSEPH, High Road, 1931, by *Adrian G. Scott*, a notable, though still medievalizing exterior of warm-coloured stone with a W tower and two large dormer windows in the low steep-pitched roof. Inside a fine and unusual effect, created by stone for the chief structural elements and whitewash otherwise, and by the introduction of two transepts in the second and fourth bay of five in all. The dormer windows correspond to them in the exterior. In the other bays small clerestory windows above the aisles with their open lean-to roof (this motif and the dormer windows are derived from Lutyens's St Jude, Hampstead Garden Suburb). To the inner aisles very low outer aisles are added. There are no capitals or bases to the piers throughout.

HARROW AND WEALDSTONE STATION: *see* at the end of Harrow-on-the-Hill.

WEMBLEY

See also Alperton, Kingsbury, Preston, Sudbury.

There is uncommonly little of historic interest in this large borough (population in 1949, 132,000). In fact the centre badly lacks shape, and the new Town Hall is placed so that it will hardly act as a new centre.

PARISH CHURCH ST JOHN, a smallish somewhat rustic building of flint, by *George G. Scott & Moffatt*, 1846. Fancy tiled roof and a very odd design for the piers.

TOWN HALL, 1935–40, by *Clifford Strange*, the best of the modern town halls around London, neither fanciful nor drab. The long-stretching front has no conspicuous climax but not one detail either that could jar. The main staircase is also far from spectacular, but airy and sensible, and the Great Hall at the back shares this character.

STADIUM, designed by *Simpson*, 1924, for the Wembley Exhibition.

EMPIRE POOL AND ARENA, by *Sir Owen Williams*, 1934, with a bold show of concrete supports.

WEST DRAYTON

Until the manor house of the Pagets was pulled down in 1750, West Drayton must have been a spectacular monument of Tudor splendour. The remaining gatehouse and straight avenue leading to it from the S are witnesses to it. Even as it is the old trees, the brick of the gatehouse, and the varied texture of the flint of the church tower form an exceedingly fine picture.

PARISH CHURCH ST MARTIN. The flint work is all restoration of 1850 with the exception of the W tower. The S porch is modern. The interior is essentially C15: nave and aisles, and arcade of three relatively tall octagonal piers, and contemporary roofs of nave and aisles (the latter on corbels with heads). If the PISCINA in the chancel is in its original position it would prove this part of the building to be C13. It is a fine, though very restored piece (cf. Hayes). – FONT. The most elaborate in the county, C15, octagonal bowl on nine-stemmed foot. The bowl has eight figured panels, five with figures of angels, one with a man with hood and dagger, one with a Pietà (of the Bohemian type of 1400), and one with the Crucifixus with the Virgin and St John. – CLOCK. The works with angle-standards as Gothic buttresses, ascribed to the early C16. – PLATE. 15 The church possesses by far the most precious piece of Middlesex: a Chalice and Paten of 1507, of exquisitely pure Late Gothic forms. A comparison with the paten of 1568 at Harrow is most instructive. Flagon and Paten by *Lamerie*, 1727. – WINDOW. A N window by *Burne Jones* to Mrs Mercer † 1878. – MONUMENTS. In chancel brasses to man of *c.* 1520 and to James Good † 1581, and wife. In S aisle an inscription plate with exceptionally fine engraved frame of early Renaissance character (Venetian segmental top) to John Burnell † 1551. – Rupert Billings- 29 ley, of H.M. Ship the *Royal George*, † 1720, with a lively relief of the ship, a three-master, at the foot (cf. the ships on such monuments as Grinling Gibbons's Cloudesley Shovell in Westminster Abbey, 1703). – Fysh de Burgh † 1793, by *Bacon*, fine and delicate with an urn on a pedestal with a seated allegory, the whole against the usual grey marble obelisk. – Fysh de Burgh, heretofore Coppinger, father of the former, † 1800, also by *Bacon*, and similar but simpler. – Catharine de Burgh † 1809, by *Bacon Jun.*, with a heavy Graecian Fides in a clumsy arcade.

ST CATHARINE, The Green, Roman Catholic, by *Alexander Scoles*, 1869. Inside, a large Spanish early C17 PAINTING of Christ nailed to the cross.

The GATEHOUSE and extensive early Tudor brick walls is 36a all that is left of the Manor House. Although much restored and with a modern parapet instead of the original upper floor or floors it is still an impressive monument; the moulded brickwork of the jambs and voussoirs and the original doors especially noteworthy.

DRAYTON HALL, the manor house of the Fysh de Burghs, appears now an uneventful stuccoed Late Georgian building but may incorporate older masonry.

THE GREEN. West Drayton is lucky in possessing a large Green with still a good deal of character, in spite of Daisy Villas, 1896, making up the S half of the E side. The best houses are at and behind the S end: THE OLD HOUSE, three-bay brick of early C18; SOUTHLANDS, well-kept

stately five-bay brick house of about the same date; and
AVENUE HOUSE, No 73, between the two, with a C18 l.
half and a C16 half-timbered r. half. N of Daisy Villas a
nice C18 house, ELMSCROFT, then a taller, more self-
assured Regency house, and several white cottages, some
gabled. Opposite, on the w side, a three-bay brick cottage
tucked away in Money Lane, and THE COPSE farther s,
apparently C18, but with a three-light C16 window still on
the SE side.

WHETSTONE

PARISH CHURCH ST JOHN, 1836 (chancel and roof 1879).
The original building small and plain with the polygonal
turrets typical of the date.

CONGREGATIONAL CHURCH, Oakleigh Road, 1900, by
E. F. Knight. An odd specimen of its date and of the fanciful leanings of the Congregationalists about 1900. Red
brick with two w turrets and a curved parapet between.
Perp w window in deep recess, its bottom part disappear-
ing behind the curved top of a lower chapel. Queer belfry
farther E.

WHITTON

ST PHILIP AND ST JAMES, 1862, by *F. H. Pownall,* small
and clumsily picturesque. Kentish rag with bell turret
outside, yellow and red brick inside. w windows by
Kempe, 1893.

KNELLER HALL (R. Military School of Music), an extra-
ordinary affair in which nearly all remains of the villa
which Kneller, the painter, built for himself in 1709–11
have disappeared. What we now see is a vast Neo-Jacobean
pile with two turrets of the Syon-House-Osterley-Park
type. Its date is 1848, its architect *George Mair.*

WILLESDEN

The borough of Willesden is now entirely part of London.
Its urbanization took place chiefly between 1880 and 1900.
Population of the parish was 27,000 in 1881, 115,000 in

1901, 184,000 in 1931, 181,000 in 1949. The borough grew out of a number of villages and hamlets, chief among them being Willesden, Willesden Green, Brondesbury, Harlesden, Neasden, and Dollis Hill. The corner of Kilburn and Kensal which belong to it will be treated in the volume of this series dealing with the County of London.

Willesden is singularly poor in buildings of architectural interest. Of the Middle Ages it possesses only the parish church, of the centuries between 1530 and 1830 only a few individual houses. The C19 also has nothing of special distinction to show.

PARISH CHURCH ST MARY. The old grey church stands in its churchyard as a solitary survival surrounded entirely by buildings of no aesthetic connection with it. It has nave, chancel, and s aisle with a SW tower attached to the aisle and a short chancel chapel. The N parts are C19. The walls are of ragstone rubble with a little flint. The best views are from SW and SE where the rough walls appear in their apparently unrestored texture. The tower is low with the SW buttresses arranged L-wise. The interior is low and on a homely scale. Two s piers are typical C13, round with simple caps and arches. The contrast to the N tower arch next to them is instructive of the development from C13 to C14. S door original with C14 blank tracery (a rarity). – FONT. One of the six of Norman date surviving in the county, tall square tapering bowl on thick central shaft with four slender subsidiary shafts, elementary abstract ornament. – Good Elizabethan COMMUNION TABLE with bulbous legs. – Charming simple IRON RAILING of C17 (?) to guard the weights of the clock; the uprights end in sunflowers. – PLATE. An elegant slim secular Cup of 1606. – The six BRASSES in the chancel floor are the chief interest of the church, varying in size and ranging from 1492 to 1609. The other monuments are minor.

ALL SOULS, HIGH STREET, HARLESDEN. An octagon, built 1879 by *E. J. Tarver*, an architect of greater importance than is usually recognized. Designed 1875. A nave

was insensitively added 1890. The octagon is large, and
the exciting timber construction of its roof in the best
English Gothic tradition is worth a special visit. Externally the centre is insufficiently stressed by a conical little
open iron lantern.

ST ANDREW, HIGH ROAD, WILLESDEN GREEN, 1886–7,
by *James Brooks*. A most typical contrast to the old village
church. Brooks's building is large and ambitious with
crossing and transepts. It displays a stately, if somewhat
dull E.E. Brick, with pointed arcades of medium height,
galleries and lancet windows in the clerestory. Straight E
end with a group of five lancets. Simple wagon-roofs and
a spectacular high altar in a style reminiscent of Orley or
such Flemish masters of the Renaissance.

ST MATTHEW, St Mary's Road, Harlesden, 1902, by *Caroë*.

CONGREGATIONAL CHURCH, Church Road, Willesden.
The free Gothic of 1900 with a nice asymmetrical SW
tower and spirelet. By *Spalding & Spalding*.

Of the village centres or the large old houses of Willesden
itself nothing can now be traced. At NEASDEN, at the
crossing of Neasden Lane and Tanfield Road, is a cottage
and an overgrown house of C18; the larger and better
houses which in 1930 still stood close to them have been
replaced by flats. At BRONDESBURY nothing requires
mention now that the Manor House has been pulled
down. DOLLIS HOUSE, where Gladstone used to stay
with the Earl of Aberdeen, is a featureless Late Georgian
house, and of the two farmhouses by OXGATE LANE, one
has also disappeared quite recently. The other is OXGATE
FARM in Coles Green Road behind the by-pass factories
and motor-servicing stations of the Roman Watling Street,
that is the Edgware Road.

For the best modern factory, the Guinness Brewery: *see*
Twyford.

WOOD GREEN

The Inventory of the Royal Commission says: 'No Monuments known', and there is indeed nothing in the borough
worth more than a cursory glance.

PARISH CHURCH, ST MICHAEL-AT-BOWES, 1843, by *George Gilbert Scott*, altered 1865 by *Curzon*, chancel and tower 1874.

ST MARK, 1889, by *Roland Plumbe*. Outside and inside red brick, of Early Gothic character, and quite clean design. It is part of the

NOEL PARK ESTATE, a 100-acre estate established by the Artisans, Labourers, and General Dwellings Company in 1889, one of the earliest examples of improved housing as applied not to the large block of tenements but to the small house. The streets are still straight, stock bricks are still extensively used, and long terraces exclusively. To that extent there is no influence yet from the two years older Bedford Park. But some streets have tree-planting, the group of larger houses by St Mark's and the school add two accents (although they are not yet inter-connected) and the terraces are not only varied by their porches, but also by taller corner houses or projecting corner houses or occasional taller gables.

L.T. STATIONS. TURNPIKE LANE, WOOD GREEN, and BOUNDS GREEN belong to *Holden's* early stations in the new and at the time quite revolutionary style which was then adopted in so many other L.T. stations. Wood Green is a less successful example; Bounds Green with its windows in the diagonals of the ticket hall block and its recessed tower is an interesting variation of the Oakwood, Sudbury Town, Northfields, etc., theme. Turnpike Lane makes use of its corner site for a pretty group with a restaurant on a curved first floor and again a recessed tower.

FISHMONGERS AND POULTERERS ASYLUM, High Road, built 1847-9 by *Mee & Webbe*; many-gabled, quite picturesque Neo-Elizabethan.

ROYAL MASONIC INSTITUTION FOR BOYS, Lordship Lane, now North Thames Gas Board. Typical example of uninspired representational scholastic Gothic Revival; 1865, by *Pearce*.

ALEXANDRA PALACE, 1875, by *J. Johnson*, one of the most extensive and most prominently placed of London buildings; there is not much else to be said about it.

WROTHAM HALL

55b Built in 1754 for Admiral Byng by *Isaac Ware* and illustrated in the 5th volume of *Vitruvius Britannicus*, that is in 1771. Ware's garden front has a detached portico of unfluted Ionic columns to which a curved two-armed staircase sweeps up, and l. and r. of the portico one more bay with a Venetian window. Lower wings with octagonal domes over the corner pavilions. Entrance side of thirteen bays in all, the wings connected by low closed colonnades with the main block. All this exceptionally pure Burlingtonian-Palladian. The entrance side has a one-sided Ionic porch and also Venetian windows. The wings were heightened in the C19. The interior was destroyed by fire in 1883, but the collection of paintings is still in existence.

YIEWSLEY

For Harmondsworth and West Drayton *see* separate entries.

PARISH CHURCH ST MATTHEW, 1898, by *Nicholson* (later *Sir Charles*) & *Corlette*. A pleasant interior with low Gothic piers without capitals and a prettily pointed wagon-roof.

EVELYN SECONDARY MODERN SCHOOL, by *W. T. Curtis* & *Burchett*, 1936. A typical example of the progressive Middlesex C.C. schools of the thirties.

GLOSSARY

ABACUS: flat slab on the top of a capital (q.v.).

ABUTMENT: solid masonry placed to resist the lateral pressure of a vault.

ACANTHUS: plant with thick fleshy and scalloped leaves used as part of the decoration of a Corinthian capital (q.v.) and in some types of leaf carving.

ACHIEVEMENT OF ARMS: in heraldry, a complete display of armorial bearings.

ACROTERION: foliage-carved block on the end or top of a classical pediment.

AEDICULE, AEDICULA: framing of a window or door by columns and a pediment (q.v.).

AMBULATORY: semicircular or polygonal aisle enclosing an apse (q.v.).

ANNULET: see Shaft-ring.

ANTIS, IN: see Portico.

APSE: vaulted semicircular or polygonal end of a chancel or a chapel.

ARABESQUE: light and fanciful surface decoration using combinations of flowing lines, tendrils, etc., interspersed with vases, animals, etc.

ARCADE: range of arches supported on piers or columns, free-standing; or, BLIND ARCADE, the same attached to a wall.

ARCH: round-headed; i.e. semi-circular pointed, i.e. consisting of two curves, each drawn from one centre, and meeting in a point at the top; Segmental,

i.e. in the form of a segment; pointed; four-centred, see Fig. 1(a); Tudor, see Fig. 1(b); Ogee, see Fig. 1(c); Stilted, see Fig. 1(d).

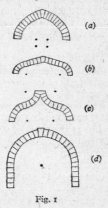

Fig. 1

ARCHITRAVE: lowest of the three main parts of the entablature (q.v.) of an order (q.v.) (see Fig. 11).

ARCHIVOLT: undersurface of an arch (also called Soffit).

ARRIS: sharp edge at the meeting of two surfaces.

ASHLAR: masonry of large blocks wrought to even faces and square edges.

ATRIUM: inner court of a Roman house, also open court in front of a church.

ATTACHED: see engaged.

ATTIC: topmost storey of a house, if lower than the others.

AUMBREY: recess or cupboard to hold sacred vessels for Mass and Communion.

BAILEY: open space or court of a fortified castle.

BALDACCHINO: canopy supported on columns.

BALLFLOWER: globular flower of three petals enclosing a small ball. A decoration used in the first quarter of the C14.

BALUSTER: small pillar or column of fanciful outline.

BALUSTRADE: series of balusters supporting a handrail or coping (q.v.).

BARBICAN: outwork, constructed like a gateway, defending the entrance to a castle.

BARGEBOARDS: projecting decorated boards placed against the incline of the gable of a building and hiding the horizontal roof timbers.

BASILICA: in medieval architecture an aisled church with a clerestory.

BASTION: projection at the angle of a fortification.

BATTER: wall with an inclined face.

BATTLEMENT: parapet with a series of indentations or embrasures with raised portions or merlons between (also called Crenellation).

BAYS: internal compartments of a building; each divided from the other not by solid walls but by divisions only marked in the side walls (columns, pilasters, etc.) or the ceiling (beams, etc.). Also external divisions of a building by fenestration.

BAY-WINDOW: angular or curved projection of a house front with ample fenestration. If curved also called bow-window; if on an upper floor only also called oriel or oriel window.

BEAKHEAD: Norman ornamental motif consisting of a row of bird or beast heads with beaks pointing downwards and biting usually into a roll moulding.

BELL-COTE: turret usually on the W end of a church to carry the bells.

BILLET: Norman ornamental motif made up of short raised rectangles placed at regular intervals.

BLOCK CAPITAL: Romanesque capital cut from a cube by having the lower angles rounded off to the circular shaft below (also called Cushion Capital) (Fig. 2).

Fig. 2

BOND, ENGLISH or FLEMISH: see Brickwork.

BOSS: knob or projection usually placed to cover the intersection of ribs in a vault.

BOW-WINDOW: see Bay-Window.

BOX PEW: pew with a high wooden enclosure.

BRACES: see Roof.

BRACKET: small supporting piece of stone, etc., to carry a projecting horizontal.

BRICKWORK: *Header:* brick laid so that the end only appears on the face of the wall. *Stretcher:* brick laid so that the side only appears on the face of the wall.

English Bond: method of laying bricks so that alternate courses or layers on the face of the wall are composed of headers or stretchers only (Fig. 3*a*).

Flemish Bond: method of laying bricks so that alternate headers and stretchers appear in each course on the face of the wall (Fig. 3*b*).

BROACH: *see* Spire.

BROKEN PEDIMENT: *see* Pediment.

BUTTRESS: mass of brickwork or masonry projecting from or built against a wall to give additional strength. *Angle Buttresses:* two meeting at an angle of 90° at the angle of a building

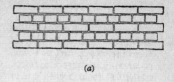

(*a*)

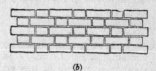

(*b*)

Fig. 3

(Fig. 4*a*). *Diagonal Buttress:* one placed against the right angle formed by two walls, and

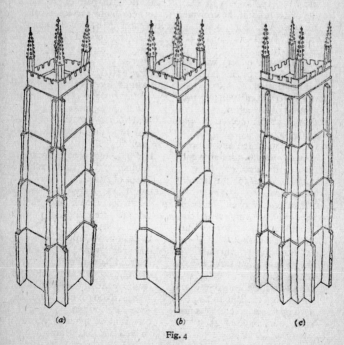

(*a*)　　　(*b*)　　　(*c*)

Fig. 4

more or less equiangular with both (Fig. 4*b*). *Flying Buttress:* arch or half arch transmitting the thrust of a vault or roof from the upper part of a wall to an outer support or buttress. *Setback Buttress:* angle buttress set slightly back from the angle (Fig. 4*c*).

CABLE MOULDING: moulding imitating a twisted cord.

CAMBER: slight rise or upward curve of an otherwise horizontal structure.

CAMPANILE: isolated bell tower.

CANOPY: ornamental covering above an altar, pulpit, niche, etc.

CAP: in a windmill the crowning feature.

CAPITAL: head or top part of a column (q.v.).

CARTOUCHE: tablet with an ornate frame, usually enclosing an inscription.

CARYATID: human figure used instead of a column.

CASTELLATED: decorated with battlements.

CEILURE: panelled and adorned part of a wagon-roof above the rood or the altar.

CENSER: vessel for the burning of incense.

CENTERING: wooden framework used in arch and vault construction and removed when the mortar has set.

CHALICE: small cup used in the Communion service or at Mass.

CHAMFER: surface made by cutting across the square angle of a stone block, piece of wood, etc., at an angle of 45° to the two other surfaces.

CHANCEL: that part of the E end of a church in which the altar is placed, usually applied to the whole continuation of the nave E of the crossing.

CHANCEL ARCH: arch at the W end of the chancel.

CHANTRY CHAPEL: chapel attached to, or inside, a church endowed for the saying of Masses for the soul of the founder or some other individual.

CHEVET: French term for the E end of a church (chancel, ambulatory, and radiating chapels).

CHEVRON: sculptured moulding forming a zigzag.

CHOIR: that part of the church where divine service is sung.

CIBORIUM: box or container for the consecrated bread. Also used to mean a baldacchino (q.v.).

CINQUEFOIL: *see* Foil.

CLAPPER BRIDGE: bridge made of large slabs of stone, some built up to make rough piers and other longer ones laid on top to make the roadway.

CLASSIC: here used to mean the moment of highest achievement of a style.

CLASSICAL: here used as the term for Greek and Roman architecture and any subsequent styles copying it.

CLERESTORY: upper storey of the nave walls of a church, pierced by windows.

COADE STONE: artificial (cast) stone made in the late C18 and the early C19 by Coade and Seely in London.

COB: walling material made of mixed clay and straw.

COFFERING: decorating a ceiling with sunk square or polygonal ornamental panels.

COLLAR-BEAM: *see* Roof.

COLONNADE: range of columns.

COLONNETTE: small column.

COLUMNA ROSTRATA: column decorated with carved prows of ships to celebrate a naval victory.

COMPOSITE: *see* Orders.

CONSOLE: bracket (q.v.) with a compound curved outline.

COPING: capping or covering to a wall.

CORBEL: block of stone projecting from a wall, supporting some horizontal feature.

CORBEL TABLE: series of corbels, occurring just below the roof eaves externally or internally, often seen in Norman buildings.

CORINTHIAN: *see* Orders.

CORNICE: in classical architecture the top section of the entablature (q.v.). Also for a projecting decorative feature along the top of a wall, arch, etc.

COVE, COVING: concave undersurface in the nature of a hollow moulding but on a larger scale.

COVER PATEN: cover to a Communion cup, suitable for use as a paten or plate for the consecrated bread.

CRADLE ROOF: *see* Wagon-roof.

CRENELLATION: *see* Battlement.

CREST, CRESTING: ornamental finish along the top of a screen, etc.

CROCKET, CROCKETING: decorative features placed on the sloping sides of spires, pinnacles, gables, etc. in Gothic architecture, carved in various leaf shapes and placed at regular intervals.

CROCKET CAPITAL: *see* Fig. 5.

Fig. 5

CROSSING: space at the intersection of nave, chancel, and transepts.

CRUCK: big curved beam supporting both walls and roof of a cottage.

CRYPT: underground room usually below the E end of a church.

CUPOLA: small polygonal or circular domed turret crowning a roof.

CURTAIN WALL: connecting wall between the towers of a castle.

CURVILINEAR: *see* Tracery.

CUSHION CAPITAL: *see* Block Capital.

CUSP: in tracery (q.v.) the small pointed member between two lobes of a trefoil, quatrefoil, etc.

DADO: decorative covering of the lower part of a wall.

DAGGER: tracery motif of the Dec. style. It is a lancet shape rounded or pointed at the head, pointed at the foot and cusped inside (*see* Fig. 6).

Fig. 6

DAIS: raised platform at one end of a room.

DEC. ('DECORATED'): historical division of English Gothic architecture covering the first half of the C14.

DEMI-COLUMNS: columns half sunk into a wall.

DIAPER WORK: surface decoration composed of square or lozenge shapes.

DOG-TOOTH: typical E.E. ornament consisting of a series of four-cornered stars placed diagonally and raised pyramidally (Fig. 7).

Fig. 7

DOMICAL VAULT: *see* Vault.

DONJON: *see* Keep.

DORIC: *see* Orders.

DORMER (WINDOW): window placed vertically in the sloping plane of a roof.

DRIPSTONE: *see* Hood-mould.

DRUM: circular or polygonal vertical wall of a dome or cupola.

E.E. ('EARLY ENGLISH'): historical division of English Gothic architecture roughly covering the C13.

EASTER SEPULCHRE: recess with tomb-chest usually in the wall of a chancel, the tomb-chest to receive an effigy of Christ for Easter celebrations.

EAVES: underpart of a sloping roof overhanging a wall.

EAVES CORNICE: cornice below the eaves of a roof.

ECHINUS: quarter round moulding carved with egg and dart pattern, used in classical architecture.

EMBATTLED: *see* Battlement.

EMBRASURE: small opening in the wall or parapet of a fortified building, usually splayed on the inside. *See* Loop.

ENCAUSTIC TILES: earthenware glazed and decorated tiles used for paving.

ENGAGED COLUMNS: columns attached to, or partly sunk into, a wall.

ENGLISH BOND: *see* Brickwork.

ENTABLATURE: in classical architecture the whole of the horizontal members above a column (that is architrave, frieze, and cornice) (*see* Fig. 11).

ENTASIS: very slight convex deviation from a straight line; used on Greek columns and sometimes on spires to prevent an optical illusion of concavity.

ENTRESOL: *see* Mezzanine.

EPITAPH: hanging wall monument.

ESCUTCHEON: shield for armorial bearings.

EXTRADOS: outer surface of an arch.

FAIENCE: decorated glazed earthenware.

FAN TRACERY: *see* Tracery.

FAN VAULT: *see* Vault.

FERETORY: place behind the High Altar, where the chief shrine of a church is kept.

FESTOON: carved garland of flowers and fruit suspended at both ends.

FILLET: narrow flat band running down a shaft or along a roll moulding.

FINIAL: in Gothic architecture the top of a pinnacle, gable, or bench-end carved into a leaf or leaf-like form.

FLAGON: jug for the wine used in the Communion service.

FLAMBOYANT: properly the latest phase of French Gothic architecture where the window tracery takes on wavy undulating lines.

FLÈCHE: slender wooden spire on the centre of a roof (also called Spirelet).

FLEMISH BOND: see Brickwork.

FLEURON: decorative carved flower or leaf.

FLUTING: vertical channelling in the shaft of a column.

FLYING BUTTRESS: see Buttress.

FOIL: lobe formed by the cusping (q.v.) of a circle or an arch. Trefoil, quatrefoil, cinquefoil, multifoil, express the number of leaf shapes to be seen.

FOLIATED: carved with leaf shapes.

FOSSE: ditch.

FOUR-CENTRED ARCH: see Arch.

FRATER: refectory or dining hall of a monastery.

FRESCO: wall painting on wet plaster.

FRIEZE: middle division of a classical entablature (q.v.) (see Fig. 11).

FRONTAL: covering of the front of an altar.

GALILEE: chapel or vestibule at the w end of a church enclosing the porch. Also called Narthex (q.v.).

GALLERY: in church architecture upper storey above an aisle, opened in arches to the nave. Also called Tribune (q.v.) and often erroneously Triforium (q.v.).

GARGOYLE: water spout projecting from the parapet of a wall or tower; carved into a human or animal shape.

GAZEBO: lookout tower or raised summer house in a picturesque garden.

'GEOMETRICAL': see Tracery.

'GIBBS' SURROUND: of a doorway or window. A surround with alternating larger and smaller blocks of stone, quoinwise, or intermittent large blocks, sometimes with a narrow raised band connecting them up the verticals and along the extrados of the arch (Fig. 8).

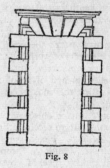

Fig. 8

GROIN: sharp edge at the meeting of two cells of a crossvault.

GROINED VAULT: see Vault.

GROTESQUE: fanciful ornamental decoration; see also Arabesque.

HAGIOSCOPE: see Squint.

HALF-TIMBERING: see Timber Framing.

HALL CHURCH: church in which nave and aisles are all equal or approximately so.

HAMMER-BEAM: see Roof.

HANAP: large metal cup, generally made for domestic use, standing on an elaborate base and stem; with a very ornate cover frequently crowned with a little steeple.

HEADERS: *see* Brickwork.

HERRINGBONE WORK: brick, stone, or tile construction where the component blocks are laid diagonally instead of flat. Alternate courses lie in opposing directions to make a zigzag pattern up the face of the wall.

HIPPED ROOF: *see* Roof.

HOOD-MOULD: projecting moulding above an arch or a lintel to throw off water (also called Dripstone or Label).

ICONOGRAPHY: the science of the contents of works of art.

IMPOST: brackets in walls, usually formed of mouldings, on which the ends of an arch rest.

INDENT: shape chiselled out in a stone slab to receive a brass.

INGLENOOK: bench or seat built in beside a fireplace, sometimes covered by the chimney breast, occasionally lit by small windows on each side of the fire.

INTERCOLUMNATION: the space between columns.

IONIC: *see* Orders (Fig. 11).

JAMB: straight side of an archway, doorway, or window.

KEEL MOULDING: moulding whose outline is in section like that of the keel of a ship.

KEEP: massive tower of a Norman castle.

KEYSTONE: middle stone in an arch.

KING-POST: *see* Roof (Fig. 13).

LABEL: *see* Hood-mould.

LABEL STOP: ornamental boss at the end of a hood-mould (q.v.).

LANCET WINDOW: slender pointed-arched window.

LANTERN: in architecture, a small circular or polygonal turret with windows all round crowning a roof (*see* Cupola) or a dome.

LANTERN CROSS: churchyard cross with lantern-shaped top usually with sculptured representations on the sides of the top.

LEAN-TO ROOF: roof with one slope only, built against a higher wall.

LESENE or PILASTER STRIP: pilaster without base and capital.

LIERNE: *see* Vault (Fig. 20).

LINENFOLD: Tudor panelling ornamented with a conventional representation of a piece of linen laid in vertical folds. The piece is repeated in each panel.

LINTEL: horizontal beam or stone bridging an opening.

LOGGIA: recessed colonnade (q.v.).

LONG AND SHORT WORK: Saxon quoins (q.v.) consisting of stones placed with the long sides alternately upright and horizontal.

LOUVRE: opening, often with lantern (q.v.) over, in the roof of a room to let the smoke from a central hearth escape.

LOZENGE: diamond shape.

LUNETTE: tympanum (q.v.) or curved opening in a vault.

LYCH GATE: wooden gate structure with a roof and open sides placed at the entrance to a churchyard to provide space for the reception of a coffin. The word lych is Saxon and means a corpse.

MACHICOLATION: projecting gallery on brackets constructed on the outside of castle towers or walls. The gallery has holes in the floor to drop missiles through.

MAJOLICA: ornamented glazed earthenware.

MANSARD: see Roof.

MERLON: see Battlement.

METOPE: in classical architecture of the Doric order (q.v.) the space in the frieze between the triglyphs (Fig. 11).

MEZZANINE: low storey placed between two higher ones.

MISERERE: see Misericord.

MISERICORD: bracket placed on the underside of a hinged choir stall seat which, when turned up, provided the occupant of the seat with a support during long periods of standing (also called Miserere).

MODILLION: small bracket of which large numbers (modillion frieze) are often placed below a cornice (q.v.) in classical architecture.

MOTTE: steep mound forming the main feature of CII and CI2 castles.

MOUCHETTE: tracery motif in

Fig. 9

curvilinear tracery, a curved dagger (q.v.) (Fig. 9).

MULLION: vertical post or upright dividing a window into two or more 'lights'.

NAILHEAD: E.E. ornamental motif, consisting of small pyramids regularly repeated (Fig. 10).

Fig. 10

NARTHEX: enclosed vestibule or covered porch at the main entrance to a church (see Galilee).

NEWEL: central post in a circular or winding staircase; also the principal post when a flight of stairs meets a landing.

OBELISK: lofty pillar of square section tapering at the top and ending pyramidally.

OGEE: see Arch (Fig. 1c).

ORATORY: small private chapel in a house.

ORDER: (1) of a doorway or window: series of concentric steps receding towards the opening; (2) in classical architecture: column with base, shaft, capital, and entablature (q.v.) according to one of the following styles: Greek Doric, Roman Doric, Tuscan Doric, Ionic, Corinthian, Composite. The established details are very elaborate, and some specialist architectural work should be consulted for further guidance (see Fig. 11).

Fig. 11.—E, Entablature; F, Frieze; A, Architrave; M, Metope; T, Triglyph

ORIEL: *see* Bay Window.

OVERHANG: projection of the upper storey of a house.

OVERSAILING COURSES: series of stone or brick courses, each one projecting beyond the one below it.

PALIMPSEST: (1) *of a brass:* where a metal plate has been re-used by turning over and engraving on the back; (2) *of a wall painting:* where one overlaps and partly obscures an earlier one.

PALLADIAN: architecture following the ideas and principles of Andrea Palladio, 1518–80.

PANTILE: tile of curved S-shaped section.

PARAPET: low wall placed to protect any spot where there is a sudden drop, for example on a bridge, quay, hillside, house-top, etc.

PARGETTING: plaster work with patterns and ornaments either in relief or engraved on it.

PARVISE: room over a church porch. Often used as a school-house or a store room.

PATEN: plate to hold the bread at Communion or Mass.

PATERA: small flat circular or oval ornament in classical architecture.

PEDIMENT: low-pitched gable (q.v.) used in classical, Renaissance, and neo-classical architecture above a portico and above doors, windows, etc. It may be straight-sided or curved segmentally. *Open Pediment:* one where the centre portion of the base is left open. *Broken Pediment:* one where the centre portion of the sloping sides is 'broken' out.

PENDANT: boss (q.v.) elongated so that it seems to hang down.

PENDENTIF: concave triangular spandrel used to lead from the angle of two walls to the base of a circular dome. It is constructed as part of the hemisphere over a diameter the size of the diagonal of the basic square (Fig. 12).

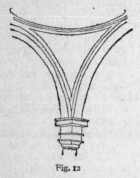

Fig. 12

PERP (PERPENDICULAR): historical division of English Gothic architecture roughly covering the period from 1350 to 1530.

PIANO NOBILE: principal storey of a house with the reception rooms; usually the first floor.

PIAZZA: square open space surrounded by buildings, in C17 and C18 English sometimes used to mean a long colonnade or loggia.

PIER: strong, solid support, frequently square in section or of composite section (compound pier).

PIETRA DURA: ornamental or scenic inlay by means of thin slabs of stone.

PILASTER: shallow pier attached to a wall.

PILLAR PISCINA: free-standing piscina on a pillar.

PINNACLE: ornamental form crowning a spire, tower, buttress, etc., usually of steep pyramidal, conical, or some similar shape.

PISCINA: basin for washing the Communion or Mass vessels, provided with a drain. Generally set in or against the wall to the s of an altar.

PLAISANCE: summer-house, pleasure house near a mansion.

PLATE TRACERY: see Tracery.

PLINTH: projecting base of a wall or column, generally chamfered (q.v.) or moulded at the top.

POPPYHEAD: ornament of leaf and flower type used to decorate the tops of bench or stall-ends.

PORTCULLIS: gate constructed to rise and fall in vertical grooves; used in gateways of castles.

PORTE COCHÈRE: porch large enough to admit wheeled vehicles.

PORTICO: centre-piece of a house or a church with classical detached or attached columns and a pediment. A portico is called *prostyle* or *in antis* according to whether it projects from or recedes into a building. In a portico *in antis* the columns range with the side walls.

POSTERN: small gateway at the back of a building.

PREDELLA: in an altar-piece the horizontal strip below the main representation, often used for a number of subsidiary representations in a row.

PRESBYTERY: the part of the church lying E of the choir. It is the part where altar is placed.

PRINCIPAL: *see* Roof (Fig. 13).

PRIORY: monastic house whose head is a prior or prioress, not an abbot or abbess.

PROSTYLE: with free-standing columns in a row.

PULPITUM: stone rood screen in a major church.

PURLIN: *see* Roof (Figs. 13, 14).

PUTTO: small naked boy.

QUADRANGLE: inner courtyard in a large building complex.

QUARRY: in stained-glass work, a small diamond or square-shaped piece of glass set diagonally.

QUATREFOIL: *see* Foil.

QUEEN-POSTS: *see* Roof (Fig. 14).

QUOINS: dressed stones at the angles of a building. Sometimes all the stones are of the same size; more often they are alternately large or small.

RADIATING CHAPELS: chapels projecting radially from an ambulatory or an apse.

RAFTER: *see* Roof.

RAMPART: stone wall, or wall of earth surrounding a castle, fortress, or fortified city.

RAMPART-WALK: path along the inner face of a rampart.

REBATE: channel or small recess cut into a piece of wood or stone longitudinally to receive the edge of some member that is to be secured in it. The depth of the channel is equal to the thickness of the member to be let into it.

REBUS: pun, a play on words. The literal translation and illustration of a name for artistic and heraldic purposes (Belton=bell, tun).

REEDING: decoration with parallel convex mouldings touching one another.

REFECTORY: Dining hall; *see* Frater.

RENDERING: plastering of an outer wall.

REPOUSSÉ: decoration of metal work by relief designs, formed by beating the metal from the back.

REREDOS: structure behind and above an altar.

RESPOND: half-pier bonded into a wall and carrying one end of an arch.

RETABLE: altar-piece, a picture or piece of carving, standing behind and attached to an altar.

RETICULATION: *see* Tracery (Fig. 19).

REVEAL: that part of a jamb (q.v.) which lies between the glass or door and the outer surface of the wall.

RIB VAULT: *see* Vault.

ROCOCO: latest phase of the Baroque style, current in most Continental countries between *c.* 1720 and *c.* 1760.

ROMANESQUE: that style in architecture which was current in the C11 and C12 and preceded the Gothic style (in England often called Norman).

ROOD: cross or crucifix.

ROOD LOFT: singing gallery on the top of the rood screen, often supported by a coving.

ROOD SCREEN: *see* Screen.

ROOD STAIRS: stairs to give access to the rood loft.

ROOF: *Hipped:* roof with sloped instead of vertical ends. *Mansard:* roof with a double slope, the lower slope being larger and steeper than the upper. *Saddleback:* tower roof shaped like an ordinary gabled timber roof. The following members have special names: *Rafter:* roof-timber sloping up from the wall plate to the ridge. *Principal:* principal rafter, usually corresponding to the main bay divisions of the nave or chancel below. *Wall Plate:* timber laid longitudinally on the top of a wall. *Purlin:* longitudinal member laid parallel with wall plate and ridge beam some way up the slope of the roof. *Tie-beam:* beam connecting the two slopes of a roof across at its foot, usually at the height of the wall plate, to prevent the roof from spreading. *Collar-beam:* tie-beam applied higher up the slope of the roof. *Strut:* upright timber connecting the tie-beam with the rafter above it. *King-post:*

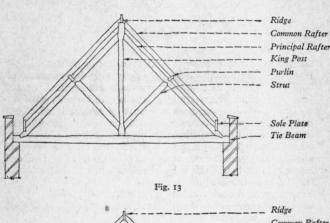

Ridge
Common Rafter
Principal Rafter
King Post
Purlin
Strut

Sole Plate
Tie Beam

Fig. 13

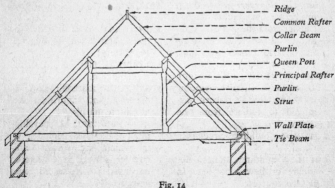

Ridge
Common Rafter
Collar Beam
Purlin
Queen Post
Principal Rafter
Purlin
Strut

Wall Plate
Tie Beam

Fig. 14

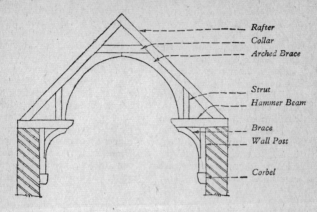

Fig. 15

upright timber connecting a
tie-beam and collar-beam
with the ridge-beam. *Queen-
posts:* two struts placed symmetrically on a tie-beam or
collar-beam. *Braces:* inclined
timbers inserted to strengthen
others. Usually braces connect
a collar-beam with the rafters
below or a tie-beam with the
wall below. Braces can be
straight or curved (also called
arched). *Hammer-beam:* beam
projecting at right angles,
usually from the top of a wall,
to carry arched braces or struts
and arched braces (*see* Figs.
13, 14, 15).

ROSE WINDOW (or WHEEL
WINDOW): circular window
with patterned tracery arranged to radiate from the
centre.

ROTUNDA: building circular in
plan.

RUBBLE: building stones, not
square or hewn, nor laid in
regular courses.

RUSTICATION: Ashlar-work of
blocks with the margins only
wrought and the faces rough or
specially rock-faced: or ashlar-
work of smooth-faced blocks
with the joints greatly emphasized (smooth rustication).
If only the horizontal joints are
emphasized it is called banded
rustication.

SADDLEBACK: *see* Roof.

SALTIRE CROSS: equal-limbed
cross placed diagonally.

SANCTUARY: area around the
main altar of a church (*see*
Presbytery).

SARCOPHAGUS: elaborately
carved coffin.

SCAGLIOLA: material composed
of cement and colouring matter
to imitate marble.

SCALLOPED CAPITAL: development of the block capital (q.v.)
in which the single semi-
circular surface is elaborated
into a series of truncated cones
(Fig. 16).

Fig. 16

SCARP: artificial cutting away of the ground to form a steep slope.

SCREEN: *Parclose screen:* screen separating a chapel from the rest of a church. *Rood screen:* screen at the W end of a chancel. Above it on the rood-beam was the rood (q.v.).

SCREENS PASSAGE: passage between the entrances to kitchen, buttery, etc., and the screen behind which lies the hall of a medieval house.

SEDILIA: seats for the priests (usually three) on the S side of the chancel of a church.

SEGMENTAL ARCH: *see* Arch.

SET-OFF: *see* Weathering.

SEXPARTITE: *see* Vaulting.

SGRAFFITO: pattern incised into plaster so as to expose a dark surface underneath.

SHAFT-RING: ring round a circular pier or a shaft attached to a pier.

SILL: lower horizontal part of the frame of a window.

SLATEHANGING: the covering of walls by overlapping rows of slates, on a timber substructure.

SOFFIT: *see* Archivolt.

SOLAR: upper drawing-room of a medieval house.

SOPRAPORTE: painting above the door of a room, usual in the C17 and C18.

SOUNDING BOARD: horizontal board or canopy over a pulpit. Also called Tester.

SPANDREL: triangular surface between one side of an arch, the horizontal drawn from its apex, and the vertical drawn from its springer, also the surface between two arches.

SPIRE: tall pyramidal or conical pointed erection often built on top of a tower, turret, etc. *Broach Spire:* spire which is generally octagonal in plan rising from the top or parapet of a square tower. A small inclined piece of masonry covers the vacant triangular space at each of the four angles of the square and is carried up to a point along the diagonal sides of the octagon. *Needle Spire:* thin spire rising from the centre of a tower roof, well inside the parapet.

SPIRELET: *see* Flèche.

SPLAY: chamfer, usually of the jamb of a window.

SPRINGING: level at which an arch rises from its supports.

SQUINCH: arch or system of concentric arches thrown across the angle between two walls to support a superstructure, for example a dome (Fig. 17).

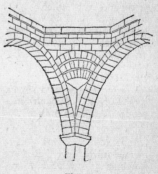

Fig. 17

SQUINT: hole cut in a wall or through a pier to allow a view of the main altar of a church from places whence it could not otherwise be seen (also called Hagioscope).

STALL: carved seat, one in a row, made of wood or stone.

STEEPLE: the tower or spire of a church.

STIFF-LEAF: E.E. type of foliage of many-lobed shapes (Fig. 18).

STILTED: *see* Arch.

Fig. 18

STOUP: vessel for the reception of holy water, usually placed near a door.

STRAINER ARCH: arch inserted across a room to prevent the walls from leaning.

STRAPWORK: C16 decoration consisting of interlaced bands, and forms similar to fretwork or cut and bent leather.

STRETCHERS: *see* Brickwork.

STRING COURSE: projecting horizontal band or moulding set in the surface of a wall.

STRUT: *see* Roof.

STUCCO: plaster work.

SWAG: festoon formed by a carved piece of cloth suspended from both ends.

TABERNACLE: richly ornamented niche (q.v.) or freestanding canopy. Usually contains the Holy Sacrament.

TAZZA: shallow bowl on a foot.

TERMINAL FIGURES (TERMS, TERMINI): upper part of a human figure growing out of a pier, pilaster, etc., which tapers towards the base.

TERRACOTTA: burnt clay, unglazed.

TESSELATED PAVEMENT: decorative floor or wall covering made up of tesserae or small coloured cubes of stone, fitted into a bed of cement.

TESTER: *see* Sounding Board.

THREE-DECKER PULPIT: pulpit with Clerk's Stall and Reading Desk placed below each other.

TIE-BEAM: *see* Roof (Figs. 13, 14).

TIERCERON: *see* Vault (Fig. 20).

TILEHANGING: *see* Slatehanging.

TIMBER-FRAMING: method of construction where walls are built of timber framework with the spaces filled in by plaster or brickwork. Sometimes the timber is covered over with plaster or boarding laid horizontally.

TOMB-CHEST: chest-shaped stone coffin, the most usual medieval form of funeral monument.

TOUCH: soft black marble quarried near Tournai.

TOURELLE: turret corbelled out from the wall.

TRACERY: intersecting ribwork in the upper part of a window, or used decoratively in blank arches, on vaults, etc. *Plate tracery:* early form of tracery where decoratively shaped openings are cut through the solid stone infilling in the head of a window. *Bar tracery:* intersecting ribwork made up of slender shafts, continuing the lines of the mullions of windows up to a decorative mesh in the head of the window. *Geometrical tracery:* tracery consisting chiefly of circles or foiled circles. *Intersected tracery:* tracery in which each mullion of a window branches out into two curved bars in such a way that every one of them runs concentrically with the others against the arch of the whole window. The result is that every light of the window is a lancet and every two, three, four, etc., lights together form a pointed arch. *Reticulated tracery:* tracery consisting entirely of circles drawn at top and bottom into ogee shapes so that a net-like appearance results (Fig. 19).

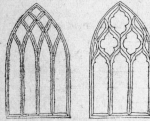

Fig. 19

TRANSEPT: transverse portion of a cross-shaped church.

TRANSOME: horizontal bar across the opening of a window.

TRANSVERSE ARCH: *see* Vaulting.

TRIBUNE: *see* Gallery.

TRICIPUT, SIGNUM TRICIPUT: sign of the Trinity expressed by three faces belonging to one head.

TRIFORIUM: arcaded wall passage or blank arcading facing the nave at the height of the aisle roof and below the clerestory (q.v.) windows. (*See* Gallery.)

TRIGLYPHS: blocks with vertical grooves separating the metopes (q.v.) in the Doric frieze (Fig. 11).

TROPHY: sculptured group of arms or armour, used as a memorial of victory.

TRUMEAU: stone mullion (q.v.) supporting the tympanum (q.v.) of a wide doorway.

TURRET: very small tower, round or polygonal in plan.

TUSCAN: *see* Order.

TYMPANUM: space between the lintel of a doorway and the arch above it.

UNDERCROFT: vaulted room, sometimes underground, below a church or chapel.

VAULT: *Barrel vault: see* Tunnel vault. *Cross-vault: see* Groined vault. *Domical vault:* square or polygonal dome rising direct on a square or polygonal bay, the curved surfaces separated by groins (q.v.). *Fan vault:* vault where all ribs springing from one springer are of the same length, the same distance from the next, and the same curvature. *Groined vault* or *Cross-vault:* vault of two tunnel vaults of identical shape intersecting each other at right angles. *Lierne:* tertiary rib, that is, rib which does not spring either from one of the main springers or the central boss. *Quadripartite vault:* one wherein one bay of vaulting is divided into four parts. *Rib vault:* vault with diagonal ribs projecting along the groins. *Ridge-rib:* rib along the longitudinal or transverse ridge of a vault. *Sexpartite vault:* one wherein one bay of quadripartite vaulting is divided into two parts transversely so that each bay of vaulting has six parts. *Tierceron:* secondary rib, that is, rib which issues from one of the main springers or the central boss and leads to a place on a ridge-rib. *Transverse arch:* arch separating one bay of a vault from the next. *Tunnel vault* or *Barrel vault:* vault of semicircular or pointed section (Fig. 20).

VAULTING SHAFT: vertical member leading to the springer of a vault.

VENETIAN WINDOW: window with three openings, the central one arched and wider than the outside ones.

VERANDAH: open gallery or balcony with a roof on light, usually metal, supports.

VESTIBULE: ante-room or entrance hall.

VILLA: according to Gwilt (1842) 'a country house for the residence of opulent persons'.

VITRIFIED: made similar to glass.

VOLUTE: spiral scroll, one of the component parts of an Ionic column (*see* Orders).

VOUSSOIR: wedge-shaped stone used in arch construction.

WAGON-ROOF: roof in which by closely set rafters with arched braces the appearance

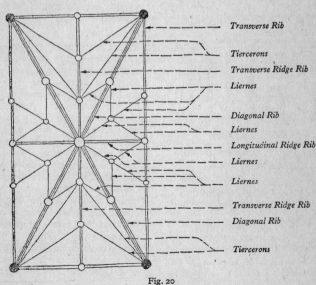

Transverse Rib

Tiercerons

Transverse Ridge Rib

Liernes

Diagonal Rib

Liernes

Longitudinal Ridge Rib

Liernes

Liernes

Transverse Ridge Rib

Diagonal Rib

Tiercerons

Fig. 20

of the inside of a canvas tilt over a wagon is achieved. Wagon-roofs can be panelled or plastered (ceiled) or left uncovered.

WAINSCOT: timber lining to walls.

WALL PLATE: *see* Roof.

WATERLEAF: leaf shape used in later C12 capitals. The water-leaf is a broad, unribbed, tapering leaf curving up towards the angle of the abacus and turned in at the top (Fig. 21).

WEATHER-BOARDING: overlapping horizontal boards, covering a timber-framed wall.

Fig. 21

WEATHERING: sloping horizontal surface on sills, buttresses, etc., to throw off water.

WEEPERS: small figures placed in niches along the sides of some medieval tombs (also called Mourners).

WHEEL WINDOW: *see* Rose Window.

INDEX OF PLATES

INDEX OF ARTISTS

INDEX OF PLACES

The references in brackets indicate the square in which the place will be found on the map preceding the title-page

NOTES

Cancro flub